# *Prentice Hall's*

# One-Day
# MBA
## in
# FINANCE &
# ACCOUNTING

## Michael Muckian

PRENTICE HALL PRESS

Library of Congress Cataloging-in-Publication Data

Muckian, Michael.
    Prentice Hall's one-day MBA in finance & accounting / Michael Muckian.
      p. cm
    ISBN 0-7352-0148-X (pbk.) — ISBN 0-13-028459-9 (cloth)
      1. Finance. 2. Accounting. I. Title: One-day MBA in finance & accounting.
    II. Title: One-day MBA in finance and accounting. III. Prentice-Hall, Inc.
    IV. Title.

HG173.M83 2000
657—dc21                                          00-029354

ISBN 0-7352-0148-X (Paper)     0-13-028459-9 (Case)

**PRENTICE HALL PRESS**
Paramus, NJ 07652

Visit us at www.phdirect.com

# DEDICATION

*To Jeanie Maria, who really makes
my numbers add up.*

# Contents

# Chapter 5 Creating the Savvy Business Plan 55

# Chapter 6 Establishing an Accounting System 73

# Chapter 7 Building A Better Budget 87

# Chapter 8 From Balance Sheets to Income Statements 105

## Chapter 9   Accounting for Merchandising Operations   119

## Chapter 10   Managing Your Internal Controls   129

## Chapter 11   Deferrals and Accruals   143

## Chapter 12   Tracking Inventory   151

# Chapter 16   Understanding the Corporation   205

# Chapter 17   Sources of Business Finance   217

# Chapter 18   The Taxman Cometh   235

## Chapter 22   Troubleshooting Your Financial System   285

## Appendix   Quarter-Hour Classroom   293

# Introduction:
# You Are What You Count

The definitions driving this volume are simple ones:

- **finance**—the science of managing money and money matters, including credit, debit and other issues as they apply to personal or professional enterprise. The heart and soul of just about every business operation on the planet.

- **accounting**—(from *accountancy*) the keeping or inspecting of commercial accounts as they relate to the financial flow of business and its strategic applications as derived from a company's financial plans and current financial position. The control mechanism by which businesses make sure their finances are on the right track.

The purpose behind this volume—to make you a better overseer of the financial side of your enterprise and more accountable for your company's or your departments' financial success or failure—is a goal that's simply stated but a little less easily attained. Accounting principles, once mastered, are reasonably and logically applied. However, their mastery takes time and effort.

But there's more. Mastery also requires a clear recognition of the importance of accounting and finance to your specific discipline. If you are the master of your own fate and manage your own company, the implications are clear: Good accounting principles correctly applied and scrupulously followed are critical to your firm's success. Any business of any size that's not following generally accepted accounting principles and financial management standards in the execution of its daily operations and strategic planning will not be in business very long.

Once we move into specialty areas, however, the rationale becomes a little fuzzier and less well-defined. If you are the very successful vice president of district sales for the Southeastern Region, the chief of manufacturing operations, or the director of materials and product distribution, why is understanding and mastery of finance and accounting principles critical to the success of your enterprise?

Quite simply, when it comes to conducting business in today's market, you are only as good as your finance and accounting abilities allow you to be.

Let me say it again another way. If you are unable to manage your operation as it adheres to and is governed by sound accounting principles—or by the scientific principles of financial management, if you prefer—then you simply shouldn't be managing an enterprise of any size or importance.

That's hard for many executives to swallow, but it's one of the basic truths of business. No matter how effective you are in the specialty field you've chosen as your life's work, finance is still the fundamental engine driving that enterprise—and that's true in the case of nonprofits as well as for-profits. If finance is the engine, then accounting principles are the drive shaft of the enterprise that keeps efforts on track and maximize all the advantages of the business.

Increased financial awareness also is more critical as the United States continues its move from a manufacturing environment to a service economy. Such a transition places fiscal responsibility into a wider variety of executives' hands. Moreover, the service environment requires a closer economic eye and greater and more continuous scrutiny for a firm to be successful.

That understanding becomes even more critical as you climb the ladder toward increased corporate and financial responsibility. In the past, it was often the chief financial officers who rose to the top and became chief executive officers. The step between CFO and CEO tended to be shorter, more direct and, in the minds of many executives, more logical.

Today the environment has broadened to include a wider array of executive types operating on a collision course with the corner office. It's no longer necessary to be a CFO or other financial expert to ascend to the top. That's because the disciplines themselves are becoming more sophisticated, and a great deal of that sophistication comes from an increased knowledge in basic and advanced finance and accounting principles.

Business executives as a whole are learning how to better master the accounting requirements behind their respective operations. That increased sophistication will have an impact not only on your future plans, but also on your present competitive stance within your industry. The vice president of sales who can better control the financial side of his or her accounts and maximize margins, discount periods and collection cycles stands a better chance to gain the competitive edge, which ultimately results in increased sales and improved market share.

The better you are at the intrinsic aspect of financial management as it affects your strategies, the more successful you likely will be. Your competition knows that, and if you haven't yet come to terms with its importance, they won't have to consider you their competition much longer.

It's a highly competitive world out there, one that requires sophisticated understanding of financial principles as they relate to business. And that's the purpose of *Prentice Hall's One-Day MBA in Finance & Accounting*.

Consider this one of the more pragmatic reference guides available to you as your educational needs evolve based on the changing business landscape. Reading this volume will not provide the full, comprehensive training required to award such a prestigious degree as the MBA. No single printed work could hope to deliver such estimable rewards. What *Prentice Hall's One-Day MBA in Finance & Accounting* can do is offer the background and some in-depth discussion in those areas critical to achieving that goal, at least as it applies to day-to-day situations.

This is a key resource for executives who want to improve the bottom lines of either their own companies or their own operations. Mastery of its principles will be critical to executives who want to move ahead competitively and plan strategically for their own advancement, and for the success of the enterprise they supervise.

To that end, this volume attempts to focus on finance and accounting within its strategic milieu, to show its applications in a less esoteric, more practical light. We'll cover some basics, including the enigmatic double-entry accounting principles, to get you grounded in the discipline. We'll also isolate and examine the transactional flow of accounting through an organization to show you that finances truly are the life blood of any enterprise, no matter what its scope, process or product. Strategic cash management also will get some significant attention.

From there we will discuss how to develop accounting systems, and the philosophy behind their implementation and use. We'll focus on accrual-based accounting and examine the component parts for such systems as they apply to different industries and applications. We'll touch on purely operational issues, such as general ledger sheet development and payroll management, as well as go over more esoteric elements, such as future forecasting, growth cycle management and troubleshooting system issues. In between, we'll talk about accounting as it relates to various types of business.

In the end, the net gain to readers should be a clear understanding of finance and accounting at a level high enough to warrant more complex speculations while at the same time providing operational tricks and tools good for immediate application. You won't quite be an MBA when you walk away from this volume, but you will be much closer than you were when you started.

If you perform diligently, you will be many steps ahead of the competition in your financial acumen and well on your way to increased levels of responsibility and growth.

And that sounds like a good investment from anyone's point of view.

—Michael Muckian

## ACKNOWLEDGMENTS

If an executive is only as effective as his financial acumen allows him to be, an author is only as good as his resources. That's especially critical on a volume such as this one.

Our thanks to Vince Market, CFO for Philadelphia Telco Credit Union in Trevose, Pa., for his guidance and counsel. With an MBA designation, Vince has all the right letters after his name to make this volume as good as it can be. His input proved invaluable.

Thanks, too, to Luis Gonzalez at Prentice Hall for championing this project and mastering the accounting process right along with everyone else who reviewed and commented on the manuscript.

Moe: My nephew just became a computer programmer.

Joe: Really? How come?

Moe: He didn't have the personality to be an accountant.

# Identifying Your Accounting Profile  1

Accountants, so the old saying goes, are the ballast required to keep the ship of business upright, balanced and buoyant in the rough waters of commerce. Noble as that sounds, however, there are few people who take comfort being referred to as "ballast." Moreover, in today's dynamic business environment, the description is no longer true.

There was a time when financial professionals were limited to strict accounting functions, wearing green eyeshades and sleeve protectors and toiling under dim yellow lamps. Their lives were dreary assemblages of lists that the accountants painfully tallied and checked against rumor and promise. If they had no discernible personalities, as some wags have said, it may have been because their daily drudgery left them little time to look beyond the ink marks they made in the general ledger.

Computers and spreadsheet software have changed all that. What was once a dour task done by hand is now quickly computed and rendered for all to see. What has emerged is a sophisticated professional who uses company finances to plan both operationally and strategically for the growth of the company. Of course, they're still responsible for financial management, but much of the accounting drudgery has been automated. Today's finance and accounting professionals can spend more time analyzing the impact of specific financial activities as opposed to merely computing their net financial effect.

## Chapter 1

## CHITS

You can't walk the walk until you learn how to talk the talk. That means mastery of terms like *debit* and *credit, revenue* and *expense* and other language specific to the accounting function. Proper financial management is all about accuracy. You first need to master the vocabulary—both independently and within context—if you're going to master the discipline. Take the time to learn the language. It will be time very well spent.

This takes today's financial professional far from his or her role as ballast in helping keep the ship of commerce upright. Today, a company's key financial leader—be it a chief financial officer (CFO), finance manager or some other trained professional—is less likely to be ballast and more likely to act as first mate. Our overall need for increased financial understanding and acumen is one factor driving this trend. We also know this because so many current chief executive officers (CEOs) began with accounting and finance backgrounds. That trend continues, but you'll also see more vice presidents of marketing, research department heads and other types joining the CFO in his or her march to the top.

If money is what your business is about—and money, or its positive byproducts, is what *all* business is about—then the financial professional is one of the most critical members of the management team, if not *the* most critical member. As you will see, revenues and expenses interlace all departments; they help hold companies together functionally and make them accountable to their goals. That means clear integration of financial principles, either in the mind of a department manager or one of his or her subordinates, is one of the most critical resources that can be brought to bear on any company's management and planning.

Company departments operate in the same way. Taking care of your line of business is your most critical function. That's what you've been hired to do and that's why you're being paid. Of primary importance in that management is the financial side of the business. If you run a department, chances are you don't have the luxury of having your own CFO. However, you need to have the same level of consciousness first and foremost in your mind. Capable executives are ready to take on the financial professional's role at a moment's notice. Only then will you see the true dimension of the business issue at hand. Objective, financially based knowledge reaches far beyond the passion or hardship that may drive what you do. That knowledge becomes an objective dimension from which you can make the right and necessarily rational judgments.

Effective business executives have finance professionals inside them ready to provide good council whenever it's needed. Decisions still may be made for less-than-logical reasons, or for reasons that seem financially unsound, often by someone at a higher level or in another operations area entirely. But, at the very least, the proper tempering of runaway initiatives has taken place and the internal accountant has had his or her say. In some cases, that makes all the difference between success and failure.

In fact, attempting to make financial sense out of executive decisions is your duty as a professional. Despite the net effect of what happens, those efforts are never wasted.

## TESTING YOUR ACCOUNTING METTLE

How good an accountant are you? You may be better than you think you are, having knowledge that's critical to the financial management of your operations, your department and your company. Try answering the following basic accounting questions to see where you stand:*

1.  What is the single, most basic formula that drives the accounting equation?

2.  Differentiate between cash and accrual accounting. What are the advantages and disadvantages of each?

---

*Answers at the end of the chapter.*

## PORTFOLIO

Because it doesn't generate revenue, accounting departments often are considered overhead items and operational expenses. Nothing could be further from the truth. The financial professionals in your firm who do their job help preserve resources while presenting trends that, in turn, may increase revenue. As a department, the accounting function is an investment that helps contribute to the bottom line.

3. What is the difference between economic income and accounting income?

4. What is depreciation and how does it impact economic performance?

5. What are the three most important financial statements used in evaluating the financial well-being of a company?

6. What are the key components of a company's statement of financial condition?

7. What are the most important elements of an income statement?

8. What are foundation principles of a cash flow statement?

9. What is meant by the phrase, "generally accepted accounting principles?"

10. What is the difference between a current asset and a noncurrent asset?

All of these questions are important to your growth as a financial professional. If you can answer any six or more, you're well on your way to financial and accounting mastery.

## CALLING ON YOUR INTERNAL ACCOUNTANT

No decision of importance should be made without checking with your internal accountant. This includes all expenditures and, especially, revenue decisions. Remember, the financial profile that defines your department or colors the balance sheet of your company is a snapshot of the success or failure of your strategic initiatives and operational plans. That profile, in turn, is a reflection of your own business acumen and may be the key criterion by which your professional success is judged.

There also are some practical reasons to master the accounting side of your operation:

- If you're running your own firm, large or small, understanding how to read balance sheets, financial statements and other financial documentation is critical to business success. Entrepreneurs who trust others to manage the financial side of their operation often run into trouble and occasionally end in ruin. No matter how good your ideas are, if no one is managing the financial side of those plans, you're headed for trouble.

- If you're running a department, your actions likely make a financial contribution and have a financial impact on every other department around you. Manufacturing's ability affects the prices of products and the company's overall overhead costs. The timeline in which the research department operates may make or break the company's ability to function in the long run. And the success of sales affects everyone in the firm. Your obligation to understand and manage company finances is in direct relationship to your department's financial impact on, and obligations to, other departments and on the company as a whole.

- A better understanding of your department's financial workings may go a long way in making the accounting department an ally rather than an opponent. It also helps you better understand one element of the way other departments operate, thus better understanding those departments.

- Finally, clear understanding of financial operations is simply good management practice. It's one of the core management skills you will need to help both yourself and your operation thrive and progress.

Remember that finances are the web linking all the various departments in your firm together in the pursuit of a common goal. Your mastery of those factors not only helps your operation, but those of the departments surrounding you. In fact, your leadership

## CREDITS

Most depart-
ment heads and
many CEOs who
find themselves in
charge of opera-
tions have had little
financial training
beyond the basics.
Yet there are ample
opportunities
through trade asso-
ciations, profes-
sional development
groups and other
organizations to
fine tune and en-
hance your financial
acumen through fi-
nancial seminars,
workshops and
classes. Take advan-
tage of as many
learning situations
as you can find. It
helps instill ac-
countability at the
department level.
You'll also see your
skills grow and
your contributions
to your firm's finan-
cial management
increase.

in this area may help fellow executives succeed as well as put you in good position when
other opportunities come along. Departments
or operations failing to master the financial
side of things may suddenly fall under your
sphere of influence once you've demonstrated
your ability to grasp the pertinent issues.
That can be as beneficial for the company as
it is for you.

## UNDERSTANDING THE
## ACCOUNTING PROCESS

Accounting practice goes back a long, long
way. The first evidence of any type of accounting system were clay tablets used to
record wages in Babylon around 3600 B.C.
There is also ample evidence that the ancient
Greeks and Egyptians used a primitive form
of accounting and financial recordkeeping.
William the Conqueror used basic accounting
principles to tally the financial resources of
his kingdom in the 11th century. The list goes
on of historical applications of what business
takes for granted today.

Those early uses, of course, were far
more primitive than the process practiced by
today's financial professionals. However, all
forms of accounting, whether ancient or contemporary, do share one aspect in common.
All are forms of a financial information system that paints a fiscal picture of business
and commerce.

In its most basic sense, accounting is the
recording of transaction information incurred
by an individual or company. Its value comes
in the data that information contains. No in-

dividual, whether a financial professional or a lay person needing some momentary accounting expertise, can hope to judge the increasingly complex situations faced by businesses each and every day with nothing but face-value information. More detailed financial accounts provide a much greater depth of knowledge that help us all over the rough spots. They enable us to make wiser plans and better execute those plans in ways that are valuable to our company, our department and ourselves.

This information is critical for the safe operation of any company. But understanding it and mastering its applications also makes a great deal of sense in the running of individual departments. In the same way a company measures the impact of its operational strategies, so, too, can individual departments measure their fiscal impact through the sound practice of economic principles.

Economic principles form the center of the financial side of your business and the purveyors of information vital to successful operations. Accounting, in a nutshell, is the compilation of financial data about transactions that affect the business. The medium most often is computer-based, but in the past has been pen or pencil on paper or even etched in clay, as the Babylonians did more than 5,000 years ago. If the numbers are accurate and the medium convenient, it matters little how the recording has taken place.

What does matter, however, is that the data is summarized and sorted in such a way that it paints an accurate picture of how the business is faring. Numbers by themselves

## LEDGER NOTES

Accounting takes its value from the fact that its data is objective and verifiable. The data is based on actual invoices, records of payments, lists of accounts receivable and other sources. Opinion, supposition and undocumented information have no place in the accounting function and should be avoided at all costs.

## LEDGER NOTES

Any company's accounting system is made up of a common information flow system that takes raw data, synthesizes it through various analysis mechanisms, then reports that information back in ways that have meaning for the various stakeholders in the process: management, investors, lenders, the government and other department heads. Understanding that flow—from source to synthesis to end user—will make the whole accounting system seem more logical, and more critical.

mean little without the proper context. Within that context, however, they can show how past financial performances and current situations will affect the future of the business. Apply trend analyses and other useful accounting tools to that data, and suddenly a picture of the enterprise emerges that is clear, concise and, most often, irrefutable.

The financial professional is not the only one who needs this data. It's really a company-wide accountability issue. Management, first and foremost, should be using this information to guide its every action. Investors in the business need a clear accounting to make sure their funds are being correctly utilized and their investment is protected from loss.

Lenders to the business need the clear picture accounting provides so they can adjust their rates and funds availability to any trends the company's financials provide. Suppliers of raw materials need to know so they can adjust their credit agreements and payment expectations accordingly. Even the government requires a clear accounting for tax and regulation purposes. And, if you're a manager of a specific department, your need for sound and accurate financial information exceeds the needs of almost all others.

## IT'S AN ACCOUNTING WORLD, AFTER ALL

Little boys and girls may still want to grow up to be doctors, lawyers and Indian chiefs, but by the time many of them have reached high school age and beyond, they have begun opting for accounting and financial professions that not only offer lucrative incomes, but also give them the power and control they seek over the business enterprises they run. Few business professionals (relative to the number who try) are able to scale the management pyramid to the top, but all who succeed fall under the influence of their company's fiscal muse. That muse, in turn, is influenced by the accounting professionals who collect the data and analyze and interpret its meaning to the company, including the company's well-being and its potential profits and pitfalls.

As you master the methods of financial management, you'll come in contact with many accountants, all of which can be classified as one of two types:

- **Accountants in industry** render their services to individual companies and sit on the staff of those companies, often at the executive level. These may include but are not limited to your firm's CFO, controller, financial vice president or departmental accountant. Their responsibilities can vary widely, but always are devoted to the company of which they are part. They manage the financial flow within one firm as well as interpret financial data and participate in that company's strategic planning efforts.

- **Public accountants** sell their services on a fee basis to other firms and the public at large, much like lawyers and consultants. They may offer smaller firms actual accounting services, but more often they come into a company as an outside auditor to review aspects of the company's private accounting efforts and verify the accuracy of its books and the propriety of its accounting practices. Public accountants often will show up and perform an audit after the close of a company's fiscal year and prior to the issuance of its annual report. It is the goal of every firm to receive a qualified report from a public accounting firm, verifying to stockholders, lawmakers and other interested parties that its books are clean and accurate and its accounting procedure is on the up and up.

## CHITS

Need a nutshell definition of accounting? Think of it as a process of a) recording, b) classifying, and c) reporting data, with a little bit of interpretation thrown in for the lay person. The first two are routine and often partially or wholly automated in most firms. It's the third step during which the financial professional earns his or her stripes.

In both cases, many accountants who plan to make the discipline their life's work take on the burden of becoming a certified public accountant, a legal designation that requires additional study and certification by state boards of accountancy. Extra effort also must be made to stay current with the industry by earning continuing education credits on a regular basis. CPA is an important designation and not meant to be taken lightly by those either within or outside the profession.

## MASTERING THE FUNDAMENTAL PRINCIPLES

In the end, we all apply accounting knowledge and principles to some degree in conjunction with our business and our personal lives. Money isn't everything, of course, but smart professionals never turn their backs on those areas in which money plays an important role.

Why should you master your company's accounting principles, understand the role and function financial management plays in your firm and cultivate the accountant within you? Two reasons come to mind:

- Understanding accounting basics and their application to your operation are worth the effort it takes to master them. Knowing how the flow of funds works and what things truly cost will help you better manage your expenses and more effectively pursue revenues. It's not enough merely to manage your department's finances. You also need to understand the way in which those funds and their flow affect the financial well-being and safe operation of the rest of the company. Understanding that makes you an ally, not an opponent, to your fellow department heads.

- Knowing the real cost and true worth of all aspects of your operations brings greater value to your management efforts. At the academic level, it's called *cost accounting,* the way in which we measure the true cost of producing products or supplying services to clients and customers. It's a way to measure direct and indirect costs so you have a better idea of the true worth of your efforts. Most importantly, it raises your understanding to a higher level and brings greater worth to the impact you have on your company's financial profiles.

True mastery of your discipline, whatever that may be, requires complete control of the fiscal opportunities and limitations that drive that discipline. Your understanding of finance and accounting techniques are the only way to make that happen. Take the steps you need to awaken the accountant within you.

*Answers to "Testing Your Accounting Mettle."*

1. *What is the single, most basic formula that drives the accounting equation?*

   The most descriptive phrase in accounting and financial management is: "Assets = Liabilities + Owners' Equity." That says it all.

2. *Differentiate between cash and accrual accounting. What are the advantages and disadvantages of each?*

   Cash accounting is the timely measure of cash receipts and disbursement. Accrual accounting is the measurement of accounting earnings by identifying periods of revenue and matching corresponding costs to those revenues.

3. *What is the difference between economic income and accounting income?*

   Economic income measures the unrealized changes in the market value of assets and liabilities. Accounting income measures the realized gain or loss resulting from the recording of accounting transactions.

4. *What is depreciation and how does it impact economic performance?*

   Depreciation is the accounting measurement for the consumption of a fixed asset. It can also be defined as the allocation of past expenditures to future time periods to match revenue and expense. Think of it as a noncash charge against assets.

5. *What are the three most important financial statements used in evaluating the financial well-being of a company?*

   The first is the statement of financial condition, known as the *balance sheet*. The second is the statement of revenue and expense, known as the *income statement*. The third is the statement of cash flows, known as the *cash flow statement*.

6. *What are the key components of a company's statement of financial condition?*

   These include assets (cash accounts receivable, inventory, plant and equipment); liabilities (accounts payable, accrued expenses and debt); and owners' equity (undivided earnings and reserves.)

7. *What are the most important elements of an income statement?*

   These include revenue (sales, fees and other income); expenses (salary and operations charges); and net income (revenue minus expenses).

8. *What are foundation principles of a cash flow statement?*

   These include cash flow from operations (CFO); cash flow from investments (CFI); and cash flow from financing (CFF).

9. *What is meant by the phrase, "generally accepted accounting principles?"*

   These principles, also known as GAAP, are the accounting guidelines required of firms owned or operating in the United States.

10. *What is the difference between a current asset and a noncurrent asset?*

Current assets are those expected to be converted to cash within one year and include things like cash, accounts receivable and marketable securities. Noncurrent assets, such as plant and equipment, will not be converted to cash within a year.

*It is one of the most beautiful inventions of the human spirit and every businessman should use it in his economic undertakings. It came from the same spirit that produced the systems of Galileo and Newton and the subject matter of modern physics and chemistry.*

*—Johann Wolfgang von Goethe*

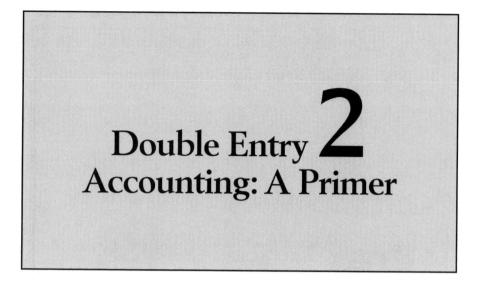

# Double Entry 2
# Accounting: A Primer

Accounting, as novices quickly discover, is much more than a series of additions and subtractions. Its mastery requires more than mere mathematical basics. The foundation of accounting lies in an algebraic equation that creates a series of checks and balances to keep your company's accounts in line.

The system, the praises of which have been sung by the poet/ scientist Goethe and others, is known as double-entry accounting. As you might guess, all transactions are entered twice—once on each side of the balance sheet, the accounting tool that displays your company's financial profile. It is the soul of your accounting system. In its simplicity one finds complex structure and application, and intellectual appreciation for the way mundane finances impact corporate and personal accounts.

Double-entry accounting quite simply helps a company balance its books, check its entries and keep true to the conceptual purposes behind its economic order. It measures the value of any transaction in the way it relates to a variety of operational functions. It records the accounting of those transactions to show its total impact on the finances of your company. Despite its complexity and the confusion it seems to cause, double-entry accounting is quite important to your company's financial well-being.

Understanding and mastering double-entry accounting is the key to your firm's financial success. No amount of effort you make toward this end is ever wasted. The net results that learning will have on the way you understand and apply accounting principles will be profound.

## ORIGINS AND CONCEPT

Exact origins of the double-entry accounting system are not known, but early application shows up in the work of the Venetian merchants of the Renaissance, who used it to keep track of purchases and sales from sea captains plying the waters of the Mediterranean. In 1494, a Franciscan monk and mathematician named Fra Luca Pacioli published the first description of the double-entry system.

A university professor, Pacioli was a contemporary of Leonardo da Vinci and worked with the artist/inventor, writing a mathematics text which da Vinci illustrated. In fact, Pacioli's dissertation on double-entry accounting and its impact on bookkeeping did not appear in any type of business or commercial text, but rather in the arithmetical part of a broader mathematical work. Whether true or not, Pacioli has been identified as the father of double-entry accounting.

No doubt da Vinci applauded the intellectual concept behind double-entry accounting, which requires that transactions be entered into financial records in equilibrium, meaning that they have the same impact on both sides of the ledger. It's this concept that gives students of finance and accounting the most difficulty when attempting to master its principles.

Despite being the core of the discipline, those without financial background may find

# CHITS

Double-entry accounting may be the soul of your financial enterprise, but accurate records are critical to saving that soul. Sloppy bookkeeping is the quickest way to undermine your company's economic success. Insist on absolute accuracy each and every time.

the concept completely baffling. Those who know the system, however, believe otherwise.

"[Double-entry accounting] organizes perceptions into a system," Goethe continues in his analysis in the novel *Wilhelm Meister's Lehrjahr*, "and one can characterize it as the first Cosmos constructed purely on the basis of mechanistic thought. Without too much difficulty, we can recognize in double-entry bookkeeping the ideas of gravitation, of the circulation of the blood and of the conservation of matter."

Perhaps, but the German poet's laudings are far from a practical description. The whole thing boils down, first, to the understanding of the concepts and terms behind transaction accounting.

## Assets, Equities, and Liabilities

Properties and items of value owned by a business are called *assets* and any rights or claims on the ownership of those assets are referred to as *equities*. The two are treated the same. For every $100 in assets, the company also must show $100 in equities. Shown mathematically, it looks like this:

*Assets = Equities*

At the personal level you might view your assets as your house and your car and your liabilities as your mortgage and your car loan. The two are intertwined and have a direct impact on one another. And each affects your personal financial profile in a specific way. So, too, in business.

Equities are divided into two separate groups as determined by either owner or

## PORTFOLIO

Accounting rules, like the periodic chart of basic elements, is something that is best memorized so that application of the principles become second nature to your accounting operation. Remember:

• On the balance sheet, assets increase debits and decrease credits, while liabilities decrease debits and increase credits.

• On the income statement, revenue decreases debits and increase credits, while expenses increase debits and decrease credits.

# CHITS

Understanding double-entry accounting is as difficult today as it was when first developed during the Renaissance or before. In his book, *An Historical Defense of Bookkeeping*, eminent accountant Henry Rand Hatfield described the double-entry system as one that was "sired 400 years ago by a monk and today damned by thousands of university students."

At least you're not alone.

creditors. Whatever is held by the owner is called *owners' equity*. Whatever is owed the creditor is considered *debt* and called *liabilities*. The basic accounting equation, now expanded, looks like this:

*Assets (Equities) = Liabilities + Owners' Equity*

In general, liabilities are shown before owners' equity because creditors have preferential rights to assets. In some cases, however, owners' equity is given a higher profile, resulting in an equation that looks like this:

*Assets – Liabilities = Owners' Equity*

Since accounting is the recording of business transactions, it's worth noting that all transactions, no matter how complex, result from changing one of the three basic elements of the accounting equation.

## Debits and Credits

From a recordkeeping standpoint, the accounting equation is most often reflected in the concept of debits and credits. These are the two sides to any company's balance sheet, which does exactly what its name implies: It helps keep the finances in balance. The debits and the credits, in fact, are the "double entries" in double-entry accounting.

The basic rule of thumb is that all debits must equal credits and all credits must equal debits. That's how the balance sheet balances. This also is shown in the *income statement,* which measures company revenue over time, and the *statement of owners' equity,* which measures the value of percentages of ownership in the firm by individuals or other organizations.

Debits and credits are most commonly reflected in what is known as the *T diagram,* so called because that's what the schematic looks like. Computers make the whole process easier, but it's still important to understand the basic concept. Debits always appear to the left of the T, credits to the right. No matter what transaction occurs, the amount of the transaction is always recorded as a debit on the left and a credit on the right. What amount you record, however, depends on how the transaction affects the debit/credit balance.

Debits and credits can't be considered increases and decreases, respectively, in all transactional cases. The accounting system is not that simplistic and doesn't work that way. Rather, the transaction patterns always manifest themselves in the following formulas:

- Debits always increase assets and expenses; debits decrease liabilities, owner's equity and revenue.

- Credits always increase liabilities, owner's equity and revenue; credits decrease assets and expenses.

Shown another way, the pattern of activity breaks down into the following diagram:

|  | DEBITS | CREDITS |
|---|---|---|
| ASSETS | Increases | Decreases |
| LIABILITIES | Decreases | Increases |
| OWNER'S EQUITY | Decreases | Increases |
| REVENUE | Decreases | Increases |
| EXPENSES | Increases | Decreases |

The pattern of increases and decreases is exactly opposite, helping balance the T diagram that frames the process. The T diagram is the most important structure in double-entry accounting.

A business perspective may help you better understand the process. Consider the following example:

Mark sells raw materials to a large manufacturing operation in the east. His contract with his clients allows for cash payment or 30 days net due, depending on the value and reliability of the client. Since Mark deals mostly with reputable firms, he almost always offers the 30-day extension to his clients. Using the T diagram, the accountant for sales at the home office records Mark's sales transaction with the delayed payment like this:

| Accounts Receivable | Sales Income |
|---|---|
| $10,000 | $10,000 |

The accountant posts the sale to accounts receivable as a debit because the account is considered an asset and debits decrease assets. The amount also is posted to sales income as a credit because credits increase income.

Once the business receives payment on that net due amount, the equation changes to show the following:

| Cash | Accounts Receivable |
|---|---|
| $10,000 | $10,000 |

Payments are recorded like this because cash and accounts receivable are both assets. The payment is a debit and a debit increases the cash account and decreases accounts receivable.

Now and again, one of Mark's clients falls into a production slump or some other form of financial hard times and Mark is required to collect on delivery of the order. What was shown as a two part transaction in the previous example now is merely one step from order to delivery to payment. A purely cash transaction is recorded like this:

| Cash | Sales Income |
|---|---|
| $10,000 | $10,000 |

The same rules apply and suddenly it becomes clear why what should be a simple transaction becomes more complex. The series of checks and balances provided by a double-entry accounting system charts the impact of transactions in a variety of ways on the financial profile of your business, helping do more than merely account for the money realized by sales and purchases.

It also helps clarify the difference between bookkeeping and accounting. The bookkeeper does just that—keeps the books on transaction activities that already have occurred. Beyond the need for accuracy and clarity in the recordkeeping process, few other skills are required. Bookkeeping is a clerical function.

The accountant, on the other hand, uses the information conceptually. Accountants are charged with interpreting the data kept in the records, drawing conclusions from the financial activity, and preparing the necessary analysis and reports for management.

Double-entry accounting is both conceptual and, as Goethe notes, mechanistic. It requires an advanced understanding of principles, but really functions as part of the bookkeeping function because its intellectual structure automatically helps balance the books if it is used right.

Our advice is to not spend a great deal of time trying to understand the algebraic clockworks involved in double-entry accounting. Instead, focus on the types of transactions and the way they impact the balance sheet. By knowing the nature of the impact, you will begin to understand the way it affects the flow of financial information through your business.

The concept may still be about as clear as mud, but its application will make more sense to you than it did before. Suddenly you'll begin to see the purpose, reason and operation with new clarity. In any event, these concepts will help you through the rest of the sections in this book.

Fair enough?

## PORTFOLIO

One of the more useful balance sheet configurations includes a third column after credits and debits that lists the running balance. The advantage to this system is that the balance is evident on any particular date at any time. Of course, your focus will stray to the regular bottom line of activity, so care must be taken to make sure the account is shown either in the proper positive or negative fashion.

*Man is a tool-using animal.*
*Without tools, he is nothing.*
*With tools, he is all.*

*—Thomas Carlyle*

# Your Accounting 3
# Tool Kit

An accountant may be considered a tradesman in the highest sense; that is, one who follows functions and uses tools to master processes. And every tradesman requires a tool kit to accomplish his or her tasks.

As this is a book that focuses on finance and accounting, we need to share some basic information to make sure we are all on the same page. However, we also have higher level issues to discuss. It's important for you to know how the system works, but we can't afford to spend a great deal of time on it. This chapter will provide four critical tools. Learn them well, because you'll need to understand their interaction in later chapters.

## UNDERSTANDING THE GENERAL LEDGER

The general ledger—that's G/L to you—is the heart of your financial and accounting system, recording all transactions that occur within the confines of the company's business. The G/L also serves as the hub around which all other transactions revolve. Any transactions entered into sub ledgers, such as accounts receivable or accounts payable, show up as part of the G/L process.

Central to that understanding is the fact that the G/L is not a single document or set of books, but an integrated accounting process in which all activities affect all other activities. Your company's G/L

23

records numerous transactions and provides reference points within the accounting system in which that data is housed. The G/L is augmented by a host of source documents—receipts, invoices, payment stubs, journal entries—all of which are an integral part of the accounting system with the G/L at its center.

All this interaction doesn't take place unless you post something to the G/L. Posting involves entering a transaction into the proper sub ledger or journal within the system and letting the results of the interaction fall where they may. When the system is automated, as most are these days, the adjustment comes automatically. That makes entry into the proper category critical. If you're careful during the posting process, your automated system will take care of you.

Of course, there are transactions posted only to the general ledger and not to individual sub ledgers. Things like merchandise returns, credit allowances extended by a supplier, asset sales, investor capital contributions, loan drawdowns and loans themselves may appear as journal entries in the G/L without posting in a specific sub ledger. Most companies do maintain subsidiary ledgers to avoid documents too voluminous to handle. But if you do choose only to post to the G/L, proceed with caution when making these additions to the books. Items carelessly posted or posted only to the G/L can wreak havoc on your accounts, knocking the whole thing out of balance. That would constitute a critical error and one to be avoided at all costs.

Setting up the G/L is a fairly simple process and consists of two parts: the balance

## LEDGER NOTES

Setting up your first general ledger? Make sure to record financial contributions from owners, partners, and investors as investments on the equity side of the balance sheet. Remember, too, to debit the cash column, since these are treated as increases in assets.

sheet, which is set up first, followed by the income statement. Both are critical tools that serve as part of the financial reporting process. Consistency in setting up these documents is important to successful accounting documentation. And documentation is one of the primary purposes of running an accounting system in the first place.

Data is added to the G/L through journal entries, a process already mentioned that is based on the provision of source documentation, such as receipts, invoices and other transaction records. No journal entry should be made to the G/L without such source documentation. Without the proper entry, payments can't be made to suppliers, nor can they be credited to customer accounts. In short, a specific financial transaction may not appear on the books, which will have a negative impact on the budget and operational expenditures of a specific department.

There's no trick to making journal entries, as long as all entries are consistent in style and information and preferably use whatever form is accepted by the accounting department. The most important issue is that all source documents be kept and available for easy access and consultation. They are among the most critical pieces of your G/L.

Another secret to successful posting to the G/L is to post similar transactions in batches. These may be transactions that cover a specific period of time, such as a day's sales receipts. They also may be transactions that cross a spectrum of similar amounts, items purchased or sold or some other logical sorting mechanism. Items are posted to a financial register then aggregated as transactions.

## LEDGER NOTES

Consider setting up a separate set of vendor files against which to cross check claims of delivery and payment. By listing all transactions with a specific company, you create a database that helps you avoid being double-billed. The files should be linked directly to your accounts payable so there's no chance for error and it should be checked monthly to enable you to better control the process and stay on top of errant vendors.

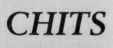

# CHITS

If you currently perform accounting by hand and plan to switch soon to an automated system, make sure the current numbering system you use with your chart of accounts is compatible with the new system's software. That will keep rekeying to a minimum.

The total is grouped by common transaction and amount, then posted to the G/L.

The bigger the batch, the easier it is for the accountant doing the batching. However, smaller batches allow for easier verification of figures when the batch fails to balance or some other need for checking exists. If your system is automated, it usually provides easy access to the items listed within the batch. Hard copy backups, especially of source documentation, are critical components of this process.

One of the most important steps in maintaining the G/L is balancing out, a process conducted periodically in which the G/L is cross-referenced to the appropriate sub ledgers to ensure continued accuracy. Revenue and expense accounts often are closed out monthly and the results reported to senior managers, board members or stockholders. Whatever the reason, balancing out these accounts on a regular basis is just good policy.

The ultimate balance comes at year-end, when it's time to close out the revenue and expenses accounts. The difference between the two accounts becomes the net income (or loss) for the year and is transferred to the owners' equity column on the balance sheet. All accounts are then zeroed out and you start the new fiscal year with a clean balance sheet.

What could be easier?

## CHART OF ACCOUNTS

Every journey—and accounting is, indeed, a journey of financial self-discovery—needs a map against which to mark its progress. As far as your accounting activities are concerned, the *chart of accounts* is that map. Moreover, it's the primary tool by which your accounting department keeps its debits and credits straight.

Specifically, the chart of accounts lists all expenditure and revenue sources in a way that makes those records easily accessible. It sorts them into pertinent categories and provides a number by which those accounts can be coded, sorted and entered more effectively into the general ledger.

The chart of accounts has three parts for every entry: an account code, a dated description, and the amount. The account code is designed to provide a numeric shorthand to code invoices, payments and other documents, as well as mesh with your automated system capabilities so that readouts of that particular description can be cross-tallied to measure impact either as an income or expense item. If your business is such that your sales force finds entertaining clients critical to making sales, for example, then assigning a specific account number to "hospitality expenses" will allow you to chart those expenses closely, better enabling you to measure their value as an investment in your sales efforts.

In addition to the account code, each item should have a date of entry and brief description to identify the expenses incurred. Knowing that a certain amount was spent to entertain clients is important; knowing where that amount was spent can help identify the time, place and client for whom this expense was incurred. This enables some careful account examination to help make sure expenses are being managed properly.

The last part is, of course, the amount spent. This completes the picture. Thus, a complete chart of account entry with detail for your company's hospitality might look something like this:

**20600       Hospitality/Client Hosting**

| | | | | |
|---|---|---|---|---|
| 9-Sept | Cecelia's | Dinner | Waxrod executives | $394.76 |
| 21-Sept | Hunt Club | Dinner | P&A Foods staff | $888.16 |
| 30-Sept | Saturn Lounge | Drinks | Service Center staff | $124.26 |
| | | | Total—Sept | $1,407.18 |

There are subsequent steps that can be taken to use the chart of accounts as a management tool as well as an accounting tool. Using the list on the previous page, you may want to assign sub accounts that further measure hospitality expenditures by a) the client; b) the product being sold; c) the type of expenditure, such as cocktails only vs. cocktails and dinner; and d) the sales associate who is doing the hosting. By creating sub accounts such as the following:

| 20600 | Hospitality |
|---|---|
| 20600-01 | Dinners |
| 20600-02 | Refreshments (drinks/snacks) |
| 20600-03 | Entertainment (please specify) |

you may be able to use sub accounts to identify whether clients require dinners or merely refreshments and whether entertainment, such as plays, sporting events and other hosted or unhosted activities, actually have more positive results on sales.

You can further subdivide clients by classifying them based on their role in your sales scenario, as in the sub account example that follows:

| 20600 | Hospitality |
|---|---|
| 20600-11 | High tech clients |
| 20600-12 | Institutional clients |
| 20600-13 | Retail clients |

Through this scenario, you may find out who is the most expensive and frequent client to entertain and measure those costs against current and potential profits to see if they are worth the investment.

Finally, the sub account system also can be used to measure the entertainment activity

## DEBITS

The biggest mistake you can make is failing to exercise discretion in setting up your chart of accounts. New accountants sometimes want to include too much detail, while those unfamiliar with the process and its purpose are happy with vague descriptions and no logical separation of accounts. Create only as many sub accounts as you need and no more. It's worth the effort.

of sales associates to see where the money is being spent and if it has an impact on the sales of that associate to those clients. Client entertainment costs are like any other business resource investment: If the return isn't significantly more than the investment warrants, then it's time to discontinue that relationship.

Your sales associate chart of accounts may look something like this:

| 20600 | **Hospitality** |
|---|---|
| 20600-51 | Joseph K. |
| 20600-52 | Mary C. |
| 20600-53 | Alex R. |

Taken together, you may have a chart of accounts that reads like the following:

**20600    Hospitality/Client Hosting**

*20600-01-11-51*

| 9-Sept | Cecelia's | Dinner | Waxrod execs | Joseph K. | $394.76 |
|---|---|---|---|---|---|

*20600-01-13-52*

| 21-Sept | Hunt Club | Dinner | P&A Foods staff | Mary C. | $888.16 |
|---|---|---|---|---|---|

*20600-02-12-53*

| 30-Sept | Saturn Lounge | Drinks | Food Svc staff | Alex R. | $124.26 |
|---|---|---|---|---|---|

In all cases, 20600 refers to a Hospitality activity. The first sub accounts—01 or 02—refer to the type of activity, either dinner or drinks. The second sub account category—11, 12 or 13—refers to the nature of the client involved. The final sub account category—51, 52 or 53—refers to the sales associate who hosts the activity.

A sort of this data may reveal over time that Alex R. has been just as successful at closing sales over less expensive drinks and hors d'oeuvres as Mary C. has been over dinners, thus saving the company hospitality-related expenditures and increasing his margin of value to the company. The same analysis might reveal that Joseph K. spends far too much time and money entertaining clients based on how his revenue figures compare to those of the other two associates. Discussion with both Mary and Joseph may help them make their time and efforts more economical and valuable to the firm.

The example also points to a basic truism that governs the establishment and management of charts of account: The detail in your chart should be just as much as you need to manage your expenses and revenue streams and no more.

Let's take the example to the revenue side. If you're a computer firm that makes 60 percent of its money selling software, 32 percent of its money consulting, 4 percent selling manuals, 1 percent selling computer covers and 3 percent managing other companies' Web pages, you may want to set up your chart of accounts as follows:

| | |
|---|---|
| **55500** | **Revenue** |
| 55500-01 | Software sales |
| 55500-02 | Consulting services |
| 55500-03 | Other activities/products |

The possible exception may come if you see one line item—say Web page development—as a fast-track item with potential for future growth despite the fact that actual amounts may be small right now. You may then want to adjust your chart of accounts as follows:

| | |
|---|---|
| **55500** | **Revenue** |
| 55500-01 | Software sales |
| 55500-02 | Consulting services |
| 55500-03 | Web pages development/maintenance |
| 55500-04 | Other activities/products |

It boils down to what is realistic for your business and your industry, with a little dash of development strategy thrown in. Too much detail and too many account breakdowns stymie the process. Too little detail and too few accounts fail to provide enough information to make good strategic and control decisions about your company's business cycle. Balance, here as elsewhere, is critical.

There are specific sorts based on the nature of the account and its cash flow that should be separated in your chart of accounts.

These include: assets, both current and fixed; liabilities, including current and long-term; owners' equity, including retained earnings; income; and expenses. Since the entries to the chart of accounts flow differently through each of these sources, incorporating this type of sorting mechanism into your program takes your company to the next level of financial management.

You might consider breaking out these critical entries into the chart of accounts in a manner similar to the following:

| Account Description | Account Number |
| --- | --- |
| Assets | 100 |
| Current | 110-149 |
| Fixed | 150-199 |
| Liabilities | 200 |
| Current | 210-249 |
| Long-term | 250-299 |
| Equity | 300 |
| Retained earnings | 400 |
| Income | 500 |
| Expenses | 600 |

Once again, by designating sub accounts for each of the attached sections, you can better manage the planning and flow of your company's financial stream.

The final step is making sure that the chart of accounts is linked to the rest of your accounting systems. Most automated systems will automatically do this. If you are operating a manual system for a small enterprise, you may have to do this yourself. In either

## LEDGER NOTES

Your chart of accounts also offers the financial history of your company. Thus, inactive or dormant accounts are still listed even though they may no longer be in use as a way to show activity that has taken place. Funds remaining in those accounts may be transferred to active accounts at the end of the year, but the account's identity may remain for some years to come. It's simply a matter of good recordkeeping.

case, the chart of accounts needs to link to the rest of the system to be effective. An entry here needs to be reflected in other components of the system, otherwise you'll have inconsistencies and, possibly, inaccuracies.

And accuracy is the single most important component of any financial accounting system, right?

## ACCOUNTS RECEIVABLE

Your G/L is made up of a series of sub ledgers that feed into the main ledger and are categorized by your chart of accounts. The most appealing sub ledger of your general ledger may be accounts receivable—or A/R—because it's like money in the bank. At least that's the theory. Accounts receivable is money owed to the company for goods sold or services already performed. The amount shows up as an asset on the balance sheet and provides value to the company against which other activities, such as loans, can be measured and leveraged.

A very small group of very small companies may be able to house this information directly in the general ledger without need for a separate accounts receivable sub ledger. But any company of any size requires a separate sub ledger to keep these amounts straight, particularly since there will be operations your system will perform that make this separation of income and assets not only preferable, but necessary.

Accounts receivable, by nature of its need for complete billing information, also functions as a fairly comprehensive record of sales and income activity. In order to be useful, the A/R should include the following information:

- the customer's name and identification information suitable to the billing process;
- a transaction or purchase description to provide necessary information to inventory or manufacturing in terms of materials or product replacement;

- the date and amount of purchase;

- the sales account to identify the general ledger account to which the transaction should be posted;

- and whether the transaction was completed based on cash payment or some other form of financial transaction.

If your firm still uses customer cards, make sure all information recorded on the card is transferred to the general ledger in a timely fashion. There's nothing worse than two sets of books that don't balance. These days, the best system is an automated spreadsheet that cross-references the accounts receivable sub ledger information to the G/L automatically so that all accounts reflect the same information.

Whether automated or manual, any accounts receivable system should reference six control points that help keep the posting and accounting for such information in line:

- Verify all A/R balances with the proper transaction documentation. All records of sales require corresponding invoices; all payments require cash receipt batches, deposit tickets or bank statements; and all credits require credit memos or other documentation.

- Record all invoice activity and remember to invoice promptly. Immediate invoicing helps better manage financial records and displays good fiscal management technique. Late or delayed

# CREDITS

Your accounts receivable should be sorted into "aging buckets," categories that indicate how long certain amounts have been due. The longer they have been due, the more attention you may want to lavish on their collection. Averaging the number of accounts and the number of aging buckets will show you how tolerant you are in awaiting payment. Don't wait too long.

invoicing does little more than delay and compromise your company's financial position.

- Make sure all invoices have been posted to the A/R by running daily or weekly tallies showing invoices compared to your posting record. They should coincide exactly. If your accounting department is multi-faceted, a section other than the one responsible for posting should run these comparisons. It's just good fiscal management.

- A good system should be able to generate a regular report on receivables that includes data on the aging of accounts, highlighting delinquencies and customers that have purchased beyond their limit. This is also the basis on which you will build your collection effort for past due and bad pay accounts.

- Even the best companies have a certain amount of credit entries to post. Your system must accommodate credits given due to payment, credit memo and journal entry. The system should also be able to address item returns, errors, amounts in dispute and, ultimately, the occasional bad debt writeoff.

- The final and perhaps most critical step is to make sure your system and its functions provide agreement among sub ledger balances, general ledger A/R balances and customer transaction records. This should be no more than a routine maintenance function.

Making entries to your accounts receivable is a fairly simple process for most systems. Each transaction is first posted to the customer's individual account. Those transactions are summarized to create an A/R sub ledger entry. The sub ledger entries are then posted to the general ledger's A/R sub-section along with any additional account information designed to offset receivables.

The following activities should be recorded in the following ways:

*Recording sales.* Invoice records—containing information necessary to form a complete record, such as transaction date, customer name and account number, item description, amount and payment terms—are always the best way to document sales. However, more sophisticated systems may keep sales transactions from appearing in the A/R until the order entry system has processed that order and generated the invoice.

Credit sales are summarized to the appropriate sales account with aggregate amounts of those credit sales batched and entered into the appropriate sub ledger account. As for the original invoices, they can be filed as part of the documentation required by the general ledger.

*Recording payments.* The amount of payments—and most are made by check—must match exactly in all forms of documentation. This includes matching into sub ledger system entries, with receipts given customers and with bank deposits made. Control totals, such as the bank deposit form, should carefully be matched with all internal documentation and sub ledger amounts. List those payments as cash and that, too, becomes a control total to keep your books balanced.

*Recording credits.* The recording of credits—credit memos, actually—acts a lot like recording payments in that they reduce the customer's balance due on any sub ledger and general ledger summary record. The entry should be made to credit the A/R and debit the original sales account. Remember that credit memos function the same as cash, so tight control should be exercised and the appropriate documentation should be required. Credits should be reviewed and approved before being issued.

*Recording merchandise returns.* Upon accepting merchandise for return, check it against description and for condition before returning it to inventory. Verify the amount in question and then credit it to the customer returning the merchandise. Then post the amount to the customer's account. This posting will reduce the balance in the A/R sub ledger with a credit; reduce the general ledger A/R account with a credit and the returns and allowances account with a debit; and increase the inventory account with a debit. Your automated system should handle this all for you in one operation.

*Managing bad debt writeoffs.* Every company has them and most companies reserve a small amount of cash to cover bad debts, unpaid bills and accounts receivable who skip town. Most likely your collections function is set up to handle bad debts that are 120 days old or more. As those accounts reach bad debt status, reduce the appropriate category as well as the bad debt reserve account by the amount of the debt.

Once you debit the bad debt reserve account, credit your A/R for the amount of the debt, since you have satisfied the amount due out of another of your company's pockets reserved for this purpose. Create the appropriate documentation to explain the debit to the bad debt account that lists customer name and number, amount, date and reason.

Bad debt writeoffs can be reinstated once payment has been made. If you're reversing a write-off entry, debit the A/R and credit the reserve for bad debt. If you're reversing bad debt expense, debit the reserve for bad debts and credit bad debt expense. And make sure you include the appropriate explanatory documentation.

## ACCOUNTS PAYABLE

In the same way there are accounts receivable—money that is owed to your company—there are accounts payable, or A/P. That's money that is owed by you to someone else for materials or services rendered to your company. Managing your A/P function is critical because it affects your credit rating and business reputation. Accounts payable offers some management options that can work to your advantage, and we'll touch on those a little later.

A/P, as you might have guessed, is another sub ledger just like accounts receivable that works in conjunction with your general ledger. There are manual A/P, and there are automated ones. No matter which you use, remember that a) A/P is supported by the appropriate documentation, in this case invoices and other demands for payment; and b) that all totals in all files and forms must match in order to keep your accounting function on the straight and narrow. As with other accounts and financial records, consistency and accuracy are paramount in A/P management.

Like accounts receivable, your A/P entries function as a transactional record. Make sure each entry contains the date the debt was incurred; the vendor to whom the debt is owed; a description of the purchase; the amount in question; the general ledger account (usually expense or assets) to which the amount will be posted; and whether this was a cash transaction or a credit transaction posted to the account.

Some companies are small enough that they operate on a cash basis, but most practice accrual accounting, a method by which financial transactions take place based on funds due in the future vs. those sitting in the bank account. In the case of A/P, accruals function as adjustment entries posted to the general ledger in anticipation of expenses to come and in keeping with the overall operational and accounting plan. As an accounting practice, this better matches income to expenses and helps your business run more smoothly.

Entries into the accounts payable sub ledger are a simple process. Purchases or transactions must be posted to the appropriate vendor account and to the accounts payable sub ledger. The summary of that sub ledger account needs to be posted to the general ledger and any other offsetting accounts. Once again, the proper documentation—such as vendor invoices—is necessary. In lieu of timely arrivals of those invoices, you may

## CREDITS

Most accounts payable systems link with a company's inventory control function. That way, when raw materials arrive at the warehouse, their financial cost is immediately posted as an amount on the A/P sub ledger and general ledger. That sets up the pattern for vendor payment without the worry of double-entry errors.

find yourself accruing the amount owed to the current period to keep it in line with offsetting revenue. That's where accrual accounting can work on your behalf.

A good accounts payable function also offers its own strategies for maximization of cash flow that is legal, ethical and within bounds of any company's accounting function. Payments should be made, not based on the date they arrive, but based on when your internal payment policy says they should be. Most bills arrive due within 30 days. Good accounting practice would dictate that those payments be made immediately prior to that 30-day limit. This enables you to use those funds for that much longer, either as leverage for some other financial transaction, as operating funds to cover other expenses, or simply allowing them to spend more time in your company's accounts and earn more interest.

The system is called "weighted-average invoice aging," and determines how old an invoice must be before the company pays it. Different types of vendors and different products may dictate longer and shorter amounts of time in terms of making payment. Your company's average weighted percent is the average time it takes to satisfy all accounts payable in all categories. That may be 30 days, 45 days or even a little longer. It's all based on internal policies, regulations (if any) affecting your industry and what the traffic will bear.

Your raw materials suppliers may demand more timely payments, while retail clients may be willing to wait. Knowing who your most critical vendors are and striking payment bargains with them may end in both a better level of service and price provided by that vendor.

One of the most critical determinants in weighted-average invoice aging are trade discounts that suppliers might offer for more timely payments. Anywhere from one to three percent may be shaved off the invoice amount for payment within 10 days rather than whatever weighted average the company normally takes. Unless interest earned on the amount or the cost of funds to run the business is greater, it makes sense to take advantage of these savings. Keep an eye out for trade discounts because they mean savings for your operation.

There are other cash management strategies where the A/P comes into play. Things like bill presentment and, especially, float strategies. We'll cover those in the next chapter.

The most important point to remember about any of this is that A/P is a money management tool, not just a bill paying function. Use it wisely and it can actually make your firm money as well as manage its outflow.

And that's what this whole topic is really all about.

*Everything in business takes longer
and costs more than you can possibly
imagine. Adjust your thinking
and your processes accordingly.*

*—Anonymous*

# From Transaction Flow 4 to Cash Management Strategies

Financial management is a series of processes that take funds from point A to point Z with as much consistency and as little variation from case to case as possible. The way money runs through an organization, and how it is accounted for in light of those systems we've already described, is known as *transaction flow*. It's not difficult to understand, but it's somewhat complicated, requiring distinct steps that need to be followed exactly in all cases in order to keep the books balanced and the flow going.

It's apparent from the outset that transaction flow is a form of funds management strategy designed to make the accounting process work for your organization. Finance departments require another type of strategy as well. That's known as a *cash management strategy*. It's how money runs to and from an organization and what a clever financial manager can do to maximize its value to the company. This is especially critical when funds don't flow evenly throughout the cycle, such as with the often seasonal nature of retail income, and cash flow must be leveraged for the sake of sound operations.

The two strategies intersect, but they don't parallel each other in process or purpose for any great stretch of the time. In fact, if you think of cash flow as a financial river—flush in some spots and dry in others—then cash management strategies would be the dams, bridges and levies designed to keep the flow constant and its value at maximum levels. The accountants and money managers are the engineers who make sure this all comes together and operates as it should, sometimes handling the "flood" of seasonal income or accommodating the dry spell that averages the flow.

That may seem a florid example, but you'll get the idea soon enough. Let's first describe the typical financial transactional flow through a company and its accounting department.

### *Transactional Flow*

- A business transaction of some sort takes place. This includes anything that affects either accounts payable or accounts receivable, anything that takes money away from the business or adds to its coffers. Things like sales, purchases, payments on accounts, debits, credits and the like fall into this category.

- Documentation of these transactions, things such as pay stubs, sales receipts, bank deposit slips, canceled checks and so forth, is passed along to the accounting department. Such documents are a critical part of the general ledger, your company's master accounting system.

- Accounting does more than merely file this documentation. Accounting analyzes each stub or receipt to see exactly how it should be accounted for and whether the transaction should be considered a debit or credit to the account. Accounting also records the account code for the company's chart of accounts so that, no matter what its balance sheet implication, it's credited to the right operation in the right department.

- Accounting creates a journal entry for each transaction, recording pertinent data in what's called *the book of original entry*. Through journal entries, accounting creates a chronology of all transactions. By including the dates, transaction description, amount and account to which it should be credited or debited, accounting has created a comprehensive transaction record tied directly to the accounting system.

- Accounting then posts the journal entry to the appropriate sub ledger and records the sub ledger reference number in the journal's posting reference column. Periodically, those sub ledger amounts are batched and posted to the general ledger.

- Once amounts have been posted to the general ledger, accounting runs a trial balance to make sure entries agree and the two sides of the accounting equation balance.

- In accrual accounting, a company operates based on a budget in which revenues and expenses are accrued to the appropriate operating period despite the presence of actual cash, whereas cash accounting requires the funds to be on hand before disbursements can be made.

  If your company operates on an accrual basis—and we'd be surprised if it didn't—adjustments must be made periodically to match revenue and expense with their proper period. Entries are made to the general ledger, bringing accounts up to date.

- At the end of each accounting period, entries are journalized and recorded to the general ledger so that the ledger agrees with the financial statements.

- Accounting follows this by preparing a worksheet to summarize credit and debit amounts for each account and calculate necessary adjustments. Accounting does this by first entering and totaling account balances in the worksheet's "trial balance" column and entering adjustments to the worksheet's "adjustments" column.

  Those balances are adjusted and entered in the "adjusted trial balance" column, the amount from which is then extended to the income statement or appropriate balance sheet columns. The income statement and balance sheet columns are then totaled. Net income or net loss is entered into both columns, the amounts from which are then recalculated to balance.

- Accounting then uses the completed worksheet to prepare the company's financial statements. Income and expense accounts are closed. Financial activity is processed, recorded and posted to the proper account and tallied. Revenue and expense totals are then posted in the proper columns on the income summary.

- Accounting then closes the balance to the owners' equity or capital account. In the case of corporations, this is called *retained earnings*. Once the amount is journalized and posted, it's checked against owners' equity as reported on the balance sheet. If all has gone according to plan, the amounts should balance.

• After any temporary accounts are closed, accounting prepares a trial balance to make sure all elements balance and the system is ready for the next accounting period. Financial statements are created and analyzed to determine the integrity and/or accuracy of transactions.

And that's it for transaction flow. But before we leave the topic, remember these three facets of transaction:

1. Every transaction either increases or decreases one or more of the elements in the accounting equation and can be stated as such.

2. The equality of the two sides of the accounting equation always must be maintained no matter what the transaction in question.

3. The company owners increase equity ("owners' equity" on the statement) with every amount invested and decrease it with every withdrawal. Owners' equity is increased by revenue and decreased by expenses.

In reality, the concept of information flow throughout your company can be seen as much more complex. Each step of nearly every process has financial implications. In the purchase of raw materials for manufacturing alone, there are a lot of individual steps that describe the business transaction that takes place preceding the movement of purchase documentation from the warehouse to the counting house. Not the least of those steps ties those purchases into an inventory management system that posts the cash value of the materials to the accounts payable sub ledger right along with posting the resources to the inventory list. You can see that going into much detail could quickly eat up the remaining pages in this chapter, as well as a good part of the next one.

Instead, we're going to devote the space we have to cash management strategies. Financial professionals know that a capable accountant can make the numbers tell any story he or she wants them to tell. But cash flow, like the river we referenced earlier, is immutable and doesn't hide the truth. Just as you understand transactional flow, it's critical to understand cash flow and the management strategies needed to successfully navigate your course.

It's also a more sophisticated funds management tool that, as we said in the previous chapter, allows you to maximize your own financial resources while still satisfying your creditors in a timely and legal fashion. Anyone—trained accountant or not—can pay the bills, and anyone can pay the bills on time and with days to spare. But a financial manager who learns to maximize the available options—including float and presentment options, not to mention obligations for liquidity—comes away with a great deal more that just a tidy balance sheet.

## DEFINING CASH MANAGEMENT

Every company needs a certain level of liquidity as a way to maximize its cash resources. But the basic thrust behind cash management is to keep the "investment" in cash as low as possible while still running the company efficiently and effectively. We say "investment" in cash because that, in a very real sense, is what it is. Cash can be invested in stocks, annuities, other business, government bonds and a range of instruments with varying rates of risk and return. A company also invests in its own liquidity needs, the return from which is the ability to pay bills, satisfy payroll and otherwise meet the company's cash flow requirements. Such investment is necessary for effective operations. The challenge, as with any other investment, is to know how much to invest. Since the financial return is nonexistent, having enough liquidity to satisfy your A/P without worry is about all you need.

English economist John Maynard Keynes identified three major scenarios under which liquidity is critical:

1. Under what Keynes described as the *speculative motive,* businesses need a certain level of liquidity to take advantage of investment opportunities and good deals that come along unexpectedly. A cheap cache of raw materials, the opportunity to open a new market or availability of some attractive real estate all might fall under this category. Companies often take care of these needs through reserve borrowing and/or selling marketable securities, but the end result is the same.

2. Under the *precautionary motive,* Keynes felt the need for a certain level of liquidity to serve as a safety net in case expenses spiked or sales fell off. However, the liquidity of current investment instruments makes this far less critical than it used to be.

3. The need to satisfy Keynes' *transaction motive* is probably the single greatest driving factor behind the need for liquidity. Simply put, companies need funds to pay bills, wages and salaries, taxes, trade debts and other costs of doing business. Again, the liquidity levels tied to certain investments, along with the rapid cash transfer abilities of electronic funds transfer systems, have muted the need for as much liquidity as companies have held in years past. Still, there is always the need for *some* liquidity.

Outside of Keynes' three points, there also may be need for some companies to hold compensating balances at the banks with which they do business for certain financial needs those businesses have. That, too, is changing, but the opportunity costs for holding cash—that is, the lack of interest income on those liquid amounts—should be kept in mind no matter how much liquidity you determine is enough for your company.

So how can you maximize those funds caught in the transaction motivation? What strategies exist to take advantage of gaps within the bill payment cycle whereby your company can earn extra and sometimes significant funds on those amounts?

## PLAYING THE FLOAT

A quick look at your personal checkbook tells you immediately that the money you know you have in your account is very different from the money your financial institution thinks you have in your account. That's because not all checks have cleared your institution even though it may be days or even weeks since you have written them out. And that's as true for your business and the checks it writes as it is for you and the checks you write.

In the case of a business, the cash balance shown on a company's books is called a *book* or *ledger balance,* while the balance shown by the bank is the *available* or *collected balance.* The amount of time between the day you write the check (affecting the ledger balance) and the day the check clears (reflected in the available balance) is called the *float.* Businesses as well as individuals can take advantage of that float if they know how to manage the time estimates within the systems affected. In the case of business, this knowledge can be very profitable indeed.

When your company writes checks, it creates a *disbursement float,* which decreases the company's ledger balance but makes no

## PORTFOLIO

Sometimes playing the float can be risky if the transaction times you estimate are not as long as you had hoped and a check appears for payment before you have enough cash back in the account to cover it. Sometimes playing the float is downright illegal. Investments made with uncollected cash can result in what might be perceived as a check kiting scheme that will result in punishment for those who do it. Cash managers should work only with collected bank balances and not the company's ledger balances; otherwise, trouble may be brewing.

change in the available balance. This condition will remain until the check's recipient presents the check for payment which, if the check is posted through the U.S. Postal Service or other delivery system, could take as long as a week getting from your office to their office. Depending on the size of the check, that could represent a sizable amount of available funds over a reasonably long float period.

If you paid for raw materials for your manufacturing process, for example, with a check for $50,000, the mathematical representation of that transaction might look something like this:

$$\text{Float} = \text{your available balance} - \text{your book balance}$$
$$= \$50{,}000 - \$50{,}000$$
$$= \$0$$

That's how it looks to your side of the operation. From your bank's perspective, thanks to the disbursement float, it looks like this:

$$\text{Disbursement Float} = \text{your available balance} - \text{your book balance}$$
$$= \$50{,}000 - \$0$$
$$= \$50{,}000$$

Until the check is presented for payment, it hasn't yet been written, from the bank's point of view. If you know how long that will take and can manage it appropriately, then those funds may be leveraged in other ways to generate other income.

This process also works in reverse. When a company or individual presents your firm with a check, it creates a *collection float*, either consciously or unconsciously taking advantage of the same cash management strategy to its advantage rather than to yours. When a check is received, it increases your company's ledger balance by the face amount. However, that amount does not increase the company's available balance until your bank has presented the check and it has been cleared by the payer's institution.

If a customer pays you $100,000 for a shipment of finished goods, and your company already has $100,000 in the bank without any float, the mathematical representation prior to the presentment of its check would look like this:

Float = your available balance – your book balance
= $100,000 – $100,000
= $0

Once the check has been received, it creates a collection float that looks like this:

Collection float = your available balance – your book balance
= $100,000 – $200,000
= –$100,000

The sum total of both the collection and disbursement floats, as you might imagine, is called the *net float*. That's the difference between your company's available balance and ledger balance. If the net float is positive, then the disbursement float exceeds collection float and its available balance is more than its ledger balance. If the available balance is less than the ledger balance, then your company has a net collection float. Knowing your float will enable you to better manage funds through the payment process.

The value of managing float comes, once again, through the gain or loss of transit costs, money not earned on income you might otherwise realize, or a delay in the payments you make. If your cash flow is substantial, then so might be your float income once you take the time to stop and figure it out.

There are three components to managing float. *Mailing time,* of course, is the time the check takes to travel from your office to the recipient's office through conventional physical transmission, such as the U.S. Postal Service or a commercial delivery service. *Processing delay* is the amount of time the receiving company takes to process your check and deposit it in the bank. *Availability delay* is the amount of time it takes for the check to clear through the commercial banking system. Any combination of these three delays can contribute to float opportunities in your cash management plan.

Let's take something as simple as your company's rent. Let's assume for this example that you pay $7,500 per month for your physical plant to a holding company in another state. Processes being what they are, the U.S. Postal Service will take four days to deliver your monthly check to your landlord's destination (mailing time). The landlord will take an average of two days to process checks and make the bank deposit (processing delay). The bank then holds your out-of-state check another two days for processing (availability delay). The total delay?

| Mailing time | 4 days |
|---|---|
| Processing delay | 2 days |
| Availability delay | 2 days |
| Total Delay | 8 days |

How much is each of those days worth? That requires some calculating on your part to determine what the average daily float would be on the $7,500 monthly rent payment that you make. The first step is simply determining the gross amount over the 8-day float period:

$7,500 rent payment × 8 day float period
= $60,000

Now, using an average 30 days to each month, divide the total float amount by 30 to get an average daily rate:

$60,000 total float value ÷ 30 days = $2,000

The average daily float on your rent, then, is $2,000 per day. That means on an average day your ledger balance is $2,000 less than your available balance. This gives you a $2,000 disbursement float and total lost opportunity cost on your rent of $16,000 (8 days × $2,000 per day.) Add to your rent any additional disbursements and receipts and calculate the daily float for each of those and you can quickly see how missed opportunity costs, from not playing the float, really can rob your company of potential revenue, or at least the use of a significant amount of funds.

The same holds true for collection floats on monies owed to you. The amounts owed compound in a similar fashion so that, while waiting for that money, you miss a valuable opportunity to leverage those funds depending on the length of the delays for mail service, processing or availability. Some financial institutions, through their collection and electronic transaction features, can help you reduce the float for a fee. Using procedures similar to those we outlined, determine lost opportunity costs based on aggregate float time compared to the fee charged by the financial institution to manage your float reduction. If the institution's fee is less, then it only makes sense to allow them to help you reduce your float and free up more cash for leverage purposes.

The rise in use of electronic data interchange—direct credits and debits to accounts through electronic paperless transaction methods—has also changed the way some companies are able to play the float. That float time between, say, payroll disbursement and when it is debited against the payroll account, has decreased dramatically with direct deposit. There is little to no float to speak of in this particular transaction, so it should not be computed as part of your float plan.

As systems improve their efficiencies, in fact, the whole concept of managing float

## PORTFOLIO

Cash concentration, combining cash resources into a smaller number of larger pools, will help streamline your company's cash management process. By mixing that concentration with the use of lockboxes—a special postal box to which payments are mailed that speeds the collection and accounting processes—you can make cash and collection management that much easier for your accounting function.

comes more into question. Is this really an opportunity for companies, given the immediacy of financial transactions? It is if there are sound management principles in place and a clear knowledge and agreement as to the average float time between you and your vendors. In all other cases, there are financial presentment strategies that provide similar opportunities that are even more efficient and effective.

Presentment strategies involve your bank or financial institution directly in managing float time, thus reducing the risk and, as a matter of fact, your company's workload to a great degree. Whereas part of managing the float was to make decisions about investments or other cash usage strategies, your bank as a business partner will now do that for you, utilizing your funds down to the last penny. You can take advantage of several cash disbursement options that may give you the leverage and advantage you seek. Here are three to consider:

- Your bank may allow you a *presentment reporting option* in which your company is required, through a separate disbursement account, to pay only those checks presented to the bank for payment that day. Funds are transferred to that account to cover those checks, usually received and reported on by noon of that day. Unnecessary funds are left in other, higher yield accounts, where they can work on behalf of your business rather than languish in wait for checks that have not yet arrived.

- Similar to the presentment account, *balance reporting* allows electronic access of the actual balance in your account via personal computer. The company accountant is allowed to transfer just as much money as necessary to pay the day's bills, with principal and interest redeposited the next day.

- The most sophisticated—and profitable—variation on this theme are *sweep accounts*. Money is placed on deposit at the bank, which then reviews the payments due at the end of each business day. Excess funds after payments are swept into interest-bearing accounts via overnight deposits, then redeposited in the company's accounts the next day. The same process occurs with excess funds; once again, they are swept into overnight interest-bearing accounts. Your company saves time and effort, pays its creditors and protects its credit rating, and earns interest compounded daily at the same time.

Anyone can deposit money into an account. Anyone can pay the bills on time. But to maximize your company's financial resources, you should be able to utilize every cent at every opportunity available to you. That, after all, is what financial professionals are paid for, to take advantage of the opportunities from which your company can significantly profit.

*Being "all things to all people" is a recipe for strategic mediocrity and below-average performance because it often means the firm has no competitive advantage at all.*

*—Prof. Michael E. Porter*
*Harvard Business School*

# Creating the Savvy Business Plan

## 5

Let's begin with a simple definition. When dealing with core competencies, it's always best to return to the basics.

In order to survive for any length of time, any enterprise needs a strategy. The word *strategy* derives from the Latin word *strategema,* familiar today as *stratagem,* and is defined as "a trick, scheme or plan for deceiving an enemy at war."

Whether or not you view your business as an offensive against the competitive forces of your industry, or some grand fulfillment of economic enterprise, matters little to this discussion. The fact is, to be successful your business needs some kind of plan to propel it forward. At the heart of that initiative is your company's corporate strategy, the specific trick, scheme or plan by which you can achieve your corporate goals and fulfill your mission.

There are various types of competitive strategies, many of which are as distinctive as the industry, company and even business unit to which they apply. At their heart, however, they all revolve around the same component. Any competitive strategy strives to establish and hold a position within its industry that is a) profitable, and b) sustainable over a long period of time against the competitive forces that threaten this position. Strategies failing to do this will lead to the failure of the business initiative they're designed to serve and, ultimately, the business unit and company that created them.

## CHIT

The core of any strategy and the heart of any business plan is the company's mission statement. It's a succinct rendering of the enterprise's goals and purposes that have been sifted, winnowed and boiled down to the strategic essence. Mission statements crystallize the company's *raison d'être*, then serve as a guiding beacon for all subsequent activities. What's *your* company's mission statement?

When asked to identify the single most decisive day of the 20th century, historians point to June 6, 1944. That was the day the Allied Expeditionary Forces invaded the beaches at Normandy, began driving the German Army back to Berlin and, subsequently, brought an end to World War II. D-Day was months in the making, but only a day in its execution. However, had Gen. Dwight Eisenhower not developed subsequent plans that took his forces beyond the beachhead and into the European continent, giving him a sustainable advantage over the competition, his army would literally have been driven back into the sea. In this case, the consequences of that failure to plan properly would have been fatal.

So, too, with business. Any strategy must move beyond the beachhead to address the long-term growth of the company and its initiatives. Failure to do so leaves the firm exposed and helpless in the face of the crossfire of competitive forces. As you establish your strategy—and subsequently build your business plan around that strategy—keep this critical thought foremost in your mind. The ability to look beyond gaining immediate market share and establishing a firm place for your product and enterprise within your industry should be the framework on which your strategy is built.

## THE KEY TO A SUCCESSFUL STRATEGY

There's another way to look at your company's competitive strategy. Think of it as your firm's *value proposition*. This, more than anything else, will be the driving force behind success or failure.

The value proposition for any product, business unit or firm—or industry, for that matter—is the definition of its ability to serve customers' needs and wants. If the cost of meeting those needs is less than the level at which customers will pay to have those needs met, then there is value for the company, its owners and shareholders.

But there must be equity on the other side of this equation as well. If those goods and services can be delivered cost-effectively to consumers at prices that maintain the profit margin while encouraging sales by providing exceptional value, then the equation is balanced and the value proposition serves both provider and consumer. Do that, and your firm will have a distinct competitive advantage and a sound business strategy.

From a finance and accounting standpoint, the impact is obvious. A sound strategy with positive implications is critical to the creation and management of your company's financial plan. The business strategy and financial plan overlay and have direct impact on the ability of each to achieve its goals. If your financial plan does not integrate with your business strategy . . . well, it may be time to start considering creation of an exit strategy because you won't be in business very long.

Finances also play a role in the two fundamental types of market strategies: cost leadership and product/service differentiation. If your position relies on being the low-cost leader in your market, your financial

## PORTFOLIO

When it comes to creating a strategy, competitive forces come into play. Michael E. Porter, a professor at the Harvard Business School and author of both *Competitive Advantage* and *Competitive Strategy* (Free Press), cites five competitive forces that can affect your business. These are the entry of new competitors, the threat of substitutes, the bargaining power of buyers, the bargaining power of suppliers, and the rivalry among existing competitors. Identify those which will have the greatest impact on your industry and watch them closely. They constitute your greatest competitive challenges.

## CREDITS

Building the financial component of your business plan requires you to identify steps that will allow you to reach your financial goals. But how do you get to where you want to go with the resources you have at hand?

- If expenses are high, look for ways to cut costs. Different industries offer different opportunities. In your case, controlled production and reduced inventory with just-in-time delivery may be one step. Changing materials suppliers may be another. More efficient use of sales staff may be a third.

- Better, more efficient use of technology can help in all areas, from production to order fulfillment to records management. If you're not making the most out of

expectations will need to be adjusted accordingly. Your company will need to move a greater volume of merchandise in order to feed its net profit expectations, which requires increased costs for greater production and distribution.

On the other hand, if differentiation is your market advantage then value, rather than cost, comes into play. Depending on the nature of your market, this may mean increased marketing costs, or the anticipation of a longer growth curve, may drive your bottom line. Your financial expectations and planning will have to be crafted to reflect this corporate goal.

Remember, however, that financial requirements help drive such goals. Need a quick influx of capital? Building market differentiation may not be the right strategy for you, since it takes effort over a longer period of time. Looking for a long-term presence with capital growth that gains momentum over time with a more profitable market life? Becoming the low-cost leader may be a strategic mistake, locking you into a sub-premium utilitarian function that will deprive you of the edge you seek.

In the end, it all boils down to the fact that your corporate strategy must be reflected in your financial goals. Building the two plans—which really are, or should be, two tracks within the same plan—is critical to your success. The financial side of the operation must be reflected in your company's strategic goals and efforts. How to build such a plan will be the focus of the remainder of this chapter.

## Identifying Your Strategy

A good strategy, whether you follow either the low-cost or differentiation scenario, is built on a foundation of competitive principles and self-awareness. Understanding your business, and the industry of which it's a part, in light of those principles could mean the difference between strategic success and market failure.

Understanding your market also is critical and so is identification of the segment(s) you wish to serve. Sometimes, by narrowing your focus to a specific segment of your chosen market, you can increase your service penetration at relatively minimal costs by focusing on the unique needs of a single service provider (small animal veterinarians instead of all veterinarians, for example). This "differentiation with differentiation" can make a huge difference in honing a sustainable competitive edge. This strategy can work very well for highly customized or expensive products and services. By distinguishing yourself as the premier provider of such products to the exclusion of all others, you may create the market edge you need.

Consider these components before you build your plan:

*1. Know thy business.* Sounds simple, doesn't it? You'd be surprised how many entrepreneurs don't understand the business they're in or, more importantly, the one they *should* be in as their market continues to evolve. Take a top-down approach and a) evaluate the industry for strengths and weaknesses;

---

**CREDITS**

*(Continued)*

the systems available, then you're wasting valuable resources.

• If revenue is dropping, look for ways to increase sales. This might include reorganization of territories, turning the sales force into commission-based entrepreneurs, improved marketing efforts and expansion into new territories.

• If your financial picture overall needs a jolt, try new ways of doing things. Try leasing rather than buying equipment, office space, or workers. Develop new products or reintroduce old ones to new marketplaces. Increase accountability by changing to a pay-for performance system.

These are the types of details that should be part and parcel of your plan.

b) identify effective competitive forces that will keep you from achieving your goals; and c) develop a strategy that meets and beats those competitors.

Consider Kinko's, which started as a quick-print service and photocopying firm for people and professionals in need of fast and cheap ink-on-paper. It didn't take long for Kinko's management to see that if a person was in need of printed materials, they might also need other basic business services such as faxing, PC availability and Internet access, and all manner of administrative support. Kinko's still prints, but it's now considered by many to be an office away from the office. The business of printing has become almost secondary to the company's *perception* as an office support services resource.

The fact that it's open 24 hours a day makes it not only the most reliable source for these services, but in some cases, the only game in town. Now that's marketplace advantage.

**2. *Know thy competition.*** Knowing the true nature of your business is critical, and so is knowing the true nature of your competition. The same rules apply when it comes to looking beyond the obvious and viewing the marketplace from your customers' points of view. That includes not only their view of your firm, but also their view of the competition.

Consider a bank that only sees other banks as competition for customer deposits, loans and investment services. If it's a community bank, then other, similar institutions may offer significant competition within the local banking marketplace. But what about large, multi-national bank holding companies that market across state lines? What about credit unions, which offer similar services, but often at a lower price?

Don't forget the mountain of credit card providers that flood customers' mailboxes by the dozens each week with low teaser interest rates. And institutions that ignore the cyberbanks proliferating on the World Wide Web—the ones that exist only electronically, thus enabling them to offer rapid-fire low-cost financial transaction services—won't be in business very long.

Truly understanding the scope of one's competition requires knowing the business you're in. Fail to do that and your business plan will fail to perform to your needs.

**3. *Know the reasons behind the way your company does that business.*** Is your company interested in cultivating the perception of quality to attract higher-level clientele, or do you produce cheap consumables in mass quantity that require volume production but lead to quick revenue growth? Knowing that will help you define the strategy critical to your firm's success. Your customers may pay extra for the time and effort you spend cultivating the next great-growth wine, but their tolerance of increased costs for a more sublime toothpaste will be considerably less. Such differentiation, of course, is not exclusively related to cost. Measure *all* aspects when making competitive decisions and deciding what niche you occupy in the business you're in.

**4. *Identify your competitive advantages.*** Every company has a few, even if it's just an entrepreneur with a brilliant idea. Find those within your scope of resources that will differentiate you from the competition and then refocus your direction to maximize those advantages. As Harvard Business School professor Michael Porter says in the quote opening this chapter, being all things to all people leads to strategic mediocrity. By attempting to hone those areas in which you have no natural abilities, you'll wind up being nothing to anyone, and that means no competitive edge whatsoever.

Some companies may find themselves stuck in the middle of a pack of competitors with no discernable advantage, either in terms of price, product or positioning. Landlocked companies will survive as long as the market is strong, but once that market begins to stumble, the faceless firms are the first to evaporate.

**5. *Identify and articulate your corporate goals.*** All companies want to grow in sales, but many fail to articulate how that growth will occur. Will you grow merely by saying you'll grow? More likely you'll grow by:

a. Reviewing and assessing the value of existing profit lines, assigning minimum performance standards that those lines must meet, and eliminating lines that fail to reach that level.

b. Identifying the company's current position within the industry in terms of gross sales, market share and growth potential and the levels at which the company sees itself within the next three years.

c. Targeting new products based on market research and methodologies to get those products to market quickly and cost effectively.

d. Basing your plans on your goals and mission. That involves incorporating your mission statement. We'll talk more about that in a minute.

True, this process takes a little time. Perhaps a lot of time. But the success level will always reflect the effort.

**6. *Identify key steps toward achieving those goals.*** These are the building blocks of your business plan, the action steps you will take to reach the goals you identified above. Every little operational step need not be identified, but the more clarity and succinctness you can bring to these steps, the greater your level of success will be.

Most importantly, your plan must articulate ownership for critical steps and processes. If everyone has responsibility, then no one has responsibility. Make sure executive and support staff realize clearly their roles and how they incorporate into the whole.

**7. *Know your mission statement, say it aloud and post it everywhere.*** Ideally, this should have been your first step, but most executives get so wrapped up in daily life that they assume an almost subliminal understanding of why they exist. Most are surprised when the true mission of the organization is analyzed.

Thus, it's practical, at least, to review the mission statement after the preliminary steps to make sure thoughts and feelings are on track. Saying the mission statement aloud promotes greater understanding and acceptance by those people who need it. What repeated recitation has done for the principles of most major religions, in fact, can work equally well for your business's goals and objectives. It can also help keep your actions on track and your company viable.

And, if you find the mission statement no longer fits what it is that your company needs to do, it may be time to change the mission.

## Units of Measure

Business plans consist of multiple steps and, sometimes, complex scenarios designed to help you reach the goals you've set. However, these are not designed to be intellectual exercises and must result in goals achieved and criteria met. Most plans contain two yardsticks by which progress can be measured:

*What financial goals can be tied to your strategy?* You may want to measure this goal not only as a whole, but also in incremental steps identifiable with each part of the plan. Individual sales goals reached or exceeded all add up to a company revenue goal, but individual goals will be more easily achieved and those responsible will understand more clearly what is expected of them.

*What is your time line for plan completion?* Like incremental financial steps, individual deadlines within the broader goal will help keep your plan moving along in an orderly and achievable fashion. Knowing where you need to be each quarter, from now throughout the duration of the plan, will help

## PORTFOLIO

One of the main reasons companies produce a business plan is to satisfy investors, lenders and other sources of outside capital whose involvement they would like to attract to their firm. Business plans are the key tool used to apply for loans, grants and other forms of funding to build or expand a business. Without a clear plan, the money sources don't know enough about a firm to make a good financial decision.

Different plans have different purposes:

• Plans that are used to attract equity investors must show ways those investors will profit from corporate success. Investors are not interested in a payback schedule; they're interested you measure progress and mark the time necessary to cover each step.

Remember the old adage: That which is measured is done. There are other methodologies for measuring progress. Time lines and financial goals should, at the very least, be part of those measurement scenarios.

The plan should also specify who is responsible for completing the steps and meeting the goals. Creating ownership of each area assigns responsibilities and develops accountabilities. Both are critical to plan completion.

## Purpose and Objectives

Business plans are the road maps by which companies identify strategic goals and the ways to meet those goals. At its best, the business plan is a distillation of days and weeks of thought and study by key players within the company and, often, outside the operational offices and cubicles that make the engine of that particular commercial enterprise run. That research then needs to be boiled down into clear goals and strategies.

Before doing that, however, planners need to identify the type of plan and the purpose for which they are preparing it:

- If the goal is to identify operational methodologies, an annual business plan is in order. Such a plan ties in well with the operating budget in identifying what the company goals are and how they will be pursued for the upcoming fiscal year. Although elements of a longer-term strategy need to be present, the key purpose of this plan is to keep the functional departments on track and make sure the financial goals are met.

• If the goal of the plan is more strategic in nature, then a three- to five-year plan is the one you need. Such a plan has many elements of operations, but its key purpose is to develop the company goals strategically over time. This broader approach is best addressed in a longer-term plan that looks at the evolution of the company, its products and goals in light of a changing marketplace rather than concentrating primarily on meeting monthly, quarterly and year-end production, sales and revenue targets.

In addition, such a plan is rarely closed-ended, but created with a rolling end mark so that, as one year concludes, the next year is added to the plan. Companies never conclude five-year plans. Instead, they use their operational (annual) plans to meet that year's goals as reflected in the five-year plan, adding another year to the rolling plan so that the company always operates with a five-year horizon. In a dynamic environment, one needs a dynamic resource. Your plan must be a constant work in progress.

## Perils and Pitfalls

A good plan requires careful construction in order to identify the right strategies and target the correct goals. But there also are perils and pitfalls that can affect a plan. Watch out for the following:

***The means is not the end.***   A plan well created can be a major strategic asset. But that plan has to exist as a living, breathing entity and its steps must be executed if its goals are to be achieved. A plan that is left on the shelf, its principles not carried out, is no plan at all.

***Accuracy is everything.***   All good plans, like all financial spreadsheets, are integrated documents. Inaccuracies within the plan—even minor ones—can cause problems through the document. Make all plan components as precise as possible and be sure all data is absolutely accurate. Even spelling matters.

***More is not necessarily better.***   Good plans gain points for inclusion of critical information. They dilute in effectiveness, however, when extraneous information is added for no purpose other than adding pages, weight or girth to the plan. Make your plan as complete as possible, but keep it succinct and easy to work with. Overwritten, bloated plans lose their effectiveness and companies refuse to wade through unnecessary rhetoric.

***Showcase management accountability.***   Make sure those using the plan understand the role management will play in the execution of plan objectives. This is especially critical when plans are used as part of the presentation to secure funding. In addition, highlighting responsibilities as part of the plan allows all involved to know who is responsible for what and holds them accountable for completion of those tasks. That often is one of the plan's most critical elements to success.

***Keep the plan objective and on task.***   Plans need to identify goals and objectives, responsibilities and measurable results. They don't need to editorialize, coerce, rhetoricize or otherwise attempt to persuade plan users through any means other than data, goals and responsibilities. Overwriting plans is the mark of an inexperienced planner and may be used to conceal failures of logic or absence of sound methodologies within the plan. Use your plan to create an operational landscape and follow the course you set through the competitive wilderness.

## WRITING YOUR PLAN

There are many ways to write a business plan and many elements which may or may not be included based on your industry, your company and its particular needs. Most plans contain the following 13 basic components:

**1. Executive Summary/Situational Analysis.** While each plan needs to be concise, it helps to front the document with an executive analysis that can, with a few minutes of reading, give executives the following information:

- An overview and explanation of your strategy: This element identifies the business by service or product; describes the company's planned direction; and analyzes the current market in light of competitive and other factors.

- Business growth and development strategies: You'll need to describe the business's current position in the market and what steps are planned to help achieve the goals.

- An overview of the organization and key personnel: Review the structure of the business and the key personnel charged with execution of the plan. Explain how the unique contributions of each will support and enhance chances of reaching the goal.

- An explanation of financial goals: What are the financial impacts of the plan and how do they leverage and affect current goals and strategies? Answers to those questions round out the executive summary.

**2. Concept.** If the summary describes the components of the business plan, the concept defines the nature of the business and its

## LEDGER NOTES

The best business plans are often found in the worst condition: dog-eared, paperclipped, wellthumbed documents that clearly have been opened and referred to time and again. The worst plans are neat, tidy documents whose pages haven't seen the light of day since they were first created. Remember that a plan is never an end in itself. A plan is a tool that must be used to be effective. Once you've created yours, don't neglect it. Use it for all it's worth.

unique position within the marketplace. The concept statement includes enough background to identify the company's purpose and unique selling proposition. Whereas the summary may deal with the breadth of the business's plan, the concept statement deals with the depth of the company's overall nature and purpose.

**3. Market/Market Segmentation.**  Knowing the company is matched or even eclipsed in importance by knowing the market for the products produced, and the market segment that the company occupies within the industry. Include enough information to allow the reader to see why the company is uniquely positioned to compete and what challenges it may face in its business execution.

**4. Customer Analysis.**  Identify the nature of the company's customers and their behavior patterns in terms of purchasing company products. Include relevant demographic data and statistics that paint a comprehensive picture of the average purchaser, along with an estimate of how many of them there may be. Include a potential average amount-per-customer sales estimate. The more comprehensive your customer profile, the more valuable this information will be to the plan.

**5. Competitive Analysis.**  Knowing your competition is as important as knowing your customer, and your plan will again need to succinctly present as comprehensive a competitive analysis as possible. Your data will be somewhat different and much of it may be unavailable or somewhat suspect depending on your source. However, if you can find parallels with other similar providers, you'll be able to chart a likely scenario that capitalizes on your company's strengths and the competition's weaknesses. This information will be critical at all phases of your development and marketing efforts.

Suppliers, too, play a role in your competitive analysis. They help drive price and availability of materials you need to produce your product. Measuring your company's relationship with them also is an important component to maintaining your competitive position.

**6. *Product/Positioning Statement.*** Positioning is the discipline that places products within certain contexts to presumably bring it value, market niche occupation and customer appeal. "The Official Airline of the Summer Olympics" is a positioning statement, designed to help the airline gain status in the eyes of consumers through its Olympic association.

Explanation of your positioning statement should describe how it will attract customers from your identified segment and describe any value-added features that such positioning will place in the customers' minds. It should also lead to a brief discussion of how that positioning will affect marketing and distribution.

**7. *Advertising/Promotion/Public Relations.*** Product positioning always guides promotional strategies, both in marketing and in public relations. This is an area where some detail is beneficial, both for the sake of the plan and for execution at a later date. Promotional investment is one of the hardest costs of any product to measure, so the more specific the plan is, the more likely it is that maximum value will be gained from your promotional dollars. Plus, it helps keep overzealous marketing efforts in line and its practitioners accountable for their expenditures.

And don't forget to evaluate your efforts in light of the five Ps of marketing: product, place, price, promotion and positioning. It's elemental, of course, but it serves as the foundation of any competitive marketing strategy.

**8. *Sales Strategy.*** Marketing and promotion investment is designed to support sales strategy, and the two components should reflect that influence in whatever plan you put together. This area also often encompasses product distribution from a *strategic* point of view, rather than an actual *fulfillment* schedule. Where you place your product and how you display it should be part of a distinct sales strategy. And that strategy needs to be reflected in this plan.

**9. *Next Steps Toward Continued Product/Market Development.*** What steps does the current plan take toward setting the stage for the next level of development? Remember, even if this is an annual operational plan, it will need strategic elements built within that will allow you to move to the next phase of your rolling three- or five-year plan. Your actions this year should set the stage for next year and the years to follow.

**10. *The Operations Side.*** How you do what you do is the focus of this section. An operations analysis may include everything from research and development to materials purchasing to warehousing, distribution, sales and collections. Keep in mind this is not an operations manual for your company. However, inclusion of key points, especially where they support the strategic initiatives, is valuable for a well-rounded plan.

**11. *Key Staff.*** Identify key executives and specialists that will make achievement of your plan's goals possible. Personal qualifications and appropriate background are helpful in creating a comprehensive document that can be used to attract outside funding. Once again, stress ownership of process and progress and hold those responsible accountable for success.

**12. *Financial Statement.*** Any good plan contains a comprehensive snapshot of the company financials, as well as an explanation of how the plan will affect them, both positively and negatively. The purpose of the plan most likely is to reduce costs and increase sales, so the anticipated impact of those efforts makes inclusion of a financial statement critical. A pro forma financial statement and scenario analysis are important components.

**13. *Payback and Exit Scenario.*** Once the goals of the plan have been achieved, how will owners and investors receive compensation? A payback and exit plan, usually targeted as the proposed date the company goes public, is a critical part of the plan whether it's being used to raise funds or merely as a report to investors. Outline those steps in your plan before you're asked and the plan will be viewed with greater trust and appreciation.

Even if your plan isn't used to raise funds, remember that an effective business plan is created for the benefit of the company, its owners, employees and shareholders. Done correctly with care and with a comprehensive approach, your business plan will mean controlled costs, increased revenues and better operating procedures for your company.

*The brain is a wonderful organ: it starts working the moment you get up in the morning and doesn't stop until you get to the office.*

—Robert Frost

# Establishing an 6 Accounting System

Accounting, as we've already defined it, is a financial information network that allows you to follow the progress of your company and manage its fiscal outcome through an organized and recognized series of financial steps and strategies. Taken at its broadest terms, this network of information and processes is your company's accounting system, the vehicle by which you report financial progress to owners, creditors, lenders and other interested parties.

While all companies differ, general accounting principles are the same no matter what the size or scope of the operation. You will need to tailor the sophistication and output of your accounting function to the nature of your business, but you'll be building on a framework similar to the ones used by IBM, General Motors and the United States government. No matter if you're an international conglomerate or a one-man band, you still need an accounting system in place to manage your finances and make sure you are fiscally capable of meeting and supporting the goals outlined in your strategic plan.

Presumably your company has some type of accounting system in place. But whether you want to give your current financial engine a tune-up or start from scratch, there are some questions you'll need to ask yourself and issues you will want to consider. First and foremost, your accounting system should be able to provide fair assessment of your firm's financial condition. Depending on your business, these issues may be many and varied, but they will at least include the following:

## *PORTFOLIO*

Good accounting systems provide management with the information they need to run the company. They also offer a logical and applicable series of procedures that enable those responsible to keep a close eye on what's happening within the firm's finances. When you put together your accounting system, you must include provisions for the type of internal controls you'll need. We'll discuss that at length later on.

- Size your accounting system to meet your management needs. Accounting systems can be as involved and complex as you want to make them. Be sure the one you set out to create offers cost-effective accounting solutions for your business. It's a delicate and important balance, but if you spend money to create accounting reports you don't need, then you've violated the entire purpose of the system.

- Keep your system flexible enough to meet the challenges and changes within your industry. Business is nothing if not dynamic and your accounting system needs to be adaptable in light of government regulations, changes in accounting principles and organizational adjustments required to meet competitive factors within the marketplace.

- Your system must provide adequate internal controls to help management monitor internal operations and keep the financial affairs of the business legal, safe and above-board.

- Since reports are the heart of accounting system output, yours must provide documents and data adequate for the company's needs. The scope and size of reports should be tailored to the size and needs of your company, but they should meet your financial information needs and requirements as part of your overall management information system.

- The system should be adaptable to the internal needs of the organization, including the human resources affected by those processes. Adaptability is the best (and sometimes the only) way to meet the company's needs at the lowest possible cost.

## INSTALLING YOUR ACCOUNTING SYSTEM

Like all operating systems, your accounting system will need to be installed before it can be put into play. But before it can be installed, it will have to be customized to fit your business and its existing procedures. This means that whoever is implementing the installation will have to know the business well enough to create a system that makes sense for current needs as well as setting the stage for the future.

And that "whoever" should consist of a team from across several management disciplines and operational levels. Your accounting system does not exist in a vacuum but has an impact on all phases of the company's operation. A team installation effort will aid understanding, application and acceptance of the system, making the system and the people who use it that much more effective.

But your system should only be installed if there is equal recognition that somewhere down the road, that system will need to change. As we said, the marketplace is dynamic and no business today can afford to be stagnant. So, too, with the systems by which it operates. Things will change, affecting the efficacy of the system you have put in place. Moreover, there are needs you will have in the near future that you may not realize right now.

This need for flexibility also will help determine the software you're using and its adaptability to change. Information technology—IT in today's parlance—has become a discipline unto itself. But it also plays a vital role in automating the accounting function. In many cases, in fact, the company's chief financial officers supervise the IT function because it is both critical and costly to the organization. Make sure your information system will do what you need it to do before you invest the time and effort on installation. The same holds true for your automated accounting system.

**CHIT**

---

The accounting system itself must be sound since it represents the heart of the organization's financial system; but it also must be able to produce useful and complete reports. It's only through those reports— which provide detailed information on specific aspects of the accounting function—that managers and executives are able to use the information the system has stored and computed to make good strategic decisions.

Install your system, but realize that sooner or later you will need to go back in and revise that system to keep pace with organizational changes. That doesn't mean you've made an error in designing your system; rather, that you haven't made an error in failing to include the necessary flexibility.

In most cases, accounting system installation consists of three steps:

*1. Analysis.* As a first step, systems analysis is used to determine company information needs, sources for that information and problems with the procedures currently used. This starts with a review of the organization's structure, its personnel and descriptions of how they perform the functions in question. Analysis also includes the study of records, forms and procedures. The purpose, of course, is to detect shortfalls and soft spots within the system as the first step toward their correction.

As part of this analysis, you'll need to study the accounting transaction flow through the organization (which we discussed in Chapter 4) and the type of reports you'll need to generate, which we'll touch on later in this chapter. Like the rest of accounting, all the pieces link together. Setting up the right kind of system components that interact the way they should and generate the information you need in the style you want is critical.

*2. Design.* The results of that analysis will lead to the creation of the system design, or perhaps a redesign of the current system. There may only be minor changes; or there may be a complete overhaul depending on the severity of the issues uncovered. Since so much of accounting has become automated, designers will need a reasonable level of knowledge about the data processing systems the company uses, the accounting regimen the firm prefers, the type of data available, and what a successful system might look like.

**3. *Implementation.*** The final stage is to implement the new accounting system's design based on information gathered during the analysis phase. Old, ineffectual procedures must be done away with and new methodologies pursued. In the case of larger companies, this may include scrapping the entire AP system in favor of one that will meet these newly defined needs. It all depends on what your analysis turns up and your designer recommends.

## ASSIGNING STAFF

A good system requires capable staff to run it. The need for technical competency, obviously, is very clear, but there's also a need for basic honesty and integrity. That, too, might seem obvious but always bears repeating where numbers, finances and accounts are concerned.

Adequate training and supervision are primary requirements for any accounting staff.

## PORTFOLIO

Good accounting systems have two types of internal controls:

- *Internal administrative controls* are procedures and records that aid administration in achieving its business goals. These would include any control mechanisms that control the business quantitatively, such as production line reports, factory safety figures, and such.

- *Internal accounting controls* consist of procedures and data that focus on financial records and reports. These would include any control mechanism designed to assure accuracy in financial recordkeeping.

*PORTFOLIO*

*(Continued)*

The presence and prevalence of internal controls will depend almost entirely on the organization. Smaller companies in which the owner has direct access to operations probably need fewer such controls than larger firms with a complex bureaucratic structure. All firms need some level of control, however. Size yours according to your needs. And make sure they support the company's strategic plan.

This is true of support as well as professional staff. It's advisable to rotate clerical staff among similar jobs throughout the department as part of your training scenario and internal control scheme. First and foremost, it broadens their cross-training opportunities and increases their understanding of the function and its various component parts. Moreover, because it requires that they maintain a learning edge to their daily jobs, it also discourages sloppiness that comes from over-familiarity, and cuts down on deviations from the prescribed operations so critical to accounting accuracy.

As part of this training, remember that good accounting practices grow from consistent procedures. Your accounting procedures manual—yes, you must absolutely have one—offers the opportunity to train employees consistently, maintains accuracy of transaction and holds staff accountable for their actions.

As part of staff's basic management, the supervisor should clearly define their jobs and their roles within the department. Any overlap of duties, particularly when they involve money, should be clearly identified and each individual should be held accountable for his or her particular part of it. It's part of management's role to make sure this happens.

One of the most important methods of helping employees remain ethical and honest and improving operational functionality involves the splitting of those functions that have several identifiable steps among several employees. This reduces the possibility of fraud, conflict of interest, inefficiency and error. It also provides an internal checking mechanism by which processes can be cross-checked prior to errors occurring. There's benefit to this for even the simplest tasks.

Take a simple bank deposit for example:

- For the sake of the business and all involved, one person should tally the checks, cash and coin and create a deposit slip.

- A second person should periodically cross check by counting the deposited amount for verification.

- A third person should note the deposit in the general ledger.

- A fourth person should make the deposit and return with the deposit slip, which should be cross-checked against the tabulations and G/L entry.

If that's too complicated or requires more staff than you have to spare, simply remember that the person who handles the money should not do the monthly reconciliation. No matter how trustworthy your employees may be, an auditor will question all aspects of your operations if you violate this one simple and easily managed precaution.

That seems like a lot of people to make a bank deposit. You may want simply to alternate the tasks listed above among several employees. If you do, plan on rotating those involved with the overall assignment from time to time so the same person is not always allowed the same critical step in the process.

# CREDITS

Learn to use your staff effectively to support the accounting system and its operation within your company. Proper adaptation to both the human resources and system structure will help you accomplish your goals at the lowest possible cost while still operating effectively.

Keep in mind this is not a question of staff honesty, but rather a procedural issue designed to improve operational efficiency. Your books are subject to audit and the auditors will question any procedures that fail to show reasonable safeguards. Your tightly wound security measures protect everyone involved from falling under suspicion should something turn out wrong.

In the same way, general operations should be separate from accounting procedures, and so should the responsibility to maintain records for both functions. In fact, accounting records should serve as an independent check on business operations. Employees who handle cash receipts should not be the same as those given access to make changes in journal reports or the general ledger. Once again, the possibility for error, fraud or both can be minimized through this strategy.

The ultimate protection of accounts and funds, of course, comes through the performance of proofs—verifying the amounts within the accounts—and formalized security measures. More than any other department within your organization, security plays an important role. Cross-referencing, as we said, is an important part of this function.

It's as simple as the lowly cash register receipt, which allows the customer to cross-check the amount charged against the listed price of the item. That amount is entered into the cash register's memory (if it's automated) and then used in aggregate to verify the amount that should appear in the cash drawer.

If the register is linked to a network, the item is often deducted from the overall inventory, which has already been verified against delivery records. The deduction from inventory creates a debit against the posted value of the item, which is entered into the appropriate report on the general ledger. It's all part of your company's accounting flow. By the time the customer is walking out the door with the purchase, its entire history as well as its full financial impact on the company, has been automatically referenced, cross-checked and posted.

Internal controls are an important part of any accounting system, and we'll talk about them in greater depth in a later chapter. Internal audit mechanisms are the key to managing such controls, whether they come in the form of employee- and management-driven efforts or audits performed by separate internal auditors. It's the auditors' job to make sure both procedures and results line up with what's expected. Despite their sometimes threatening nature, auditors are an important part of the safety and soundness equation.

## TYPES OF ACCOUNTING

There are a variety of types of accounting, some of which we've already discussed. Here's a more comprehensive list because it helps to be familiar with the differences:

- *Financial accounting* is the recording of transactions for business and as part of any economic unit. The process generates reports for use as management tools and is expected to adhere to generally accepted accounting principles, also known as GAAP. Corporate entities are required to use financial accounting procedures to prepare their annual reports and their profitability and financial status for shareholders.

- *Managerial accounting* uses historical and estimated data to manage daily operations and plan managerial needs accordingly. Unlike financial accounting's broader scope, it deals with specific issues and alternative courses of action. Managerial accounting takes place at the department level and often falls

## DEBITS

When it comes to financial professionals within your company, the worst mistake you can make is to confuse accounting with bookkeeping, a sin that is rarely forgiven.

- A *bookkeeper* is responsible for recording business and transaction data in a prescribed manner and according to established rules. In many companies this is a clerical position and one that increasingly is being replaced by automation.

## DEBITS

*(Continued)*

• *Accountants* direct
and review the
work of those
bookkeepers, de-
signing the sys-
tems in which they
work and utilizing
the reports they
produce. Some ac-
countants for
smaller organiza-
tions may actually
do some book-
keeping work, but
this is quickly be-
coming the excep-
tion rather than
the rule.

under the supervision of the company's
CPAs and accounting department
liaisons.

• *Tax accounting,* as you might imagine,
deals with tax preparation and recording and consideration of improper filing
procedures. This requires a special body
of knowledge regarding federal and
local tax requirements and is considered
an accounting specialty.

• *Budgetary accounting* presents the financial plan through a certain period of
time. Sometimes considered part of
managerial accounting, budgetary accounting compares actual operational
totals with the predetermined plan.

• *Social accounting,* both more esoteric
and strategic than standard accounting
practices, measures the financial impact
as based on demographic trends and activities of specific population segments.
The financial actual and planned impact
of changing traffic patterns within a city
is social accounting. So are changes in
workforce makeup and income as well
as the general social migration of different population segments and what it
might mean to civic operational costs.

• *International accounting* deals with international business and requires a comprehensive knowledge of the financial
and social customs of the countries and
population segment's with which the
company is doing business. This includes a knowledge of the country's

laws, tax scenarios and general accounting principles.

## Cost Accounting

One of the most significant types of specialty accounting is cost accounting—the attempt to accurately determine and control all costs related to a business function. This is particularly important in a manufacturing setting, where a wide variety of fixed and variable direct and indirect costs add to the true cost of producing merchandise. By considering all these costs in the financial profile of an item, a company can price more accurately and earn greater profits overall. Cost accounting is, quite simply, critical for the survival of some industries.

The basis of cost accounting is perpetual inventory procedures, which measure all aspects of production from acquisition of raw materials to the production and distribution of merchandise. Controlling accounts and subsidiary ledgers are maintained for materials, works in progress and finished goods in these systems. The balance in each account reflects inventory on hand, no matter how that inventory is defined.

All expenditures that are part of the manufacturing process begin in a work-in-progress account, then move to the finished-goods account. Eventually they enter the cost-of-goods-sold account. It all seems somewhat complicated and unnecessary to some. But the value of the merchandise changes as it moves through the production cycle and the

### PORTFOLIO

Cost accounting takes into account both direct and indirect costs for materials and labor. In automobile manufacturing, direct materials costs would be the steel used in the body, the rubber in the tires and the glass in the windshield. Indirect materials would be the utilities that run the lights and heat in the manufacturing plant, the grease and oil that lubricate and fill the machinery necessary for assemblage, and other related materials that do not end up in the car itself.

Direct labor would involve the assembly line workers and their immediate supervisors.

PORTFOLIO

*(Continued)*

Indirect labor would be time spent by human resources filling the assembly line positions, the accounting staff that does the cost accounting during production and the executives who oversee the entire factory.

The lesson to learn here is to account for all components in the manufacturing processes in order to understand the true cost of production.

value of those changes must be reflected accurately on the company's books. Remember, those books must reflect accurately the value of the company. As the manufactured merchandise moves through the production line, it increases in value which, in turn, increases the company's value.

Cost accounting systems are further broken down into two basic types. Both systems are widely used and whether one is better than the other depends on your type of operation and your accounting department needs.

The *job order cost system* provides a separate financial record for the cost of each quantity or product that passes through the factory's production line. Industries that manufacture to fill special orders or produce different lines of product for stock are the most likely to use the job order cost system. Batch production of products also is accounted for in this way. The costs incurred in completing a manufacturing task would look something like this:

**Special Order AB12 (500 units)**

| | |
|---|---:|
| Direct materials cost | $9,666 |
| Direct labor charges | 13,054 |
| Industrial overhead applied | 2,550 |
| Total cost | $25,270 |
| Cost per unit | $50.54 |

The *process order cost system* is best used for companies that produce a continuous line of merchandise, products that are created in mass quantities and not necessarily distinguishable from each other. Costs are gathered by department or process and accounted for in that way. Rather than charging individual job orders direct and indirect materials and labor, the costs are charged by departments and then divided by the number of units produced to determine the cost per unit.

Thus, the production of, say, automobiles becomes a series not of products, but of assembly line procedures that are measured by the number of units passing through that procedure. Accounting for the brake drum assembly in an automobile assembly line, for example, would look something like this:

**Brake Drum Assembly—Work date 12/31/01**

| | |
|---|---|
| Direct materials cost | $16,500 |
| Direct labor | 24,610 |
| Industrial overhead applied | 8,450 |
| Total cost | $49,560 |
| | |
| To Axle Assembly Dept | $49,560 |
| Cost per unit: $49,560 / 500 = $99.12 | |

Either cost accounting process works, but one may work better than the other. Choose the one that's right for your type of operation.

*Actually, I have no regard for money.*
*Aside from its purchasing power,*
*it's completely useless*
*as far as I'm concerned.*

*—Alfred Hitchcock*

# Building a Better Budget 7

Accounting processes, for those who don't practice them every day, may seem vague at best and sometimes appear diabolical to managers without the proper background and training. Despite appearances, all of the various accounting steps exist for a reason and are part of an inter-related process that leads to sound financial management. The biggest challenge often comes in applying the theoretical to the real, and that's where many a manager has hit the wall.

Understanding and applying the budgeting process will help you understand the application of other financial principles. The operating budget serves as the link between theory and reality. And, quite honestly, it's the way most managers are introduced to the accounting process within their organizations.

Budgeting also is a strategic link between your department and the goals of the company. You don't exist in a vacuum, but are part of the company's overall operation. Just as your management style must coexist peacefully within the operations and guidelines of company policy, your financial strategy must make sense within the context of your company's master plan. That makes a sound departmental budget critical to operations at a variety of levels.

This chapter will walk you through the basics of budgeting while taking a broader, more strategic view of the process at the same time. Managers who have the ability to master the concept at both levels will gain not only better financial control of their departments, but will also play a more valuable role in determining their firm's destiny. And that's always a good investment in your own professional development.

## THE BUDGET:
## DEFINING THE CONCEPT

If you're already managing a department, or even if you're just managing to spend less than you earn, you have the rudimentary skills and the basic applications experience to create and manage a budget. You may have established your first personal budget by banking your babysitting money or keeping close tabs on paper route earnings. We've all been exposed to budgeting to some degree and we all understand more about the underpinnings of good budget development than we may think.

From a business perspective, your department's budget represents a blueprint of action, a statement of your plans for the future represented in financial terms. From your position as area expert, do you see a bull market ahead? Are there steps to climb before reaching that next sales plateau? Will the competition send you back to the drawing board for newer and better ideas and products? All that information is reflected in a departmental and company budget, and it's all plainly accessible for those who know how to find and use it.

Although time period and start dates may vary, 12 months is the most common cycle and the most practical time frame for budgeting, with 24 months popular in some

### BY DEFINITION

What is a budget? Webster defines it as "the cost or estimated cost of living or operating during a prescribed time period." Accountants see it as a formal statement of management's plans for the future expressed in financial terms. Both are correct, and both are budgeting.

industries. The annual budget covers all four quarters of a company's operating year and conveniently correlates with the tax cycle. In today's dynamic business environment, anything too much longer is wishful thinking at best. And shorter time periods lack the perspective needed to judge the rough spots in the road that may lie ahead.

However, the budget may be divided into shorter components to better manage the flow of funds or the development of new products and strategies. Most companies assess budget performance on a quarterly basis and some do it weekly if funds availability or some other factor requires more frequent examination. Subdivision doesn't change the nature or need for an annual blueprint, but it does offer tighter control when it's necessary.

Most businesses operate with two budgets. The *capital budget* pertains to fixed assets and measures the worth and financial evolution of higher-ticket items such as real estate, computer systems and other major equipment, expenditures and purchases. The *operating budget* measures the actual cash flow activity of day-to-day operations. From a manager's perspective, this is the more critical of the two budgets because this will impact your cash flow and affect your ability to do things within your department.

Your personal budget may be designed to keep you just ahead of your creditors or it may be sophisticated enough to include an investment component with an eye toward building reserves for future use, such as retirement or a major purchase. Business budgets tend to be a little more complicated than those you mastered when counting quarters from babysitting jobs, but the philosophy is very similar.

Departmental and company budgets predict sales, investment revenue and other earnings (income) along with production and operating costs (expense). The difference between the two is the estimated profit or loss of a product line, a department or the overall company. In addition to its strategic component, the budget is the tool by which you can predict those numbers, enhance revenues and reduce expenses. The budget mirrors the company's strategic goals, providing a clear expression of the financial effect that those strategies may cause. And it helps set the goals for revenues and/or expenses as well as determining accountability for meeting those goals.

## LEDGER NOTES

Cost control is a major facet of budgets and a major responsibility of departmental managers. It's one of the first budgetary components a manager learns, but does little good if the manager hasn't had a hand in drafting that budget. All those responsible for managing a department's finances should have a hand in developing its budget. They'll feel greater ownership about both process and result, and will be more effective in implementing the plan they've helped create.

Your budget is that simple in concept, and that critical in application.

### Budgeting: What's My Type?

Budgets, as a part of the business planning process, come in several makes and models, each with its own specific purpose. Long-term budgets, which evaluate and set financial goals for a longer window of five to 10 years, are considered strategic budgets and operate as part of the company's overall strategic plan. Short-term budgets of roughly one-year's duration or less reflect the financial side of operational goals and have more direct application to day-to-day activities. Most operations have both types of budgets. Smart managers review them regularly—sometimes continuously, depending on business conditions—and adjust them periodically as needs arise.

The short-term budget is what most managers expect to master first because it most directly relates to their core responsibilities. Its outcome is also more easily predicted. Designed to measure a year of production and earnings, it's a key controller of the ups and downs of operations and allows for adaptations in expenditures designed to increase revenue or reduce expenses.

The fact that the budget covers a 12-month time frame gives it somewhat of a strategic nature, allowing you to take both a proactive and reactive approach toward preserving a positive bottom line, if that's your goal. But its primary purpose is to anticipate and react to business changes within the coming year.

Longer business cycles require a longer term budget to reflect their growth and anticipate changes over time. Most basic business operations run their courses within the standard budgetary year. Most strategic initiatives unfold over a longer period of time and often are the result of several years' worth of short-term growth initiatives. The long-term or strategic budget interacts at a higher level with your company's strategic goals, tracing a much longer financial profile that reflects those long-term goals.

The strategic budget plays a very different role from that of the operational budget. Its numbers may appear more general and less precise in their units of measure. Together the two budgets provide a necessary and more comprehensive approach to financial management critical to long-term success.

Not all companies may want or need a strategic budget. Many operate just fine budgeting from year to year, applying what they've learned to the following year's operational budget and thus creating a satisfactory strategic component within the context of their annual operational approach. Yours may be just such a company. If so, be thankful that your life is that much simpler.

However, if your company:

- is involved in major capital acquisition strategies that result in depreciation scenarios carried out over periods of years;

- pursues extensive research and development activities that result in incurring years of expense before realizing one red cent of revenue; or

- has significant building and development plans, the results of which will be extensive capitalization scenarios and amortization of expenses over a long time frame;

then a strategic budget not only may be more appropriate, it may be critical to the successful execution of any or all of those strategies.

By its very nature, the strategic budget identifies and measures the financial impact of long-term strategies on the company's economic well-being. What's good in concept ultimately may be bad for business. The strategic budget is the barometer by which those decisions can and should be made.

## Setting the Stage for Budgeting

The act of budgeting appears to be a simple one: the manager identifies (or is given) financial goals for his or her operation; estimates basic expenses to accomplish these goals; and puts the two opposing forces (revenue and expenses) into a spreadsheet, hoping that the first guess is the best one. Usually, it isn't.

Successful budgeting relies less on the spreadsheet exercise and more on the thought and planning that goes on prior to any numbers being crunched. It's the issues beyond the numbers, rather than the numbers themselves, that govern the creation of a successful budget. Consider the following questions before you sit down with your calculator and/or PC spreadsheet:

***What goals will my budget and those of the other departments reflect?*** Because "profitability" is a key component to most businesses' success, that may be the single driving factor. But profitability isn't always defined as short-term capital gain. More often, profitability falls under the heading of current client service and future market share growth, including new product development and new customer acquisition. Expenditures this year in pursuit of higher goals next year will definitely affect short-term capital gain. But that investment may make better finan-

## DEBITS

The key to budgeting, like the key to life, is to keep all things in balance. Managers who budget to keep costs low may not invest enough development dollars into the expense side of their budget to realize revenue goals. Cutting essential costs to have a good bottom line on paper is not an effective way to budget.

cial sense and be more in line with company goals in the long run than concentrating on short-term profit.

**Will company objectives be plainly visible in my budget?** Remember that a well-articulated budget contains clear representation of goals and methodologies specific to your industry. Broad-brush growth in a short-term budget does little to aid those who need to understand or to pursue that growth. If the objectives of your budget match the goals of the company, then those goals should be clearly evident, thus more easily achieved. That makes your budget more of a strategic tool and less of a mere recitation of numbers.

**Does my budget identify tactics by which those objectives will be achieved?** If the budget is well-articulated and prepared with organizational goals in mind, it will also include a financial reflection of the tactics by which you will reach those goals. If your department's goal is increased market share, then the results of that increase will be reflected in projected revenue for that business segment. It's likely, too, that there will be corresponding marketing expenses, as well as some possible R&D costs for refining or adapting products to meet the needs of that market share. Evidence of such tactics contributes to the budget's strategic nature while enhancing its role as the tool by which these objectives will be accomplished.

**Has my budget outlined the procedures necessary to achieve the goal?** Remember that procedures are to tactics what objectives are to goals. If the overall goal is market dominance for the product you produce, the objectives likely will be to establish footholds in the various niches that comprise the market. Your tactics, then, will focus on ways to penetrate and ultimately dominate those niches, as well as ways to knit them together for the full market dominance you seek. Your procedures will be the steps by which those tactics are executed.

If your company produces pencils, your goal may be to dominate the public school market throughout the U.S. Your objective, then, would be initial percentage penetration in all major public school districts, followed by second- and third-tier penetration based on the size of the district and potential pencil consumption. The tactics would measure key components, such as quality, price and packaging, and determine the best balance of all three. Once the proper ratios have been determined, subsequent steps would include producing the product to the appropriate specification, outlining the sales and marketing strategy, and delivering the product to those markets within the time frame and via the method that provides the highest level of customer satisfaction, thus the greatest potential for income.

Can your budget measure all that? It will if you take the right approach and bring the right level of awareness, information and understanding to the budget-creation process.

## BASIC BUDGET COMPONENTS

This may seem rudimentary, but it's important to note that all budgets, strategic or operational, contain two basic categories: revenues and expenses. It's your job as manager to learn these sections fully and come to know their implications completely. It can be as important as memorizing your children's names. (Well, almost.)

Traditional budgets first show the revenue, including income from sales, investments, sponsorships, licensing fees and any other sources. Sales revenue is generally the most significant and most important.

Revenue should be divided into key product lines or sources with an eye toward understanding the impact of those sources without

## BY DEFINITION

Your budget comprises numerous components, but its physical manifestation most often is seen as the financial statement. It's also reflected in the income statement and balance sheet. Generally developed on a spreadsheet, the financial statement displays budgeted and actual revenues and expenses for one or more years and serves as a snapshot of your financial condition at any given time.

drowning in the minutiae of listing acquisition methods. Keep your income lines clear and understandable, but divide them into logical, reasonably-sized components. In most cases, revenues will be the higher of the two bottom-line numbers, particularly if the company wants to continue operations.

Our pencil company would show earnings primarily from basic product sales. It also might show income from franchise fees paid for distribution rights granted in certain areas of the country. If the pencil brand were ever to become a household icon and its name and image used on other products—much like the Crayola Crayons brand—then licensing fees for this image also would be counted in this category.

The other part of the budget focuses on the expense side and accounts for all the costs of all the steps and materials necessary to produce, market and distribute those pencils. Included in expenses would be manufacturing and raw materials costs, marketing and sales expenses, and distribution costs. Sales commissions, executive salaries and any kickbacks to school districts for allowing the placement of the product also would be noted here.

The budget measures revenue and expense expectations—what the company thinks it will earn and what it thinks it will spend in the production and distribution of pencils at the level necessary to achieve its financial goals. Revenue should balance against expense with a net margin that reflects the company's earnings objectives. With rare exception, a company that doesn't budget for greater revenue than expense won't be around very long.

## CHIT

Different strategies for different companies and types of budgets exist and yours likely will coincide with what your firm expects of your department. If you lack a strategy, one of the most rudimentary is to budget expenses at the high end of its projected range and budget revenues at the low end of its range.

Presumably, you've already budgeted with a positive bottom-line margin in mind. By sticking to the far end of each respective range, you've

And you can't make up a negative margin in volume, either.

## Top-Down Budgeting

The art of budgeting is an exercise in logic and hope, realism and optimism. It begins with an industry analysis, market share evaluation and sales forecast. Different components can be accumulated and plugged into the appropriate spreadsheet when and where you find them. However, many companies pursue a more strategic approach to budgeting based on goals. They tend to create the following budget components in the following order, adjusting each to accommodate the needs of the other:

- The *sales budget,* which comprises the lion's share of revenue for most companies, usually comes first. This is the revenue component that serves as the foundation on which other budget components are based. The sales budget usually includes the quantity of forecasted sales of each item and the price of that item. The data is then sorted and classified by sales area or representative, with the past year's data included somewhere for comparative purposes. The past year's actual or projected sales are the starting point. Company goals, mixed with marketplace realities, drive the amount by which this number will increase or decrease. The amount of back orders, competition and remaining product in the warehouse will affect this number.

**CHIT**
*(Continued)*

also created an internal margin that can pick up some of the slack if your expenses run high or revenue falls below expectations. No system is foolproof, just as no business environment is without turmoil. As long as you use this double-cushion approach judiciously and keep your numbers realistic, chances are you won't come down as hard as often.

- Once the sales budget has been established, the *production budget* is developed. The number of units necessary, along with the price of manufacture and the required year-end inventory, all help determine the production budget. Current inventory sitting in the warehouse should be subtracted from the production budget's costs.

By establishing the sales budget first, we've designed a system that is goal-driven rather than cost-driven. This seemingly backward way of budgeting may make meeting the bottom line a little more challenging, but in the long run paints a better financial scenario for any company pursuing growth.

- The *direct materials purchase budget* comes next and operates much like the production budget. Estimates should include materials for the desired number of units to meet financial goals and maintain the desired year-end inventory. Again, the value of raw materials in stock should be subtracted from this amount.

- Estimating the *direct labor cost budget* to produce products comes next and operates in tandem with direct materials cost. Manpower will have to be measured in tandem with materials, inventory and sales goals for a realistic picture of actual estimated expenses.

- Along with materials and labor, you may have to create a *factory overhead costs budget*. Unlike materials and manpower, which are directly attributable and variable with the number and type of products produced, factory overhead will include related light, heat and facilities costs, supervisors' salaries, plant maintenance, insurance and property taxes and other costs that are more general in nature to the production process.

- The *cost of goods sold budget* comes next and combines the three previous expense categories—direct materials costs, direct labor costs and factory overhead costs—to identify the cost of goods sold. Divided by the number of units produced and compared to actual sales price, this will give you a good

## LEDGER NOTES

Traditional budgets are not without their alternatives. Some businesses engage in flexible budgeting. A flexible budget is really a series of smaller budgets strung together and designed to measure variations in activity over a given time period. This is especially valuable in manufacturing and in businesses with strong seasonal activity.

idea of both production expenses and net margin per unit for the work you do and products you produce.

- In addition to the cost of goods sold, there's also an *operating budget* that needs to be prepared. This adds marketing, sales, distribution and any other general expenses to the mix. While not technically considered part of the cost of goods sold, it is a very real part of the expenses scenario.

Those steps define the basic operating budget for the measurement and flow of expenses and revenues. There may be need for the development of a *capital expenditures budget,* which measures the expense of equipment and facilities, the cost of which will be amortized over a period of years. There also is a *cash budget,* which measures the anticipated revenue and expense flow. This allows for better funds management, enabling you to create cushions where you need them and invest excess liquidity when the opportunity arises.

What at first may seem a simple process can grow very complicated. But those complications enable you to exercise greater control and to better manage resources in pursuit of your strategic goals. And that, after all, is what budgeting is about.

### A WORD ABOUT EXPENSES

Budgeting is an exercise in control, and effective budgeting means being able to use all the tools available to you. One of the most critical is also one of the simplest. That's understanding the difference between fixed and variable costs.

Take our pencil company, for example. Their goal last year may have been to produce 10 million units for sale or distribution, with a guaranteed half-million units warehoused at year end. Using their current facilities, that required 100 employees working with a half million pounds of wood, carbon, rubber and sheet metal over a period of 1,000 hours of manufacturing time.

Since all those costs are dependent on the number of pencils produced, those are variable costs that may be subject to change in the future dependent on the number of pencils the strategic plan calls for. If sales increase, so do variable costs to accommodate demand.

Those pencils were produced and warehoused in the company's Dayton, Ohio, plant with standardized operating costs based on the size, capabilities and nature of the physical plant. It took two-dozen line managers, a half-dozen middle managers and the equivalent of two executive-level staff to oversee the operation. Since those costs exist irrespective of the number of pencils produced, those are fixed costs that do not vary whether the production line produces one pencil or one million pencils. An increase in sales likely won't ratchet up these costs significantly enough to increase the per-unit costs.

This is a cardinal rule to remember in creating a budget and the subsequent management of that budget. Your fixed-cost investment is the foundation of your expense scenario. It has to be because it's the most difficult to change. In good times, that becomes a positive factor. If your company suddenly suffers a marketplace setback, the reverse is true. Your rent or real estate taxes won't lighten just because the market wants less of your product. Nice as it might be, life doesn't work that way.

Variable costs can be your swing factor and should be used to leverage expenses against revenue. If product begins to accumulate in the warehouse and your market doesn't seem to be consuming at the expected rate, you can soften the blow to the revenue side by reducing the amount of materials ordered, the number of hours line employees work or, in very hard times, the number of employees.

If such conditions are necessary and your executive staff is involved in also overseeing other, more profitable operations, they

## BY DEFINITION

Virtually all budgets contain a line item called "overhead," but few budgets define those costs. Overhead can include staff salaries and benefits, facilities and utilities expenses, administrative support departments, property and payroll taxes, and other indirect expenses. Knowing what's included in your company's overhead line item will help you budget more effectively.

likely won't be reduced in number or earnings. Also, it's unlikely we would be able to reduce facilities or equipment overhead unless the downswing proved permanent. Those costs are fixed in place for the length of the budget cycle. You may be able to soften them, but you likely won't get rid of them entirely.

There also are semi-variable costs, such as marketing and sales. In hard times, those costs can be trimmed, but they shouldn't be cut entirely if you plan on reversing the down trend. There requires shrewd judgment on your part to know when to spend and when to pull back.

The bottom line? With rare exception, the higher your production run, the lower your per-unit expense thanks to the nature of fixed and semi-variable costs. That means greater net profit and a stronger financial profile for your company.

Just take a look. It's all there in your budget.

## DEVELOPING YOUR BUDGET

From an accounting standpoint, budgeting follows a required format. There may be variance in style and content within your company. Expenses and revenue may be accrued over the duration of the budget, for example, and then those accrual amounts applied throughout the year to even out the funds flow into and out of your department. In almost every case, revenues are estimated first, followed by expenses. For most companies, it's the same exercise in subtraction (revenues − expenses = net margin) that you learned in grade school.

Budgets generally are best illustrated in a financial statement that shows the following units of measure of your financial performance:

- the *current budget,* articulated into understandable references, which measures anticipated revenue and expense;

- the *previous budget or year-end actual figures,* usually from the prior year, which shows a line-by line comparison charting business cycles, represented by increases or decreases in revenue or expense. This is a critical strategic component that provides context for your goals and strategies for this year's financial performance;

- the *year-to-date performance,* as posted to the general ledger. These are actual figures that show your financial well-being at a precise moment in time. Remember that if you're using accrued numbers rather than actual sales, your performance figures may be based more on expectation than actual performance;

- and, finally, *quarter or annual projections,* a line-by-line comparison that measures revised anticipated performance against marketplace realities. These numbers may be the most critical from an operational perspective, especially when compared to budget. It not only shows how close your planning was to reality, but forces you to consider or accommodate performance weaknesses that could sink your ship.

Let's take a look at a top down financial statement that measures budget (both current and previous), and year-to-date performance. (See Table 7.1.)

By comparing the actual performance column to the budget, this manager can better adjust expenses to meet sales shortfalls, thus coming closer to bottom-line goals. That addresses the operational needs of the department. Quick comparisons between the previous

Table 7.1: Financial Statement

Positively Pencils
Period Ending 12/31

| Revenue | Budget | Actual | *Previous Yrs. Perf.* |
|---|---|---|---|
| Standard No. 2 | $165,000 | $158,750 | $110,099 |
| Novelty Pencils | 16,550 | 18,750 | 19,900 |
| Erasers, Boxes | 95,500 | 118,000 | 88,650 |
| Other products | 235,000 | 278,000 | 195,000 |
| Total revenue | $512,050 | $573,500 | $413,635 |
| *Expenses* | | | |
| Manufacturing | 155,750 | 164,900 | 148,900 |
| Salaries/Benefits | 210,775 | 231,010 | 219,150 |
| Marketing/Sales | 58,800 | 46,900 | 26,685 |
| Other costs | 36,000 | 41,550 | 3,200 |
| Total expenses | 461,325 | 484,360 | $397,935 |
| *Net Margin* | $50,725 | $89,140 | $15,700 |

year-end-actuals and this year's budget will describe the soundness of the department's strategy.

And all the information necessary will be available and clearly stated for use when next year's budget cycle roles around.

## Factoring the Human Equation

The budget is the financial reflection of your department's and your company's overall business strategy. But a budget also reflects the expectations and desires' of the department responsible for setting the sights and striving for the goals articulated in the numbers. Management—middle or upper—that fails to factor in the human equation does a disservice to all involved in the process. That failure also compromises—perhaps significantly—the department's ability to reach the levels described in the budget and achieve department or company goals.

Your budget will work only under the following circumstances:

- *Budgets must set optimistic but realistic expectations.* Revenues that will never be reached or expenses that can't be maintained will do little more than frustrate the managers and undermine their ability to reach stated goals. In the same vein, budgets that require minimal reach will waste managers' efforts and do little to stimulate initiative and corporate growth.

- *Budgets must be well articulated in order to be effective.* Budgets whose goals aren't specifically defined or backed up with sound development strategies are little more than numbers on paper. Their ability to influence company or departmental growth is weak at best. Budgets must be based on sound strategies designed to help reach the necessary levels of financial growth.

- *Budgets must be active tools used throughout the year.* No well-defined budget merely sits on a shelf. An effective budget is a continual resource, a barometer for the department's and the company's financial progress. It should be checked regularly and the information it provides should be noted and analyzed.

- *The unexamined budget is not worth using.* Budgets are not pristine documents carefully created for their esthetic value. Budgets are meant to be reviewed, questioned, scrutinized, analyzed and adjusted based on market influences and strategic changes. To that end the budget, as well as the thinking behind it, needs sufficient levels of flexibility. Budgets are not ends in themselves; they exist to help the company reach its financial goals.

- *Above all, budgets are guidelines, not gospel.* Both budgeters and the people supervising them would do well to remember that budgets are, at best, educated guesses. They must be based on logic, research and strategic necessity, but no one budgets with pinpoint accuracy. Treat a missed margin as just that, and use the information learned from that miss to make the necessary adjustments and get back on track.

Remember, the year has four quarters. There will almost always be another one.

*If he works for you,
you work for him.*

*—Japanese proverb*

# From Balance Sheets to Income Statements

The chief value of any accounting system is to keep close track of the company's financial activity and, through a series of checks and balances, to make sure the efforts being made by professionals and support staff at all levels within the company hierarchy are aimed at assisting positive financial progress and a solvent bottom line.

In order to make this happen, the company's finance department needs to produce periodic reports that reflect this activity. Keep in mind the reports are not an end in themselves. Rather, the reports are mileage markers and signposts along the road to achieving a company's strategic and financial goals.

As we've said before, reports can be as varied and as numerous as those goals demand, but two reports are critical to all companies financial progress:

- The *balance sheet* is a financial snapshot in time. At any given point, it can accurately measure the company's financial progress and alert company officials to perils and pitfalls, along with growth and positive trends.

- The *income statement* is a report with longer-term implications and one that reflects operating results for a certain period of time. Quarterly financial statements are not uncommon, but the document must be produced at least yearly to coincide with the budgeting cycle.

Accounting departments also produce a report called *statement of cash flows* to report financial progress to those outside the company—shareholders, partners and others who have a financial stake in the firm. We'll discuss those statements in a later chapter.

For now, an introductory discussion of balance sheets and income statements should suffice. This also will reinforce some basic accounting concepts reflected in the statements that will help you understand the process more fully.

## BUILDING A BALANCE SHEET

It's also sometimes referred to as a *statement of financial position,* but the more common term is balance sheet. It's a list of the firm's assets, liabilities and owners' equity on any given date. The balance sheet should be headed with the name of the company, title of the document and date for which the statement is prepared. That's standard operating procedure when it comes to building a balance sheet.

The body of the statement contains three sections devoted to a company's assets, liabilities and owners' equity. Readers should be able to tell at a glance what the company's financial position is from the way the balance sheet is arranged. The example shown below demonstrates the proper format.

A quick glance at the following statement shows that V. Market & Son, Inc. has $111,375 in resources and that these assets are

---

**V. Market & Son, Inc.**
**Balance Sheet**
**December 31, 20xx**

| Assets | | | Liabilities | | |
|---|---|---|---|---|---|
| Cash | | $4,000 | Accounts Payable | | 23,500 |
| Accounts | | | Mortgage Payable | | 41,500 |
| Receivable | | $4,500 | Total Liabilities | | $65,000 |
| Inventory | | $2,500 | | | |
| Land | | $6,600 | Owners' Equity | | |
| Building | $100,000 | | Vincent | | |
| (Less | | | Market | | 34,780 |
| Depreciation) | | $48,125 | Christopher | | |
| Equipment | 75,000 | | Market | $11,595 | |
| (Less | | | Total Libilities | | |
| Depreciation) | | 45,650 | and Owners' | | |
| Total Assets | | $111,375 | Equity | | $111,375 |

| | | |
|---|---|---|
| **V. Market & Son, Inc.** | | |
| **Balance Sheet** | | |
| **December 31, 20XX** | | |
| | | |
| **Assets** | | |
| Cash | | $4,000 |
| Accounts Receivable | | $4,500 |
| Inventory | | $2,500 |
| Land | | $6,600 |
| Building | $100,000 | |
| (Less Depreciation) | | $48,125 |
| Equipment | 75,000 | |
| (Less Depreciation) | | 45,650 |
| *Total Assets* | | $111,375 |
| | | |
| **Liabilities** | | |
| Accounts Payable | | 23,500 |
| Mortgage Payable | | 41,500 |
| *Total Liabilities* | | $65,000 |
| | | |
| **Owners' Equity** | | |
| Vincent Market | | 34,780 |
| Christopher Market | | $11,595 |
| *Total Liabilities and Owners' Equity* | | $111,375 |

being financed from two sources: creditors ($65,000) and owners' equity ($46,375). The right side of the balance sheet can also be referred to in total as *Equities* and subdivided into *Creditors' Equity* and *Owners' Equity*. The fact that the two sides of the statement balance is referred to as the *Accounting Equation*. As we know from an earlier chapter, the two sides must balance. That's why it's called a *balance sheet*.

The sample balance sheet may do an even better job of illustrating what the various accounting classifications mean:

- A business's *assets* are economic resources that can be defined in monetary terms. These include obvious assets such as equipment, real estate, and liquid assets, as well as less tangible assets like accounts receivable, which represent money owed the firm. These always are listed on the balance sheet with the most liquid assets first, then descending in cash availability from there. Assets are always recorded at actual cost or acquisition price (book value) or as part of a depreciation scenario. Generally accepted accounting principles do not allow for the upward valuation of assets. They require accounting at the lower of cost or market price.

- *Liabilities,* also known as creditors' equity and listed on the right of the balance sheet, are financial obligations the company has to outside agents, such as vendors, landlords and others to whom the company owes money. Liabilities are listed in the order they will come due, with short-term notes heading the list. Longer-term debts, such as mortgages, follow.

- *Owners' equity* usually is listed below the liabilities and comprise the business's net assets. That means owners' equity represents the amount left after the liabilities have been subtracted from the assets. At one time this was called net worth, but that term is not considered viable because it implies value. There certainly is value to the business owner when it comes to personal equity, but the owners' equity is still a draw on the resources of the business as a separate entity and must be treated as such on the balance sheet.

## How Transactions Affect the Balance Sheet

Different transactions have different impacts on the balance sheet, as you might imagine, and all transactions must be recorded. The standard equation is:

$$\text{Assets} = \text{liabilities} + \text{owners' equity}$$

Total assets must continue to equal total liabilities to keep your balance sheet in balance. Anything you do to one side must reflect the appropriate changes on the other side. The following general guidelines will help you understand the impact changes will have on the balance sheet:

*Revenue:* The term *revenue* refers to increases in the owners' equity through income earned by providing goods and services in exchange for payment. Revenues are added to the *Assets Received* side of the equation, then attributed to *Owners' Equity* on the liability side. From an accounting standpoint, revenue is earned at the time those goods and services are provided. Amounts for items purchased by customers on credit are added to *Accounts Receivable*. Once those items are paid for, those amounts are converted to *Cash*. No additional amount is entered, however, because it already has been entered in another category.

*Expenses:* *Expenses* are the cost of doing business, of producing and distributing the goods and services that lead to the *Asset* side of the equation. The cost of doing business, including manufacturing expenses, as well as daily operational costs and depreciation, all occur as a part of producing revenue and all are listed as expenses.

Expenses must be accounted for during the same period as their accompanying revenues because they reflect the cost of producing that revenue. That's called *accrual-based accounting,* which we'll describe in a minute. V. Market & Son Inc. pays an annual mortgage of $41,500, or about $459 per month. No matter when the amount is paid, one-twelfth of the total rent should be assigned to each month as part of the expenses for producing the company's revenue.

It's important to note that cash expenditures made in support of revenue goals do not have an impact on owners' equity. If the owner withdraws funds from the company, that amount reduces owners' equity, but is not listed as an expense, which are costs related to the direct effort to earn revenue. As a rule, owner contributions to the business increase owners' equity, while withdrawals decrease it.

In the same way, revenues to the company increase owners' equity and expenses decrease it. The goal of any business is to increase owners' equity by earning profits, or net income. That net income is determined by subtracting expenses from revenue. What's left is considered owners' equity.

If V. Market & Son increases its cash holding from $4,000 to $8,000, that additional revenue would be reflected by an addition of $4,000 to the owners' equity column on the right side of the balance sheet. Since the equity split shows 75 percent ownership by Vincent Market and 25 percent ownership by Christopher Market, those totals would most likely jump to $35,780 and $12,595, respectively.

*Accrual accounting:* The revenue and expense discussion relates to companies that practice *accrual accounting.* In accrual accounting, expenses incurred are matched to the revenue which those expenses have produced. This creates a meaningful net income figure for the period to which those numbers relate and helps balance assets and liabilities. This occurs regardless of whether the bill for those expenses has actually been paid or the funds from that revenue have actually arrived. Like so much of accounting procedure, the presence of cash is irrelevant to the operation. This also is true in accrual accounting.

*Cash accounting:* Other companies practice *cash accounting,* in which the actual presence of funds drives the recordkeeping function. Service industries, such as law firms, may choose to practice cash accounting because it offers certain tax advantages and is easier in some ways to manage. However, financial statements for companies that operate on a cash basis can distort the firm's true net worth. Because of that, companies that operate on a true cash basis are either very small or very rare.

## A Smattering of Balance Sheet Sample Transactions

Knowing the theory behind balance sheet transactions is one thing; seeing how it works in practice is quite another. Here are a smattering of samples to show you how the balance sheet for V. Market & Son, Inc.—a manufacturer of custom jukeboxes—progresses through the daily course of doing business.

*Transaction A*
V. Market & Son decides to build 12 new jukeboxes on speculation for an emerging market in another city. This requires expenditures of

---

**Balance Sheet**

**Assets**

| | |
|---|---|
| Raw Materials | $3,350 |
| Equipment (Less depreciation) | $6,500 |
| *Total Assets* | $9,850 |

**Liabilities**

| | |
|---|---|
| Accounts Payable | $9,850 |
| *Total Liabilities and Owners' Equity* | $9,850 |

---

$3,350 for raw materials, as well as an investment in another $6,500 for a new piece of assembly equipment. Those costs are reflected on the balance sheet of this particular enterprise, shown above.

*Transaction B*
The salesperson for V. Market & Son visits the neighboring city and manages to sell 10 jukeboxes at $2,500 each. Five are sold for cash; five are sold on a time payment with the balance due in 90 days. The two remaining jukeboxes stay in the company's inventory.

---

**Balance Sheet**

**Assets**

| | |
|---|---|
| Cash | $12,500 |
| Accounts Receivable | $12,500 |
| Inventory | $5,000 |
| *Total Assets* | $30,000 |

**Liabilities**

| | |
|---|---|
| Accounts Payable | $9,850 |
| Labor | $7,840 |
| Sales Costs | $1,100 |
| Owners' Equity | $11,210 |
| *Total Liabilities and Owners' Equity* | $30,000 |

*Transaction C*

Company ownership decides from its test marketing that this new type of jukebox has market appeal. V. Market & Son invests its recent earnings in another piece of assembly equipment that will allow the assembly of twice the number of units in one third the time. The cost of equipment ($6,500) is the same, but the cost of materials to produce 24 jukeboxes has doubled ($6,700).

| **Balance Sheet** | |
|---|---:|
| **Assets** | |
| Raw Materials | $6,700 |
| Equipment (Less depreciation) | $6,500 |
| Total Assets | $13,200 |
| | |
| **Liabilities** | |
| Accounts Payable | $13,200 |
| Total Liabilities and Owners' Equity | $13,200 |

*Transaction D*

The 24 jukeboxes have been assembled, still identified as having a market value of $2,500 each, for a total of $60,000. The cost of labor is cut by one-third due to the new machine ($5,175). The difference between the actual costs of materials and equipment

| **Balance Sheet** | |
|---|---:|
| **Assets** | |
| Inventory | $60,000 |
| Back stock | $5,000 |
| Total Assets | $65,000 |
| | |
| **Liabilities** | |
| Accounts Payable | $13,200 |
| Labor | $5,175 |
| Owners' Equity | $46,625 |
| Total Liabilities and Owners' Equity | $65,000 |

($13,200) and labor ($5,175) and the jukes' retail value ($60,000) is added to owners' equity.

*Transaction E*
The salesperson for V. Market & Son takes a three-city sales trip and manages to sell 25 jukeboxes (including one from the previous production round) at $2,500 each. Eighteen are sold for cash; seven are sold on a time payment with the balance due in 90 days. One jukebox stays in the company's inventory.

| Balance Sheet | |
|---|---|
| **Assets** | |
| Cash | $45,000 |
| Accounts Receivable | $17,500 |
| Inventory | $2,500 |
| *Total Assets* | $65,000 |
| | |
| **Liabilities** | |
| Accounts Payable | $13,200 |
| Labor | $5,175 |
| Sales Costs | $2,700 |
| Owners' Equity | $43,925 |
| *Total Liabilities and Owners' Equity* | $65,000 |

At this point V. Market & Son may have taken its equity and gone on an extended vacation. Or perhaps they invested either in real estate or the stock market. In any event, you can see how such transactions progress and how they are reflected in the balance sheet.

You can also see how the balance sheet—which in this case combines some elements from income statements to better create a scenario—can tell a narrative and describe a strategy that goes beyond the mere recitation of numbers if you're perceptive enough to pick it up. V. Market would only risk limited capital on this new design and was sure to establish an equity base in this product area before stepping too far out on a limb and jeopardizing his other juke box lines and designs.

Chances are V. Market did none of the above, but rather used his investment in equipment and research into more potential markets to produce more jukeboxes at a cheaper rate, since he now needed to make no further equipment expenditures. Based on Transaction F, we can assume the following cost-per-unit:

| Materials | $279 |
|---|---|
| Labor | $215 |
| Sales | $112 |
| Total cost per unit | $606 |

Based on a retail value of $2,500, it's easy to see how well V. Market is paid for his handiwork and why he and his son are in the jukebox business. Continued iterations of the original scenario would yield greater investible profits, all of which are added to the owners' equity. The financial scenario clearly identifies V. Market's market strategy, which is in turn a clear reflection of the company's financial strategy.

V. Market's action, along with a series of balance sheets reflecting the different steps in the process, are the best and really only way to understand the importance of financial statements. Financial statements must be viewed in some kind of context or in relation to other balance sheets in order for them to make sense and provide the perspective necessary to add value to the equation.

V. Market's action illustrates the two key facets of any company that financial statements are designed to measure:

- Is the company *solvent*? Lacking other information about V. Market & Son, one would have to assume based on what we've seen that the company is very solvent.

- Is the company *profitable*? The same issues apply and we know, at least, that the custom jukebox product line offers V. Market & Son a very healthy profitability indeed.

## INCOME STATEMENTS

The balance sheet is a very informative tool, but periodically it's important that you prepare an income statement to round out your financial information profile. The income statement is a tool that shows revenue and expense for a certain period of time without using the cross-functional transaction of the balance sheet. For those more interested in the result of financial transaction than the relation of financial transactions themselves, the income statement is the plainer, more accessible of the two tools.

To prepare a financial statement for June, 20XX, for V. Market & Son Inc., we would first list all the financial transactions that have occurred and their positive and negative impact on the company's bottom line:

| | | |
|---|---|---|
| 1. | Capital contribution (owners' equity) | +$43,925 |
| 2. | Mortgage payment (June) | −$1,458 |
| 3. | Sales | +$25,000 |
| 4. | Labor | −$5,175 |
| 5. | Sales expense | −$2,700 |
| 6. | Insurance and utilities | −$668 |
| 7. | Cash withdrawal by owner | −$4,000 |
| | Ending capital balance | $54,924 |

From this list, we can identify revenue of $25,000 (3) for jukebox sales. We also see expenses of mortgage payment (2), labor costs (4), sales expense (5), and insurance and utilities (6). Contributions (1) and withdrawals (7) by the owner are not considered direct expenses.

The income statement for V. Market & Son Inc., would look something like this.

---

**V. Market & Son Inc.**
**Income Statement for June, 20XX**

| | | |
|---|---|---|
| **Revenue** | | |
| Sales | | $25,000 |
| | | |
| **Expenses** | | |
| Mortgage payable | $1,458 | |
| Utilities and insurance | $668 | |
| Cost of goods sold | | |
| Labor | $5,175 | |
| Sales expense | $2,700 | |
| | | |
| *Total Expenses* | | $10,001 |
| *Net Income* | | $14,999 |

# STATEMENT OF
# OWNERS' EQUITY

When producing the income statement, we purposely left out both contributions and withdrawals made by the firm's owners, Vincent Market and Christopher Market. Those need to be summarized in the statement of owners' equity, another document that is periodically produced to provide a comprehensive financial snapshot of the firm.

This statement interacts with the income statement through the inclusion of the net income line item from the previous document. That activity is shown thus:

---

**V. Market & Son Inc.**
**Statement of Owners' Equity**
**for June, 20XX**

| | |
|---|---:|
| V. Market and C. Market, Capital, June 1, 20XX | $—0— |
| Add: Capital contributed in June | 43,925 |
| Net income for June | 14,999 |
| | 58,924 |
| Less: Capital withdrawn in June | 4,000 |
| V. Market and C. Market, Capital, June 30, 20XX | $54,924 |

---

As the sequence shows, earnings for the month were added to the owners' initial capital investment. The monthly withdrawal taken by the owners was then subtracted and a total capital position for the month determined. That's the statement's bottom line.

The statement of owners' equity is one more tool by which you can follow your company's financial stream as well as manage your company's development strategy. If V. Market's strategy is to build a strong capital position, solid earnings and minimal withdrawals for the period helped support this goal. If, on the other hand, his strategy was to reinvest in new business development, this statement would show that he didn't do a very good job during this period, choosing instead to amass capital.

Your strategy should drive your financial results, not the other way around. If what you see in your mind's eye is not what you get when you produce your balance sheet, income statement and statement of owners' equity . . . well, it's time to go back to the drawing board.

*Merchants have no country. The mere spot they stand on does not constitute so strong an attachment as that from which they draw their gains.*

*—Thomas Jefferson*

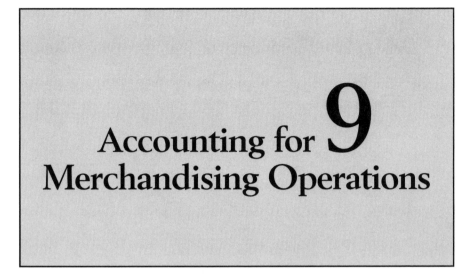

# Accounting for Merchandising Operations 9

Business is made up of chains of transactions that result in the movement of raw materials through the manufacturing, sales and distribution processes, winding up as finished products in the hands of consumers. Throughout the process, at numerous turning points in the life of both the product and audience, comes the merchandising step.

*Merchandising* is the purchase of goods for resale to customers. It is the act of selling objects—a lamp shade, five pounds of potatoes, a jet aircraft—rather than services. As such, it requires its own accounting procedures. The fact that merchandise purchases can be made through a variety of means (cash, check, credit card, and layaway) makes what at first appears to be a fairly simple concept quite complex in its accounting practices. When you pull in policies and procedures for merchandise returns, the whole process becomes even more cumbersome.

There are a lot of different steps in accounting for merchandising. This chapter will talk about the accounting needs for a variety of merchandising options. The text will consist less of concepts and more of examples. It's the best way to show how the process can work in your business.

## KEEPING TRACK OF PURCHASES

The most basic accounting step is the actual purchase of merchandise. These transactions often are identified in the general ledger as "purchases" and sometimes "purchases of merchandise," although the shorter title is preferred.

Purchases for *cash* can be shown as follows:

March 21    Purchases            750
                 Cash                      750
            Purchase from Wazoo Electric

However, in most businesses purchases are made *on account*. That transaction is shown as follows:

June 16     Purchases            325
                 Accounts Payable       325
            Purchase from Grand Canal Designs

## UTILIZING DISCOUNTS

A lot of companies offer cash discounts for bills paid within a certain period of time, often 10 days from receipt. The percentage savings is small—usually 2 to 5 percent on a purchase—but the savings can add up. In accounting nomenclature, this is referred to as "2/net 10" or "5/net 10" depending on the size of the discount. A 2 percent savings on a $50,000 balance due is $1,000. Assuming you have the cash, it is well worth the effort to pay within 10 days; it maximizes your financial resources and maintains your preferred credit status.

### BY DEFINITION

When it comes to understanding terms, remember that the *merchandiser* is the buyer of materials for resale and the *manufacturer* is the seller. You may operate at either end of the equation, but knowing the difference will help you master the process

Such savings are called *purchases discounts* and can be a critical part of your business's financial plan. If you're on the granting end of purchases discounts, then you must account for them in the right way. Let's follow the transaction we began above:

```
March 31    Accounts Payable        750
                Cash                        735
                Purchases Discount (2%)      15
                Invoice from Wazoo Electric
```

The 2 percent purchases discount ($15) is considered to be "cash" and added to the credit side of the diagram above.

What about returns? When merchandise is returned and a refund requested, some type of document must be added to the general ledger to support the transaction. (Remember, the G/L is not a single document but a series of entries, statements and documentation supporting the transactions posted to the account.) The request for refund usually results in the generation of a *credit memorandum,* which documents the return and shows the financial impact of that return.

The proper way to account for a return is to debit accounts payable and credit purchases return, a contra or offsetting account that deducts from the purchases account. The return of merchandise purchased in our earlier example would be illustrated thus:

```
March 21    Accounts Payable        750
                Purchases Returns
                    and Allowances          750
                Debit Memo 261: Purchase from
                Wazoo Electric
```

If the merchandise is returned prior to billing for the amount and there is a purchases discount in the works, the return is subtracted from the initial amount prior to the application of the discount. If not, you'll find yourself refunding the full purchase price after having collected the discounted price. A debit memo illustrating that approach would look something like the following:

| | | |
|---|---|---:|
| Sept. 15 | Invoice 3606 (dated Sept. 12) | $11,365 |
| | Debit memo #63 (dated Sept. 16) | 299 |
| Balance of account | | $11,066 |
| | Purchases discount (2% of $11,066) | 221.32 |
| Balance due | | $10,844.68 |

Assuming the payment was made on terms of net due in 30 days (often shown as n/30), then the bookkeeping for this transaction would look like this:

| | | | |
|---|---|---|---:|
| Oct. 15 | Accounts Payable | 10,844.68 | |
| | Cash | | 10,844.68 |
| | Purchases discount | | 221.32 |
| | Payment of invoice 3606 less Debit Memo #63 | | |

Once again, the purchases discount amount is shown on the right side of the diagram.

## ACCOUNTING FOR SALES ACTIVITY

Sales is the life's blood of most businesses and constitutes the major percentage of most firms' revenue. Proper accounting for those sales, while not difficult, is critical to keep the books balanced and the finances in order. What's important, however, is knowing how to account for the different types of sales:

• Sales paid for with *cash* and *bank credit cards* are recorded like this:

| | | | |
|---|---|---|---:|
| Feb. 14 | Cash | 563.50 | |
| | Sales | | 563.50 |

If there is a service fee for the credit card purchase, it should be debited to an expense account.

• Sales paid for with bank credit cards, like MasterCard, are treated like cash. Merchandise sold on account results in a debit of accounts receivable and a credit to sales:

```
Feb. 14    Accounts Receivable          563.50
             Sales                                  563.50
                Invoice 1119: V. Market & Son
```

• Some sales may be paid for with non-bank cards which require a report to the card company before payment is issued. The sale creates a receivable with the card issuer from which a service fee often is deducted:

```
Feb. 14    Accounts Receivable          563.50
             Sales                                  563.50
                American Express card sales

Feb. 18    Cash                         513.50
           Collection Expense            50
             Accounts Receivable                    563.50
           Cash receipt from American Express for sales 2/14
```

## Showing Sales Discounts

If the buyer receives a discount for early payment of an invoice or for some other reason, these are called *sales discounts*. They're treated as a reduction in the amount of the sale itself and shown through a sales account debit. This becomes an offsetting account for sales.

Using our example from before, let's consider this a sale that offers a 3 percent discount for payment within 15 days, with the balance due in 30 days.

```
Feb. 14    Cash sale                    563.50
           Discount (3%)                 16.90
             Accounts Receivable                    546.60
                Invoice 1119: V. Market & Son
```

## Posting Sales Returns Or Allowances

When dealing with the public, you always have to be prepared for the return of merchandise purchased, also known as the *sales return*. There are also reductions given from the list price of an item.

## LEDGER NOTES

Managing merchandise transportation costs becomes a matter of *when* ownership of said merchandise is transferred from the seller to the buyer. If ownership transfers to the buyer when the merchandise is received by the shipper, the buyer pays for transportation. However, if that ownership doesn't transfer until the buyer receives it, then the seller pays the freight. The first is called FOB shipping point and the buyer should debit that cost to a "transportation" line item on the expense account and credit to cash. When the seller pays delivery, those costs are reported as an expense of sales.

These are called *sales allowances*. In either case, these often result in a *credit memorandum,* which shows the amount the buyer is credited.

The effect of a return or allowance will be a reduction in sales revenue, along with a reduction either in cash or accounts receivable. Debiting the sales account will result in a showing of net sales, which means transaction specifics, such as the volume and itemization of returns, won't appear. In addition, returns often come with attendant costs, such as shipping, packing and handling charges. Reserving for these proposed costs is critical to an accurate budget.

Some companies also utilize *trade discounts,* reductions in the list price that have no corresponding accounting obligations. In other words, inventory are not valued at list prices, but at the actual sale price of the merchandise. Something listed for $49.95 in your catalog that sold on special for $29.95 would not require a $20 sales discount entry in your books, since your books would not reflect the printed list price. Instead, that amount would simply appear as the sales price in the company records.

### Sales Tax

Many states charge a sales tax, levied at the time of purchase, charged by the seller and paid by the buyer either at the moment of transaction in a cash sale, or added to the account in a charge. The seller would account for the sales tax as follows:

| Feb. 14 | Accounts Receivable | 597.31 | |
|---|---|---|---|
| | Sales | | 563.50 |
| | Sales Tax (6%) | | 33.81 |

The buyer who was charged the sales tax would record the transaction similarly, but without separating the tax from the cost of the merchandise:

| Feb. 14 | Purchases | 597.31 | |
|---|---|---|---|
| | Accounts Payable | | 597.31 |
| | Invoice 4141: Grand Canal Designs | | |

## FINANCIAL REPORTING

All of this comprehensive recordkeeping will do your operation no good unless you are prepared to report your findings. The report, which should show the state of your operation, will then be used to update the company's general ledger. Different companies have different procedures by which they report their merchandising operations. Here's a sample procedure for you to consider:

- Prepare a general ledger trial balance using a worksheet.
- Review accounts and gather all data necessary to make the appropriate adjustments.
- Add adjustments to the worksheet and complete the trial balance.
- Use worksheet data to prepare the financial statement.
- Journal the adjusted entries and post to the general ledger.
- Journal the closing entries and post to the ledger.
- Prepare a post-closing trial balance to the ledger.

Once that's done, you need to determine the cost of merchandise sold for the reporting period. In most cases, this is as simple as determining the total cost of merchandise, then subtracting the value of the remaining inventory. The difference will be the cost of merchandise sold for that period.

## LEDGER NOTES

Merchandising operations use one of two types of inventory accounting systems. The more popular of the two is the *periodic* system, which records revenue on the date of sale but does not record the cost of goods until a physical inventory is taken, often at year-end. Under the *perpetual* system, both the sales amount and cost of goods sold are recorded at the same time; the accounting record is then used to show the inventory on hand.

For example, if your company purchases $245,000 worth of merchandise for the period January 1–December 31 and, at the close of that period, you have $64,000 worth of merchandise left, your cost of goods sold during that calendar year will be $181,000. The $64,000 worth of merchandise left over becomes the basis for the new inventory and its value is added to new merchandise purchased under the heading *merchandise available for sale*. At the end of the next year, the process is repeated, thereby keeping a rolling inventory of goods.

From this point, the next step is developing a trial balance and making adjustments necessary to the accuracy of that balance. Once that's taken care of, it's time to move right to the financial statement.

That's one of three more tools you need to know, by the way. We've referred to them before and it's important you understand the difference between an income statement, a balance sheet and a cash flow statement:

- The *income statement* summarizes the company's revenue and expense for a certain period of time, such as a month or a year, and usually highlights sales revenue.

- The *balance sheet* lists assets, liabilities and owners' equity in the business as of a specific date, usually for the month for which the figures are reported.

- The *statement of cash flow* offers a look in time at the company from the perspective of cash inflows and outflows.

We'll refer to these throughout the rest of this book. Sometimes they interact with each other; other times, they stand alone. Each has its own usage and it helps you to understand the differences among the three early, whether you're the head of a merchandising operation or not.

*Money talks.*
*The more the money,*
*the louder it talks.*

*—Arnold Rothstein,*
*accused of fixing the 1919 World Series*

# Managing Your **10** Internal Controls

If we could penetrate the shadowy side of the lives of our employees, those dark recesses they take care not to show their friends, their coworkers and certainly not their supervisors, we might be surprised at the amount of dishonesty we'd find.

Office supplies wander home in briefcases and purses. Expense reports list meals that were never eaten and tips that were never left. Inventory disappears or is never delivered. Durable goods, raw materials and larger items, including computers, ride home with workers after hours and on weekends. Funds are embezzled or payments simply never make their way onto the books or into the company bank account.

Not a pretty picture, is it? That's not to say all employees are dishonest. But many, given the right opportunity, can rationalize their way into a great deal of trouble if controls haven't been put in place to deter their actions. We're human beings, after all, and subject to weaknesses of judgment and, occasionally, lapses in honesty. No one's perfect, and companies that operate as if we were, exist in a fool's paradise and run the risk of significant financial loss.

Every company, firm, partnership and operation, no matter how large or small, needs an effective system of internal controls to protect its assets. That's true of for-profit corporate giants and not-for-profit fundraising operations. Even the business side of churches and synagogues need to have internal control mechanisms to protect the contributions of their members. Those that don't have such

## *LEDGER NOTES*

Firms of any size usually have their own internal auditors—sometimes several of them—whose job it is to review procedures and make sure they are compliant with a) the company's internal controls policy, and b) the requirements of any formal regulatory body that oversees their industry. The auditor(s) sometimes report to either the company's chief executive officer or chief financial officer, but more often than not report to some outside source, like the firm's board of directors, to avoid any conflict of interest or undue influence that might arise from reporting to one of those other departments.

controls run the risk of hosting the slow drain in assets that, left unchecked, could turn into a raging torrent of loss. Needless to say, that's bad for the organization's financial well-being, but it also has a negative impact on employee morale and respect for leadership overall. The harm can run much deeper than you might anticipate.

## YOUR TOP CONCERN: DETERRING DISHONESTY

Homes and businesses that are protected by electronic security systems—and even many that aren't—proclaim that protection loudly by displaying stickers prominently on doors and windows. Their goal isn't to catch criminals red-handed, it's to prevent them from breaking and entering in the first place. The same logic applies to internal control systems. They're like the lock on your door and the sticker on your window. You don't want to allow employees the option for dishonesty and then catch them in the act; rather, you want to show dishonest employees up front that you're prepared to meet their challenge and to make it as difficult as possible for them to succeed in stealing from the company.

Call them preventive measures, if you will, or perhaps preemptive action. Those steps often are the most economical and may well be the best investment you make in establishing your internal controls. Potentially dishonest employees who know you will be watching likely won't run the risk of committing theft or fraud unless they are truly stupid or truly desperate—and then there are other signs to alert you to potential problem areas. Take preventive steps first and announce your intentions clearly and forcefully. The majority will listen and your flow of problems will be significantly reduced.

The whole effort starts with a well-developed security plan and a commitment from management to support the plan and its requirements. Such a plan may be drafted by corporate officers with or without outside consulting help. If your company is staffed by seasoned professionals who are honest and committed themselves, they may be able to spot the soft spots and weak areas that need shoring up. Contributions from multiple departments is the best way to gain staff support and broaden the plan to cover all major functions. That's a critical part of protecting your assets.

## MANAGING ACCOUNTING CONTROLS

Employee theft can be highly detrimental to your company's asset value. But a greater area of danger comes from the finance side of the operation. Corporate embezzlement is growing at an alarming rate, making both your accounts receivable and accounts payable vulnerable through clever manipulation by unscrupulous staff. Accounting controls are the most critical part of your company's internal control mechanism. By its very nature, your accounting system, especially systems linked to other areas of operation, such as inventory, provides built-in mechanisms to track assets and cross-check for questionable activity. That makes your accounting department the key component to your internal controls program.

Internal control plans may vary, but all contain, to some degree, the following four components:

• The plan must provide for a separation of operational functions within departments, especially in accounting or other functions with a close control of assets. Inventory control should be separated into physical assets management and recordkeeping for those assets, while those handling cash should be charged with the responsibility of recording cash amounts into the general ledger. It's a simple process that not only can make operations easier and more effective, but can also protect those assets and the individuals involved from the temptation of theft.

• Staff experience must match the responsibilities given. Whoever is charged with managing your company's internal controls needs to at least have an aptitude if not specialized training in such management. Too often smaller companies assign it merely as another task to an overloaded executive's roster of duties. An internal controls plan inadequately managed is almost worse than no plan at all. Make sure those given the responsibility are up to the task.

• Like any other accounting operation, strong policies and procedures, along with effective recordkeeping and data management, are critical for an effective internal controls program. If you've already been following good accounting principles, you may already have an adequate framework on which to build your program. If not, your most important work still lies ahead. Be sure whatever you do covers all known contingencies and exceptions as well.

• We've implied it before, but let us say it again more directly: Keep all transaction recording and asset custody separate. If one employee handles the paperwork and another signs the checks, records credits and acts in other ways that affect the value of the company's assets, you set an effective stage for loss prevention.

## The Cost of Security

There's a cost to everything, including your program of internal controls. If your operation is so small or so secure that the cost of internal controls would be greater than the loss of assets they would be designed to protect, you may consider not bothering with such a thing. If there are few assets to siphon off, then it may not be worth the cost and effort. Someone we know once ran a college poetry magazine that had so few assets that they almost weren't worth protecting. The cost of occasional issues walking out the door or cash subscription payments disappearing weren't worth the costs of building a system.

But if the potential for harm is great, then it's worth the expense to put a comprehensive system in place. In addition to preserving assets, good internal controls affect the perceived professionalism and market value of any company, large or small.

One of the least expensive and most effective means of protection available is the purchase of a fidelity bond for critical, cash-handling or asset-managing employees. Purchasing a bond guarantees comprehensive research into the employee's past (no insurer will bond a person whose past shows evidence of wrongdoing) as well as providing protection against future activity. If a bonded employee does embezzle funds, the bonding agent will pay the company as well as pursue the wrongdoer. That's an excellent resource to have on your side.

## AVENUES TO EMBEZZLEMENT

For as well-structured and comprehensive as your accounting system is, each of the various components offers different avenues for fraud and embezzlement. Understand the impact on each of these areas, or be prepared to pay the price.

***Accounts payable:*** When it comes to targeting operations, accounts payable can be the most easily and most often threatened part of your accounting system. There are no liquid assets available, but savvy embezzlers quickly realize they have an entire arsenal of opportunity awaiting them in the area responsible for the greatest outflow of funds. Vendors may bill for services never provided while insiders help them collect the cash. Those same insiders may be savvy enough to alter the invoices so that more money is paid than owed, then have their outside accomplice siphon off and share the

## CHITS

The key to embezzlement, from the embezzler's point of view, is to be able to rationalize illegal actions. Employees who work hard and feel under appreciated may think the money is owed to them, while those with chemical dependency or gambling problems may simply need extra funds to survive. We've heard about an embezzler who siphoned off funds and gave them all to his church. But even for a Robin Hood, such an action constitutes theft.

extra funds. Although it requires greater accounting acumen, this is much the same as dipping into the till.

There are still boiler operations that prey on unsuspecting companies, claiming false orders for shipments that never arrive and demanding payment for goods that were ordered by someone who already has left the company. In the effort of efficiency, ignorance or confusion, well-meaning employees often pay these bogus claims and outside embezzlers get away with your company's precious assets, thanks to the unsuspecting collusion of employees.

The logical step is to segment the payment function so that more than one person is involved with recordkeeping and disbursement. If one individual reviews and approves disbursement and another cuts the actual check, chances are better that errors and embezzlement opportunities will be fewer.

Once the process has been concluded, remember to reconcile all accounts payable sub ledgers and ledgers and vendor account records. Stamp paid invoices PAID and void all unused checks. The strength of any accounts payable system is its paper trail. Take advantage of it and don't forget to account for all links within the chain.

Good procedures also help control opportunities for fraud. Try the following steps and see if they apply to your firm:

• Warehouse staff accepts deliveries and unloads the stock while the warehouse clerk verifies delivery information against the invoice and enters shipment information into an inventory program linked to accounting.

• The invoice amounts are entered by accounting staff into accounts payable after comparing the invoice to the purchase order. Two signatures may be preferred to verify accuracy of the shipment.

• A third party delivers the preprinted checks to accounting for payment of the invoice that accompanied the shipment. In the case of a pre-established payment schedule, checks will be cut as that schedule indicates.

• The chief financial officer or controller reviews the work done by the accounting staff and signs the check for shipment to the vendor.

You'll note that no less than six individuals were involved in the merchandise acceptance/invoice approval process, assuring no undue influence by any single individual and eliminating the opportunity to falsify records or inflate payment to the vendor.

***Accounts receivable:*** Where revenues are logged into the company records is another gateway for the embezzler. Separation of payment handling and recordkeeping duties is as critical here as it was for accounts payable. The person making the sale is not likely the one who enters the sale in the general ledger. If that's not true for your company, make a change to see that it is.

There are three specific issues affecting accounts receivable: a) receivable assets must be properly recorded; b) payments must be properly recorded; and c) receivables must actually exist. If your business faces seasonal revenue swings, watch closely for contra trends that may indicate something is amiss.

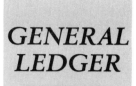

# GENERAL LEDGER

For many businesses, petty cash is a thing of the past. In most cases, the amount in question is under $1,000, the lowest level of dollars threatened, but one that often takes up the greatest amount of time in management. These days company credit cards have removed both the hassle and threat of petty cash for most firms.

Some companies still operate with petty cash. If you're one, remember control is necessary, but it shouldn't exceed the relative value of the asset in effort or importance. Follow these procedures and you should keep yourself out of trouble:

## GENERAL LEDGER

*(Continued)*

- Establish your fund for a specific amount, then reimburse as needed when cash is taken out to bring the total back to the agreed upon amount.

- Appoint one individual as keeper of the cash; appoint a second individual as disbursement officer.

- Require an approval voucher from management for every amount that comes out of the cash box (or cash drawer). Unless a voucher goes in, no cash can come out because the vouchers and cash on hand must total the agreed upon amount. Make the keeper of the cash responsible for that reconciliation.

The separation of sales and accounting functions is the key to the first challenge; otherwise, it is easy for someone in the firm to sell merchandise, goods or services to an outside party without recording that sale in the company records. Other control mechanisms include the daily reconciliation of sales balances. The total must equal the amount from cash sales and customer purchases credited to accounts receivable less credit memos posted to those receivables. Periodic reporting to management of excessive account aging and/ or writeoffs, growth beyond the working capital projection or shrinkage beyond the bank's collateral requirements also should be noted.

When it comes to receiving and logging payments, a solid separation of duties should exist between the two functions. Some firms have individuals outside of accounting receive the checks, prepare the bank deposit and create an accounts receivable package for accounting that contains invoice stubs, check copies and a check receipt log. That keeps the process moving while allowing dual control over postings to the accounts receivable ledger.

Verifying receipt of receivables is a periodic activity done on a spot check basis to assure that the records are correct. Banks sometimes require this if receivables are used for collateral. Letters to randomly chosen customers asking for verification of the amount owed usually will do the trick.

***Inventory:*** Inventory management is an area especially sensitive to misappropriation. Goods and supplies that disappear in the night can add up quickly, costing the company money and leading to other fraud-related problems. The answer is simple: Commit to scrupulous recordkeeping, preferably tied back electronically to the accounting function, and institute careful handling of the merchandise. Utilizing a perpetual inventory management system with the appropriate number of checks and balances will help you keep closer tabs on all activities.

Remember, too, that inventory—whether finished goods or raw materials—changes as it progresses through its life cycle within your walls. Because of that, inventory should not move without some type of in-process documentation that not only tracks its status as a fiscal entity, but helps you better manage its movement to reduce the frequency of loss.

*Payroll:* Payroll theft does not refer only to the armed robbery of a Brinks truck, but rather the slow trickle that can be caused by employees who falsify time sheets or punch another worker's time card long after he or she has vacated the premises. Fictitious employees or retention on the payroll of employees who have left is another way workers have managed to milk the system of additional funds. Without close attention, you can begin to lose money quickly.

A regular payroll audit of personnel is one way to assure that those claiming wages have actually earned them. This involves review of time cards against employment sheets by someone who knows the employees and can spot a ringer. This also requires periodic checks of the work force throughout various

## GENERAL LEDGER
*(Continued)*

• Replace vouchers with new cash as needed. Vouchers then become part of the general ledger. As you replace vouchers with cash, be sure to reconcile the amount. This should be done by a third party.

• Minimize your use of petty cash to reduce the likelihood of misplacement or theft. Unless your business does a lot with petty cash—neighborhood recyclers pay cash to consumers for aluminum, brass and other refuse, for example—make your petty cash supply only as large as you need it.

And if you are that neighborhood recycler, pay for any refuse that totals over a certain amount—$20, for example—with a company check.

## LEDGER NOTES

Every company goes through its operational and financial ups and downs, but consistent problem indicators can signal that fraud may be a factor. The following problem signs, when several exist at once or over long periods of time, may signal trouble:

- The company has multiple bank accounts and more than it needs.

- Those bank accounts are not routinely reconciled by someone outside the cash transactional flow.

- Bank accounts have excessive balances or banking relationships are poor.

- Emergency borrowing has become a way of life.

- Cash movement, both inflow and outgo, continually surprises company officers.

- Short-term investment yields are below market rate.

shifts to make sure those reporting time can be accounted for. A final method is regular reconciliation from pay period to pay period with ample explanations of payroll amount swings within the shifts.

***Investment of funds:*** Excess cash sometimes becomes short-term investments, which opens another area of scrutiny and possible abuse. If your company follows this tack, make sure the person responsible for that investment is capable and qualified to do so. The officer investing the cash should not be the one recording the transaction, since the same opportunity for abuse exists.

Finally, make sure the investing officer doesn't have a personal trading account at the same brokerage firm in which he or she is investing cash on behalf of the company. Such dual interests may lead the broker in directions you don't want him to go. Stop-gaps and safeguards do exist, but it doesn't pay to take chances.

### WHEN SECURITY IS BREACHED

Even the best, most conscientiously designed systems can be breached by smart employees who have mastered the necessary skills to circumvent your protective measures. Your first step is to make sure the following components have been put in place:

- You have notified employees that you have installed and are using internal controls, but you have not given them the details of those procedures. The more information they have to work with, the more likely it is they will find a chink in the armor and learn how to exploit it.

• You have divided recordkeeping and cash (or accounts) handling operations so that you have a natural system of checks and balances in operation at all times. This is the single greatest problem area affecting the success of internal controls.

• Management staff is committed to maintaining the operational criteria of these controls as a critical part of their day-to-day job. In addition, you have created a system that requires the participation and support of all major departments.

• Your accounting system can be used as a forensic tool to spot errors and irregularities, not just as a means for explaining your company's financial picture. If you aren't utilizing that facet of your accounting system, you are letting a powerful tool slip through your hands.

Fraud investigation, also known as forensic accounting, is becoming a significant activity for many accounting and consulting firms who are brought in when company officials have reason to suspect wrongdoing. Unlike the auditors, who assume the company they are auditing is being honest, forensic accountants are more skeptical and more critical, assuming the likelihood of wrongdoing. Quite often, they are right.

Forensic accounting is very much like detective work. It also differs in that it takes a very narrow focus, often of a single department or function, whereas an audit reviews

## CHITS

According to industry statistics, a surprising number—nearly two-thirds—of all embezzlers are women. But most investigators say that's not surprising at all. Often male managers will put women in the position of handling the books and tend to trust them more. These tend to be low-paid secretaries or bookkeepers who see their male bosses taking home large salaries for doing what appears to be very little. Some rationalize that they're overworked and underpaid and figure they're entitled to help themselves.

# LEDGER NOTES

Just about all employees who embezzle rationalize their way into the crime. While situations differ, there are several distinct signs that can help you identify potential embezzlers. These include:

- marked personality changes in an employee;
- financial pressures on an employee;
- employee's apparent inability to manage money;
- an employee who appears to be living beyond his or her means;
- an employee with outside business interests;
- poor corporate internal controls;
- rising business costs;
- too much control vested in a few key employees;

the entire firm's financial well-being. Its goal is to root out a specific instance or instances of fraud and provide enough evidence for the company owner to seek restitution, if not pursue criminal prosecution.

Fraud tends to be very localized within a company. That requires extensive interviewing and research by the forensic accountant, most of whom receive specialized training in interview techniques. Examiners listen to what is said, as well as what is not said, by company employees they interview. *How* things are said is another facet, as well as whether the information corroborates with that gained from other interviews. The suspect is usually the last to be interviewed so the investigator can corroborate existing testimony and utilize previously collected evidence.

Investigators recognize the existence of a "fraud triangle" that enables the employee to steal. There must first be an opportunity, a loophole through which he or she can gain access to funds. Second, the embezzler must be able to rationalize his or her fraudulent activities. Finally, there must be a need or greed factor driving the action. There is no typical profile of an embezzler, but there are standard trouble signs. Embezzlers are often characterized by alcohol or drug dependency problems, gambling debts, or the need for money to finance an extra-marital affair. In some cases, they're just plain greedy and want to improve their standard of living.

Companies of all types are targets for embezzlement, but the public sector gets hit much more often than the private sector, with not-for-profit agencies and churches being hit the hardest. In those cases, it's a matter of too little in the way of controls and too much in the way of trust that allows the thieves to help themselves to assets.

## MORE PREVENTIVE MEASURES

Some companies have gone the route of policy development to help set the stage for employees and protect against fraud. Ethics policies that direct a promise of honesty and require an employee signature may not deter hardened criminals, but they may help those with a dubious sense of honesty from making a mistake.

Even those with a high level of scruples may accidentally run afoul of the firm by accepting gratuities or kickbacks from vendors for making purchases or providing favors. While they think they may be doing this in the best interest of the company, kickbacks skew the competitive nature of the vendor bidding process and also profit the employee at what could be the expense of making higher priced or inferior quality purchases. Like the ethics policy, a gratuity policy will help keep well-meaning employees from making what could be a serious error—collecting a bonus for themselves that doesn't come from the company's coffers.

It's all part of a well-developed and well-maintained system of internal controls, one that can mean greater loss prevention. But it can also add to staff morale and the sense that the company is secure and well-run. That in itself is value enough to establish such a system.

*LEDGER NOTES*
*(Continued)*

• lax management awareness; and
• failure to pre-screen new hires.

In addition to your financial obligation to shareholders, your company is also legally responsible for fraud prevention efforts. Firms that flagrantly ignore those measures could have its assets seized by the government if the employee is convicted of a federal crime. That's in addition to the monetary loss the firm has already suffered at the embezzler's hands.

*The way of accounting is right in its own eyes. Funds deferred maketh not the balance sheet sick.*

*—Proverbs: The Variations*

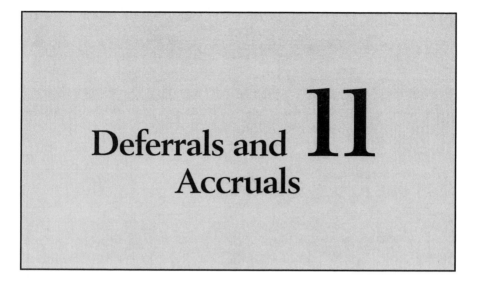

# Deferrals and Accruals 11

Understanding accounting procedure is really a very simple thing. In an organized, cogent and mathematically correct fashion, your numbers person(s) receives and records revenue and logs and pays expenses, at all times measuring through generally accepted accounting principles the net effect those actions have on the complex financial equation that forms your company's economic profile. Once the proper system is in place, there should be no particular challenge other than keeping up with accounts receivable and payable and making sure all the right numbers hit the general ledger, right?

What happens if expenses are incurred before revenue is realized? It doesn't matter whether you have the cash on hand to pay the bills. From an accounting standpoint, those two transactions should occur in the same time period and offset each other in order to balance your accounting equation. We live in an imperfect world, however, and oftentimes related transactions occur months apart. Fortunately, through the use of adjusting entries called *deferrals* and *accruals,* income earned and expenses incurred during the same period can be dealt with in the various ledger accounts, allowing you to accurately determine net income for the period without the presence of actual cash. If ever there was a purpose or rationale for the accounting system and its rigors, this may well be it.

We've mentioned it before: There are two types of accounting. Small companies with revenues of less than, say, $5 million, can operate either through cash accounting or accrual accounting. Larger

## *DEFINITION*

The essence behind the need for accrual accounting is a little thing called the "matching principle." Simply put, your revenues must match with the expenses incurred to produce them in the same period in which they were earned. This is true even if the actual cash won't be in your hands until some time in the future. The "matching principle" is a critical driver when it comes to balancing your books.

companies use accrual accounting as part of what is known as generally accepted accounting principles. The two, while having their root in similar operations, are really very different.

Small companies can elect to recognize and record transactions at the time cash changes hands. If you're a small pay-as-you-go construction firm, for example, you may choose not to record the purchase of a load of lumber until such time as you pay the bill to the lumber yard. From the standpoint of your books, until you actually cut that check, nothing has happened, even though you may have carted away the wood and even built the structure. You likely won't have recorded it into your accounts payable sub ledger before that. For that matter, you may not even have an accounts payable sub ledger.

Accrual based accounting, on the other hand, records transactions on the day and date those transactions occur, "matching" revenue and expenses to the period in which the transaction took place. If you're a large contractor in the middle of a building project picking up a truckload of supplies, you're incurring both expense (the purchase) and revenue (the project for which you are being paid) at the same time. You'll want to match income and expenses to the period in which each was incurred for a wide variety of reasons, not the least of which is a measure of earnings productivity. That's where accrual accounting comes in. The transfer of cash, as a matter of fact, is incidental to accounting for the transaction.

Which method to use? That depends on the nature of your business. If the purchases you make will be paid for in the future, or if the sales you make will not see the cash right away, then it makes sense to follow an accrual accounting approach to your business. If your operation is small and cash changes hands when goods and services are rendered, cash accounting might be suitable. It removes the step of setting up and utilizing accounts payable and accounts receivable sub ledgers. In fact, you can pretty much account for your business out of the company's check register.

For the sake of most businesses, however, let's concentrate on accrual accounting. That requires clarifying a few definitions first:

• A *deferral* delays recognition of an expense that already has been incurred and revenue received for the purpose of recognizing it in the period appropriate to the transaction. A tenant may pay a year's worth of rent in order to secure some type of discount, but the landlord won't recognize the full amount of that rent paid on the date of receipt. Rather, the landlord will defer that income, recognizing one-twelfth of the total each month during the duration of the lease.

Even though the money has been received, banked and perhaps even spent, from an accounting standpoint, recognition of those funds will be deferred until such time as they are earned. That would be for the month in which they apply to payment of the terms of tenant's lease. By deferring the full payment and applying as appropriate to the expenses that it covers, the landlord is able to get a true picture of his financial situation, enabling him to better manage his assets.

• An *accrual* is an expense not yet paid or revenue not yet received even though the transaction may already have taken place. Insurance premiums that are paid quarterly for coverage that already has been given fall into this category. As with deferrals, the value and impact of the transaction must be recognized at the time of that transaction whether or not the funds realized through that transaction have been distributed and/or received.

Accrued expenses also may appear on the balance sheet as accrued liabilities. Generally speaking, they're listed under current liabilities and subject to payment within the year. Accrued revenues may be treated as accrued assets. Classified as current assets, those funds are usually due in shorter order.

The accounting rule of thumb: Earnings for any given period result from identifying revenues and then matching appropriate expenses to those revenues. Unless both components are present, you haven't accounted for those earnings properly.

Within this realm, there are four distinct applications. Under deferrals, there are prepaid expenses and unearned revenues. Under accruals, there are accrued liabilities and accrued assets. Let's consider how each might appear on your company's books.

## ACCOUNTING FOR PREPAID EXPENSES

The cost of any purchase, any portion of which was not used during the accounting period in question, is considered a prepaid expense. That is to say, the unused portion is considered a prepaid expense. Rent paid in advance is considered an expense for the period to which it applies. Remaining rent paid that falls outside the accounting period is not recognized as an expense until such time as it applies. Thus, if a tenant prepays two year's worth of rent, one-half of that amount is considered an expense at the end of the first year; the remainder becomes an expense as each month in the new calendar year progresses.

At the time of payment, the amount may be debited to either an expense account or an asset account. The choice is yours and differs only in procedure and application. Just make sure that you treat similar expenses in the same way throughout your accounting system. Generally, these expenses include such things as prepaid insurance, rent, advertising and even interest on financial accounts.

If you choose to record prepaid expenses as assets, they are considered a debit to that account even though all or part will be used during the accounting period to which the entry applies. The adjusting entry of the amount of value that was used during the accounting period should be entered as a decrease of the asset and corresponding increase of the expense. The remainder does not appear on the balance sheet until the end of the accounting period.

If you choose to record prepaid expenses as an expense, you will debit those funds to an expense account rather than to an asset account, even though all or part of the payment will be expected to remain at the end of the accounting period. Once that amount is determined, the accounts are adjusted accordingly. The unused balance, upon being recognized as an expense, changes in nature through an adjusting entry that decreases its value as an expense while adding its value as an asset.

Either methodology may be used when dealing with prepaid expenses and, to some degree are interchangeable. In either case, the amount reported as expenses on the income statement or assets on the balance sheet will not be affected by the system used. We would suggest, however, that whatever system you apply to whatever portion of the transaction might be appropriate, it should be used the same way from year to year to preserve the integrity of your historical accounting data.

## HANDLING UNEARNED REVENUES

Every time you subscribe to a magazine and pay for that subscription a year in advance, the funds received by the publisher are unearned revenue. Any money received for goods and services not yet rendered is considered unearned revenue and hits the balance sheet as a liability until such time as it is earned. Then it appears on the income statement. Any type of payment in advance, from insurance premiums to tickets for a Broadway show six months down the road, is considered unearned revenue.

Unearned revenue can be handled either as a liability or as a revenue, similar to the way prepaid expenses are handled. By crediting it as a current liability on the balance

## CHIT

Unused deferrals, recorded as prepaid expenses, will at some point need to be transferred from the asset account to the expense account as their value is realized. The most efficient way that also assures proper allocations is through reversing entries, which reduce the possibility of error while transferring the entire balance immediately. It's also a way to eliminate the need for earlier adjustment procedures.

# LEDGER NOTES

*Reversing entries* are optional procedures, but they go a long way in simplifying transaction analyses and reducing errors in transaction recording. When they're applicable, reversing entries should be used. Consider them for the following transactions:

• when an accrued asset has been recorded;

• when an accrued liability has been recorded;

• when unearned revenue has initially been recorded as revenue; and

• when a prepaid expense has initially been recorded as an expense.

sheet, you're agreeing the service for which you've received payment needs to be rendered during the next accounting period. If you credit the amount to a revenue account as cash received, then the subsequent transfer of funds when the service is rendered will be reported to the income statement.

Assuming the unearned amount will be earned during the next period, it can be transferred to an income account through a reversing entry immediately after the account is closed. Subsequent payments made during following accounting periods can be treated the same way. Without the use of the reversing entry, however, you may wind up with balances in both the income and liability accounts. That will never do and will require some scrutiny and analysis to avoid further confusion.

Either system may be used in handling unearned revenue, or both systems may be used for handling separate accounts. Again, for historical purposes, keep your use consistent from year to year.

## MANAGING ACCRUED LIABILITIES

Certain expenses—payroll, for instance—accrue on a daily basis, but are usually recorded only when it's time to pay them out. This means the amounts of these expenses accrue as both an expense and a liability, hence the joint terms *accrued liabilities* and *accrued expenses*.

Once you reach the end of the accounting period for which these liabilities (expenses) apply, their amount must be recorded by an adjusting entry that debits the expense account and credits the liability account. Separate items may require separate accrued liability accounts. However, in the case of numerous items, you can lump them all into one account. But, in all cases, the reversing entry will be the method by which you can make the change.

## MASTERING ACCRUED ASSETS

By the time you reach the end of your accounting period, it will be necessary to record assets from all transactions in the general ledger. During that same period, however, it's fairly common to record some types of revenues as funds roll in. That could well mean at the end of the accounting period there is revenue left unaccounted. Thus, the amount of that revenue needs to be recorded by debiting an asset account and crediting a revenue account. Those funds make up the general category known as *accrued assets* and *accrued revenues*. Once again, use reversing entries to make this change.

Using accruals and deferrals isn't difficult and the options for use vary. If yours is a larger company, you really have no choice. But that's not a bad thing. These are accounting tools that can go a long way in keeping you on the right financial track throughout the year and making your operations less cash dependent. For virtually all businesses, it's really the right thing to do.

Even if you're just paying for your lumber as you go.

*For want of a nail, the shoe was lost.*
*For want of a shoe, the horse was lost.*
*For want of a horse, the rider was lost.*
*For want of a rider, the battle was lost.*

*Now* that *makes a case for inventory control.*

*—Apologies to George Herbert*

# Tracking Inventory 12

All companies, no matter what business they're in, have inventory. The grocer has canned goods, General Motors has automobiles and even consulting firms operate from an inventory of ideas. That's the stuff of which profits are made and it also constitutes some of the most tangible assets your company or any other firm has.

But there's more to the inventory question than the number of boxes, stacks of raw materials or racks of finished goods taking up space in your warehouse. Inventory has fiscal as well as physical dimensions. In order to maximize its value to your company—a value that changes as materials go through various stages of manufacture and distribution—you have to understand how to account for and handle that inventory. Tight inventory control that minimizes loss while maximizing worth will help your understanding and protect the value of your inventory investment.

First, let's identify what inventory is in light of your operation. It's more than merely the goods ready to purchase that your firm offers the marketplace, a common misconception by members of the public and many business people as well. Specifically, inventory breaks down into three "product" tiers:

- *Raw materials and supplies* used to produce the goods you take to market are part of your inventory. Since you likely paid money to attain them (remember that even catching fish from a stream has a cost equivalent in time and materials) they have

## CHIT

Accountability by key staff is the most effective way to manage inventory. Whether we're talking about your CFO's responsibility to make sure the inventory accounting system is effective and operational, or your warehouse manager's responsibility for merchandise that walks away at night, you'll find that inventory with accountability attached tends to be a more reliable asset.

a cash value. They also have an investment value because of what they will become once the work your company performs on them has been completed.

- *Goods currently in the process of completion* also constitute a level of your inventory. Car chassis on their way to becoming automobiles have a very different inventory value than the raw steel from which they were created because time, skill and manpower was invested to bring them to the chassis stage. In addition, if that inventory were stolen or destroyed, it would cost more to replace a chassis than merely the purchase of more steel.

- *Completed goods ready for customer purchase* constitute the most familiar tier of inventory and the one with the greatest cash value to the company. Completed goods represent the culmination of raw materials mixed with the intellectual property (ideas) your company owns that enables it to produce the goods, along with the cost of the labor it takes to turn raw materials into finished merchandise.

This inventory tier system exists in virtually every company in operation. Even if your firm is in the business of providing raw materials—say lumber—to another level of manufacturer, you still have an inventory that consists of source materials (trees purchased), inventory in process (the cost of cutting down, transporting and milling those trees) and finished inventory (the lumber you sell to builders, homeowners and other buyers).

Recognition of the value of each of those steps is recognition of the value of that inventory and how it plays into the net worth of your company's assets.

## CREATING AN INVENTORY CONTROL SYSTEM

Like any other company asset, your inventory needs to be managed in order to have its worth protected and its value maximized. What makes this even more critical is that inventory, by its nature, is an asset in process that increases in value from the time the materials enter the door until they leave as finished goods. That makes it difficult not only in terms of valuing that inventory, but also in keeping track of it as it moves through channels of production. Current computer technology has made that process a littler easier, but you still need to establish a comprehensive inventory control (I/C) system to manage your goods.

The system's purpose, first and foremost, is to track the evolution of inventory during its transfer from raw materials to finished merchandise. Keeping tabs on materials at various stages so that the purchase matches the number of finished items expected to be produced from it also is important. If, for example, 250 pounds of steel are used to produce an auto chassis, then a ton of the stuff should produce eight chassis. If your inventory control shows that only five are being produced from each ton, then there is some problem with production efficiencies or roughly 750 pounds of steel is being diverted from each ton for other purposes. Good inventory control can help track and aid in the investigation of such discrepancies.

Tracking inventory flow and controlling materials in process are two more ways by which your I/C system can help you manage this important set of assets. By the description of the process, you know that such a system helps compute the cost of goods sold by answering the following questions:

- What is the cash value (cost) of the raw materials that arrive in the warehouse? This is the basis of the value you give to your inventory.

## DEBITS

Balanced inventory values, like balanced books, are the secret to management of this critical asset. The numbers and merchandise must match. If the book value is lower than physical inventory, chances are you have an accounting error. If the physical inventory falls below what you have recorded, it may also be an accounting error, but it also could be theft. Keep tight control and watch for breaks in the chain.

- How much value does the manufacturing process add to the cost of the original materials? Included in this process, in addition to production, is all the time and labor spent handling those materials as well, which means lack of efficiency on your part can increase costs without increasing value either to the company or to the customer.

- How many phases are involved in the manufacturing process and what costs are associated with each of those phases? Inventory ages, which changes its value. Unless you're dealing in fine wines, that aging doesn't add value, but costs the company money. Delays in production and/or excessive and unnecessary procedures associated with materials handling raises costs without increasing value.

- What ancillary value is acquired by the finished goods that is only evident under the microscope of a good I/C system? That's really the answer to the issues raised above. Close inspection may reveal sources of value of which you weren't aware before.

There may be other variations, or you may find the whole process a little more cumbersome and expensive than might be necessary or economical if you run a small operation. But the main point remains: If you don't understand the cost of the steps it takes to produce the goods you sell, you can't properly price those goods either in line with your preferred strategic plan or your true economic needs. If not carefully handled, you may find you're unable to sell competitively in your market or that, in attempting to beat that competition, you've priced yourself right out of business. Neither is a preferred scenario.

## Choosing Your Inventory System

There are two types of inventory systems that you can apply to your operation:

- Under a *periodic inventory system,* revenue from a sale is recorded at the time the sale is made. No entry is made of the actual cost of the materials sold, which means you must conduct a *physical inventory* of assets to determine the cost of the inventory at the close of each accounting period, most likely the fiscal year.

- A *perpetual inventory system,* on the other hand, uses accounting records that continuously list the amount and value of inventory. Subsidiary ledgers are maintained for each type of material you list in inventory. Increases to those ledgers are recorded as debits, while decreases count as credits. The account balances are referred to as *book inventories.* Despite their supposed accuracy, you will still need to take a physical inventory at least once a year and then compare that inventory against the book inventory records. Adjustments are made to the book inventories based on the quantities on hand.

As you might guess, perpetual inventory systems are more costly and time consuming to maintain, while still requiring annual physical inventory. Grocers and other high-volume merchants of low-cost items tend to favor periodic inventory systems for that very reason. Sellers of high cost items, such as office equipment and luxury goods, are more likely to use a perpetual inventory system.

We're going to spend most of our time on the periodic inventory system, since crossover needs are similar and this system is more widely used by businesses of most types.

## CHIT

Some inventory isn't worth the value that is placed on the books. If your inventory is obsolete, spoiled, damaged or outdated, it may only be sellable at a price below cost. If that's the case, that inventory should be valued at *net realizable value,* or the sales price less any direct cost of disposition, such as sales commission. That's called *lower of cost or market* and will give that inventory a more realistic and achievable worth.

## COUNTING THE STUFF

The first step in inventory development is determining the amounts in each category, which means counting the stuff. That also will be part of your internal controls and/or company audit function. Whether you can count by the item or the pallet-load, whether the stuff needs to be weighed and measured, or whether the crew has to come in at night so as not to interrupt daily operations, you need to know exactly how much stuff you have on hand before you can get a full inventory. This usually takes place at the end of one accounting period and prior to the beginning of another.

Depending on the nature of your business and the needs of your inventory control system, you may have a special method by which you take your inventory. Most businesses operate with two-person teams; one recites the inventory before his or her eyes, and the other records it in an inventory book or some other data-capture technology like merchandise bar coding. In the case of high-priced merchandise, a third person who is not a member of any team verifies and signs off on the quantity, as well as doing random verification of all inventory team ledgers. That's necessary because inventory is a key asset. In the same way you need to protect liquid assets through various accounting control mechanisms, you also must protect your hard goods and raw materials for the same reason.

Remember, too, to count only merchandise and supplies owned by the company on the inventory date. Items waiting to be shipped that have already been sold and/or paid for aren't subject to your company's inventory.

The exception would be materials to be shipped for sale on consignment. Even though the company will not have physical possession of those materials, it will retain ownership until such time as the items are sold through the merchant to a third-party buyer. Thus, they should remain in your inventory.

Components of a good inventory control system also require a transaction record, which already should be part of your general ledger, that accounts for the different values assigned during the purchase of raw materials, materials in process and finished goods. These records (even for internal transactions) should contain the following:

- The date of transaction, critical for bill payment and process tracking.

- The person responsible for the transaction. In the event costs and numbers don't align, you'll want to know who to go to with questions.

- The names and numbers of each inventoried item. This goes without saying.

- The origin and destination of items moved. This is most critical for keeping track of inventory items in process that will be moving physically as well as fiscally within the company.

## COSTING THE STUFF

Once you've inventoried your goods, it's necessary to apply a cost to those goods. That's the purchase price, of course. But the actual cost also should include shipping and handling charges, tariffs and duties paid on the goods and any other cost that can be attached to your acquisition, warehousing and sale of the merchandise. Applicable discounts on the sales price should be deducted from that sales price, or treated as a gross discount on the category of merchandise overall. That's how things are done under a periodic inventory system.

Consider the dealer of cuckoo clocks purchased in Switzerland for $30 each. There was a $5 shipping charge for each clock plus another $5 in duties and tariffs. Once the sale was made the purchaser paid his or her own shipping and handling charges, so the hard dollar obligations end there. But this particular shipment was sold wholesale to a large dealer of clocks at a 20% discount taken from the sales price. What, then, is the inventory value of each clock?

| | |
|---|---|
| Price of cuckoo clock | $30 |
| Shipping | 5 |
| Duties/Tariffs | 5 |
| SUBTOTAL | $40 |
| Less 20% discount | (8) |
| TOTAL INVENTORY VALUE | $32 |

But what if those cuckoo clocks were purchased in larger quantities at different times of the year, when Swiss market conditions, the value of the Swiss franc and customer demand affected your cost? Suddenly, your computation above goes out the window when the base cost vacillates from shipment to shipment between $30 and $55 per unit. That changes the way you account for your merchandise. You have to determine the cost of goods sold before you can accurately price or account for those goods. When this happens, there are four ways to manage product valuing within your inventory system:

**1. Inventory average costing.** As you might expect, this method accumulates the total cost per units of items purchased during the accounting period, then averages them across all purchase prices to come up with an average value. The larger and more inconsistent the price of goods purchased, the more efficient this method becomes. Here's how it applies to our cuckoo clock dealer:

| Date | Item | Number/Unit Cost | Total Cost |
|---|---|---|---|
| Feb. 6 | Cuckoo clocks | 50 units @ $30 | $1,500 |
| Feb. 20 | Cuckoo clocks | 65 units @ $42 | 2,730 |
| Mar. 15 | Cuckoo clocks | 48 units @ $49 | 2,352 |
| Mar. 30 | Cuckoo clocks | 30 units @ $55 | 1,650 |
| TOTALS | | 193 units | 8,232 |

Average per unit cost: $8,232 / 193 = $42.65

If the number of units remaining at the end of the accounting period is 60 units, then the inventory value of those remaining units would be (60 × $42.65 =) $2,559.

**2. Lower cost or market value.**  One of the problems you want to avoid is inflating your company's assets by unrealistically valuing your inventory. First of all, it won't stand up to auditor scrutiny; secondly, if you're forced to liquidate those assets you won't be able to pay shareholders off at the amount promised in your inventory evaluation, a situation sometimes known as "cooking the books."

Evaluating inventory at the lower of cost or market is a very conservative approach that makes it nearly impossible to unrealistically inflate inventory values. Items are valued at the lower of the purchase cost of materials or present market value. This works especially well when attempting to assign inventory value to items with wildly fluctuating values, such as stocks, precious metals or gemstones, or even vintage collectibles.

**3. First-In, First-Out (FIFO).**  In most businesses that don't deal in perishables, like produce, or date-stamped items, it's almost impossible to know which purchase lot—thus, which price scenario—applies to a specific unit of goods. FIFO is an accounting mechanism that assumes that the older merchandise is sold first. Nevertheless, the cost of all units in inventory are computed at the price most recently paid.

Thus, on April 1, our cuckoo clock importer would compute the value of each clock at $55—the most recent price paid—despite the fact that some of his inventory was purchased for as low as $30 per unit. That would change the gross value of the 193 units from an averaged value of $8,232 to a FIFO-derived value of $10,615.

In an era of rapidly rising prices, FIFO allows for a lower cost of goods sold, thus increasing the net income—and subsequent tax liability—at a faster rate. This also results in higher inventory balances on the balance sheet, greater working capital and lower cash flows. This could apply artificial standards to your net income, so be judicious in your use and understanding of this method.

**4. Last-In, First Out (LIFO).**  This method, just the opposite of FIFO, assumes the last items in are the first items sold. The value of our 193 cuckoo clocks, when assigned the low $30 price per unit at which the first shipment was purchased, now changes from an averaged value of $8,232 to $5,790.

When prices are rapidly increasing, LIFO increases the cost of goods sold, thereby reducing the net income and offering a tax advantage to companies that need or want it. Declining prices increase income. The process also lowers taxes by lowering net income, as well as reducing working capital and inventory balances as shown on the balance sheet.

LIFO can soften fluctuations in the business cycle and is often the best strategy in a period of rising prices, but must be handled with care. Since evaluation reflects earlier prices, LIFO can paint an unrealistic picture of the value of your inventory.

Remember that the method by which you value your inventory has a strategy in and of itself and can be used to your company's financial advantage. Consider the following methods and strategies under the following situations:

• During periods of inflation or rising prices, FIFO will result in the highest profit margins in determining inventory evaluation. However, if the cost of goods sold continues to rise, that advantage will eventually be lost. In an era of declining prices, the effect is reversed and FIFO produces the lowest level of gross profit. FIFO has been criticized for simply mirroring inflationary and deflationary trends, but that also means the cost of inventory replacement is about the same as your balance sheet evaluation.

• LIFO can be used during inflationary periods to raise the cost of merchandise sold and lower the amount of income taxes owed. The strategy also more closely matches replacement costs, since unit costs more closely match those of the items being replaced. Companies interested in a tax saving strategy can lean heavily on the reduction in net profit realized through LIFO scenarios, using the savings to their advantage. During deflationary periods, the effect is just the opposite, with LIFO methods yielding a higher level of gross profits. Unfortunately, LIFO value don't always match merchandise replacement costs, a common criticism of the strategy.

• Average costing of merchandise, quite obviously, is a compromise between the FIFO and LIFO methods. Averaging neutralizes the ebbs and flows of actual costs as well as their impact on replacement costs. If your inventory valuation strategy is to not have a strategy, average costing may be the best way to go.

Choose the method that best fits the needs of your company, but make sure that choice has been made for the right reason and that it matches your overall business strategy.

## ACCOUNTING FOR THE STUFF

Taking careful inventories of materials and goods is critical to measuring assets. You also have to account for inventories correctly on your books. As always, proper accounting methodology is important in having your inventory recognized for its true worth.

From its most basic level, inventory is merchandise available to be sold and should be indicated as such. At the end of the accounting period, that merchandise will have to be divided into two categories depending on whether it has been sold or not. The cost of merchandise still in inventory will appear on the balance sheet as a current asset; the cost of merchandise sold will be reported on the income statement as a deduction from net sales to yield gross profit. If you're not careful and inaccurately list the inventory amount, you could misstate both the gross profit and net income. That means the amount reported both for net assets and owners' equity on the balance sheet also will be in error. Clearly, it's critical that you do this right.

There's even more potential for harm during the next accounting period, because the inventory at the end of the first period becomes the inventory for the beginning of the following period. If errors are carried over from period to period, problems could escalate. However, they will cease at the end of the second period. The course will reverse

## GENERAL LEDGER

Many companies have moved toward "just-in-time" inventory practices, both on the receiving as well as distributing end. Just like its name sounds, just-in-time inventory management means goods are available when needed and not a moment before. From a physical aspect, this keeps you from tying up your precious floor space with materials you don't yet need or goods you haven't yet sold.

itself and sort itself out, assuming no other errors are incurred. Such problems won't occur during a third accounting period.

From a fiscal standpoint, however, just-in-time means that precious cash isn't tied up in merchandise, allowing you the opportunity for extra earnings on those funds from overnight investment accounts and other short-term options. Just-in-time strategies have been used to effectively manage inventory and all that that means, but it also has had a positive impact on companies' bottom lines.

## LIFE IN THE PERPETUAL INVENTORY LANE

We talked at length in this chapter about tracking and accounting for inventory under the periodic system involving FIFO, LIFO and cost averaging. The perpetual inventory system has its own set of requirements that helps make it a more effective program for some businesses.

The perpetual inventory system is the more comprehensive of the two systems and links directly via your computer network to your database. Computations made in your perpetual inventory system immediately have an impact on other areas of your financial picture as appropriate. It's a more complex system to set up and maintain, but far more effective in helping you control inventory on a daily basis.

Under the periodic system we described earlier, the inventory at the beginning of the accounting period reflects the inventory on hand at that date. Further inventory purchases are recorded in the purchases account, with subsequent sales recorded in the sales account. The cost of merchandise sold isn't determined on a per sale basis, but rather at the end of the accounting period. At that time, a physical inventory is taken and two adjusting entries are made, one to remove the beginning inventory entry from the merchandise inventory account and another to add the revised inventory in its place. The adjusted balance of that inventory is reported on the balance sheet and the cost of goods sold determined at that point. This cost is then reported on the income statement.

Under the perpetual system, increases and decreases in inventory function similarly to increases and decreases in cash. As in the periodic system, the amount of inventory is entered at the beginning of the accounting period. Sales are still recorded in the sales account, but the cost of goods sold is debited to the cost of merchandise sold account and credited to merchandise inventory. This allows the merchandise inventory to perpetually disclose accurately the amount of merchandise on hand at any given time. At the end of the period, the balance listed in the merchandise inventory account is reported on the balance sheet and the balance in the cost of merchandise sold account is reported on the income statement.

The control feature and the ability to produce automated inventory records are probably two of the most important features in the perpetual inventory system. An ongoing, accurate record enables you to cross-check through conducting a physical inventory at any time. If shortages are discovered, they can be investigated immediately instead of waiting until the end of the accounting period. A record of shortages should be made to an inventory shortages account and credited to merchandise inventory for the cost of the loss.

A perpetual system is also a more easily tapped source of interim reports to compare primary and sub ledger balances to keep close tabs on inventory activity. The automated recordkeeping also allows for a more comprehensive record of sales and returns that credit and debit the appropriate accounts in the general and sub ledgers. In addition, these reports can be used to help determine the optimum level of merchandise and aid in "just in time" inventory replenishment, which allows your company better, more effective use of its cash.

## THE SECRET TO EFFECTIVE
## INVENTORY MANAGEMENT

What's the secret? Like any other aspect of business, the secret to inventory management is MANAGEMENT. By treating your inventory seriously, both as a fiscal and strategic asset, and using the tools and techniques at your disposal, you'll find yourself in a better position to understand the value of your company by truly understanding the value of these important assets and using them to the best possible advantage for your firm.

Inventory is your company's stuff, to be sure. But it's that, and a whole lot more.

*Never invest your money in anything that eats or needs repainting.*

*—Billy Rose, entertainer*

# The Fiscal Side **13** of Physical Assets

In the previous chapter, we described your inventory's role in your operation as an asset to your company. That's all very true, but there's also another level of asset that goes beyond both liquidity and inventory. Depending on the firm and the industry, these may be known as long-lived assets, plant assets or fixed assets. All three terms refer to the land on which your business sits (if you own it), the building in which your company lives (if you don't lease it) and the equipment with which your business operates (which has distinct value from the largest piece of machinery right down to the smallest piece of office furniture).

There's no firm and fast definition of what constitutes fixed assets, no minimum life cycle that moves the materials out of the realm of "supplies" into one of more permanent status. (As a point of reference, the Financial Accounting Standards Board, also known as FASB, defines assets as future probable economic benefits.) Rather, the defining characteristic has to do with usage. A fixed asset must be something that has repeated uses—such as a printing press or an office chair—and is expected under ordinary circumstances to last more than a year.

That's not to say, of course, that the asset needs to be in constant or even periodic use. The emergency generator your company purchased, installed and tests once every six months just in case there is a power failure is considered a fixed asset with a depreciable life even if the power never fails and the piece of equipment is never used. It's all wrapped up into the equipment you need to operate your business, and that falls into the fixed asset category.

## COSTING YOUR FIXED ASSETS

From both an operational and bookkeeping standpoint, you'll need to start with an accurate accounting of your fixed asset's true cost before you can begin to calculate its true depreciation values. Consider the following when costing out your assets:

• In the case of new equipment, machinery and other purchases necessary for running your business, an asset's true cost includes all expenditures necessary to put the asset in place and make it ready for use. In the case of the office chair we referred to earlier, that would include the price of the chair, sales tax and shipping charges, if any, to set the chair next to the desk with which it will be paired. In the case of the printing press, the true cost would include unit price, sales tax, and shipping to be sure. It also would include the cost of any installation charges, insurance on the piece while it's in transit, and expenses for any special installers who might accompany its delivery. If a foundation needs to be poured to support the press, those costs also should be added to the price. FASB ruling 34 also allows for lost interest tied up in building projects to be counted.

• In the case of your physical structure, all costs related to the construction and development should be considered part of the value. This includes everything from architect fees through construction fees right down to the

---

*GENERAL LEDGER*

When assessing the value of previously owned equipment, include any costs of repair and refurbishment needed to make the equipment ready for use. This does not include repairs due to negligence or vandalism or any cosmetic repairs. The key here is that repair must be associated only with getting the equipment up and running to meet your company's needs.

finishing contractors, insurance on the building during its construction and, if applicable, the cost of any security required to protect the site. Even the interest paid on loans required to finance the structure may be considered part of the construction fee. Once again, costs that contribute to the development of the asset necessary to make it ready for use fall in this category.

• The same holds true for the real estate on which the physical plant sits. The purchase price and all related broker fees and closing costs come under the value of the land, as do other fees connected with the legalities of the purchase and securing the title. Reconditioning the land for use, including the razing and clearing of old buildings and landscape work, should be added to the cost, as should the assumption of any delinquent taxes on the property that you might assume in acquiring its ownership.

Sidewalks, parking lots and other exterior accouterments that attach to the building and are designed to last the life of the building can be counted as part of the building and its value. Public improvements to the street or curb and gutter for which the building owner is liable, however, fall under a different account.

## DEFINING DEPRECIATION

We know the one constant in the universe is change. That's true of your fixed assets, too. Real estate, gemstones, fine art and wines may be the only assets that appreciate in value. All others decline in value as their opportunity to provide service declines with age. That being true, the cost of these declining assets must be valued properly over the effective lifetime of the asset. The process of this periodic cost expiration is called *depreciation*. For the truly technical, it's also defined as the systematic allocation of the capitalized cost of an asset to income over the life of its use. Or think of it as the replacement cost of an asset. That works, too.

Depreciation is further refined into two specific categories:

1. *Physical depreciation* covers wear and tear on a fixed asset from use or from the elements. As the asset ages and its functionality declines, it physically depreciates until it no longer is

## DEBIT

Proper depreciation is critical to assessing the true value of your company's assets. But beware of making the following two mistakes:

• The term *depreciation* has two meanings. One relates to the declining value of a fixed asset, while the other refers to the declining market value of an asset. The two likely will not equal each other in value, so make sure you understand what it is you're attempting to compute.

serviceable in the capacity for which it was designed and for which you purchased it.

2. *Functional depreciation* occurs when the asset becomes inadequate to meet the demand or obsolete in its use. Equipment designed to produce long-playing records for the most part has fallen into this category, along with other electronic components. But it's the personal computer industry that tops out here. Functional obsolescence also is reached when there is no longer any demand for the product the fixed asset produces, or when newer, better equipment can produce the product more cheaply or quickly.

What makes the distinction and depreciation activity important is the often unstated belief that virtually every business, no matter how large or how small, thinks of itself as a going concern and operates as if it were going to be in business forever. That's probably not true, but it does provide the necessary framework needed when analyzing depreciable assets. Moreover, it dictates that those assets be depreciated not in terms of market value, but rather in terms of usefulness to the future of the enterprise. That makes a big difference when it comes to factoring asset value on your company's books.

### Determining Depreciation Value

Once a fixed asset has run its course in service to your company, it likely will be time to retire or replace that asset. Some assets still have value once they're retired, while others don't. Determining the likelihood of this value is as much a function of accounting as it is of the marketplace and your ability to resell the asset.

There are three components to determining depreciation value when it comes to measuring your fixed assets:

- First and foremost is the original cost of the item. That's the amount you paid when you made the purchase and, as you'll remember, includes the per unit cost, sales tax, shipping, installation, insurance and other costs associated with acquisition.

- From the original cost of the item and after its period of worthwhile contribution to your company, you may come up with a residual value. Also known as scrap or salvage value, the residual value is the amount at which the marketplace values the used asset and what they may be willing to pay for it. If you expect the office chair you bought for $100 to last for five years and then fetch $10 at a garage sale, the $10 is your best guess at a residual value.

- Once you've taken your best guess at residual value, you can subtract the amount from the purchase price of the asset and that will determine your depreciable cost. An office chair that you purchased for $100 and then sold five years later for $10 has a depreciable cost of $90.

Once that's been determined, that cost will have to spread over the life of the asset.

## DEBIT

*(Continued)*

- As a noncash expense, depreciation accounting does not provide for liquidity to replace the item being depreciated. Once it's used up, you'll have to find the cash to replace the asset. Since depreciation expense, like most expenses, does not require an outlay of cash for the period, there is no slush fund created to buy a replacement. You'll have to reserve for that under separate activities in your cash account.

We assigned that chair a residual value of $90 and said it would last five years. That brings the periodic depreciation expense to $18 per year which, after five years, will equal $90. From an equation standpoint, it looks like this:

*Initial Cost* – *Residual Value* = *Depreciable Cost*
$100 – $10 = ($18 + $18 + $18 + $18 + $18) or $90

Of course, the chair may last six years, prompting you to alter your estimate. No one knows for sure what either the final residual value or depreciable value will be until such time as the appropriate transaction takes place. For the purpose of your accounting procedures, however, your best guess is as close as you may be able to come. Smaller units of measure, such as months, may help you better pinpoint these values accurately. Management policy about the life of a fixed asset also may help increase accuracy. Your company may use different methodologies at different times for varying reasons. The choice is yours—or your accounting department's, anyway—but it should be used consistently from year to year so that historical comparisons are consistent in the same account over time.

Currently, there are four common methods of determining depreciation:

**The straight-line method:** This method is used in almost 90 percent of all cases due to simplicity and equitability. It is by far the most common method for depreciating fixed assets because it most closely replicates the matching principle we talked about earlier. The office chair in the previous example was depreciated at the most basic level of this strategy, with a certain amount assigned as depreciable value each year for five years. You may also assign this depreciation on a percentage basis or vary it based on the actual time or perceived value involved. In the case of our office chair, the depreciation value was literally 18 percent per year, or 1.5 percent per month. If the chair were purchased in July, its first year's depreciation may constitute the full 18 percent, or it may be just 9 percent (1.5 percent per month for six months).

***Units of production:*** Under the units-of-production method, depreciation is computed as a variable rather than a fixed cost and is based on the amount of actual use a fixed asset receives. This would be hard to compute for our office chair, but may not be for a company car that a sales person takes out on sales calls. Assume a sales price of $20,000 with a residual value of $5,000. That leaves $15,000 in depreciable cost to be divided up over the three-year depreciation period. That looks like this:

Initial Cost  – Residual Value  =             Depreciable Cost
  $20,000    –     $5,000    =  ($5,000 + $5,000 + $5,000) or $15,000

Under the units-of-production method, however, we would assume depreciation on a per mile basis. Assume the sales person logs 20,000 miles per year or 60,000 miles for the three-year depreciation period. That depreciation equation would look more like this:

$$\frac{\text{Cost: \$20,000} - \text{Residual Value: \$5,000}}{\text{60,000 miles}} = .25 \text{ per mile depreciation}$$

Thus if the sales person logs 54,675 miles during his or her three-year service with the car, that means a total vehicle depreciation of $13,668.75. With any luck, the resale on the vehicle will net an additional $1,331.25—the difference between the original and actual depreciation rate—for a sales price of at least $6,331.25. In any event, adjustments can be made once final numbers are firm.

***Double declining balance:*** The double declining-balance method of depreciation takes a very different approach to determining depreciation value. In fact, the question of residual value doesn't even come into play. Instead, the life of the product is computed and then the yearly percent value doubled. That doubled value is converted to the cash value, computed and then subtracted at that rate for the life of the asset. Consider our early printing press example, valuing the press and its shipping, installation, et al., at $1 million. Under the declining balance method spread over a five-year period, the equation looks like this:

| Year | Cost | Accumulated Book Value Depreciation | Annual Book Value Beginning/Year | Rate | Depreciation | End/Year |
|------|------|------|------|------|------|------|
| 1 | $1M | ___ | $1 Million | 40% | $400,000 | $600,000 |
| 2 | $1M | $400,000 | $600,000 | 40% | $240,000 | $360,000 |
| 3 | $1M | $640,000 | $360,000 | 40% | $144,000 | $216,000 |
| 4 | $1M | $784,000 | $216,000 | 40% | $86,400 | $129,600 |
| 5 | $1M | $870,400 | $129,600 | 40% | $51,840 | $77,760 |

For each year, we have depreciated a new annual book value and depreciated that book value by 40 percent—twice the actual percentage determined by the number of years of useful life. At the end of five years, this process has left us with a residual value of $77,760.

**Sum of the years' digits:**  Under the sum-of-the-years'-digits method, we utilize the number of years that will make the depreciable life of the assets and then apply increasingly lower fractional levels of depreciation as the asset ages. In figuring this method, you create a fraction, the denominator of which is determined by adding the total of the years. The numerator is the actual aging year of the asset. This fraction acts upon the depreciable value of the asset once the residual value is subtracted from the purchase price.

By example, we'll use a five-year depreciation scenario for the depreciation amount of $15,000 depreciable value for the salesperson's car from the earlier example. Once that amount has been determined—in this case a book value of $20,000 at the beginning less the residual value of $5,000—you apply the sum-of-the-years'-digits method like this:

| Year | Cost Less Residual Value | Rate | Depreciation for Year | Accumulated Depreciation at End of Year | Book Value at End of year |
|------|------|------|------|------|------|
| 1 | $15,000 | 5/15 | $5,000 | $5,000 | $15,000 |
| 2 | 15,000 | 4/15 | 4,000 | 9,000 | 11,000 |
| 3 | 15,000 | 3/15 | 3,000 | 12,000 | 8,000 |
| 4 | 15,000 | 2/15 | 2,000 | 14,000 | 6,000 |
| 5 | 15,000 | 1/15 | 1,000 | 15,000 | 5,000 |

Of course, $5,000 is the residual value and drives the equation above. How do these systems compare?

- The straight-line method provides uniform depreciation over the life of the asset. It is the simplest and easiest method of the four.

- The units-of-production method can vary the asset's value considerably, but offers some flexibility when the straight-line method isn't quite as appropriate.

- The declining-balance and sum-of-the-years'-digits are both referred to as accelerated depreciation methods because they provide for a high depreciation the first year of the asset's use and declining value for that use as the asset ages and the term of depreciation lengthens. Some assets that decline in production or value over time may be better served by these methods.

## Recording Depreciation

A large part of making depreciation work on your fixed assets is recording it properly. Most companies record it on a monthly basis and close out their books with an end-of-year adjustment. Those entries are usually made to an *Accumulated Depreciation* or an *Allowance for Depreciation* account, a contra asset account that permits the original purchase cost(s) listed on your books to remain unchanged, while allowing those depreciated costs to find a place on your balance sheet so they are available for tax purposes.

The exception to the rule comes when an asset is sold or written off for scrap. In this case, both the cost of the asset and its accumulated depreciation are removed from the books at the date of disposal. That doesn't mean you can't still take the depreciation on that item for the period in question, but it must be done prior to disposal of the asset. This also means that your interest in this asset has ended when it comes time to compute the depreciation for other fixed assets.

## DISCARDING FIXED ASSETS

Eventually, all fixed assets run the course of their usefulness. Computers become outmoded, equipment ceases to function properly, facilities no longer meet your company's needs. You will find yourself

# GENERAL LEDGER

Once you've established your fixed assets, such as your company's building or plant, you can add to those assets through a capital expenditure. That's what you'd do if you wanted to build an addition on the building to increase production capacity. Capital expenditures, designed to spread across multiple accounting periods and over several years, are usually debited to the asset account or the accumulated depreciation account. Expenditures benefiting only the current period are called revenue expenditures and are debited to the expense account. The acid test, once again, is in whether the expenditure increases efficiency, adds capacity or increases the life of the asset.

discarding fixed assets eventually and you need to know how to account for that disposition.

The rule of thumb for all types of dispositions—writeoffs, sales and trades—is that if the asset has been fully depreciated, no loss need be shown on the books. The asset has run the course of its book value and can be disposed of without having a financial impact of any kind. Of course, the asset's book value will need to be deleted. This is done by debiting the full amount from the appropriate accumulated depreciation account and crediting the asset account.

Keep in mind, however, that fully depreciated assets that are still useful to the firm should not be removed from the books just because they have completed their depreciation cycle. They're still working assets of your company and preemptive removal from your books will cause problems with your ledger, especially when it comes to property tax evaluation. As long as you're using them, keep these assets on your books until such time as you do dispose of them.

Here's how you deal with fixed assets that are "written off" (in effect thrown away), sold and traded in on newer or different equipment.

• If a fixed asset has run its course of usefulness and is discarded, it must be fully depreciated to have no financial impact on the firm. For accounting purposes, fixed assets are considered nonoperating items. If the asset is discarded prior to being fully depreciated, the depreciation balance should be considered a loss and reported in the "other expenses" section of your income statement.

Likewise, if you realize a gain on the disposal of the asset—say it is sold for scrap or parts—then any revenue is recorded on the other income section of the income statement. The phrase "gain or loss on asset disposition account" usually appears at the bottom of the financial statement.

• If a fixed asset is sold, it's treated much the same as a disposal, except that income from the sale needs to be recognized on the income statement. This is especially true if the asset has been fully depreciated, but is subject to several requirements if the asset is not. Sales that are made for greater than book value are recognized as gains; sales for less than book value are considered a loss.

• Old equipment occasionally is traded in for new equipment. The trade-in allowance for the old equipment is deducted from the price of the new and handled in whatever payment fashion to which you've agreed. Chances are, the trade-in allowance won't be an exact match for the book value on the old equipment and adjustments have to be made. In case of the trade-in price exceeding the book value, however, generally accepted accounting principles don't allow you to recognize that difference as a gain, since your company's primary revenue occurs from the sale of the item it produces, not from horse trading equipment. If the trade-in price is less than book value, however, you may immediately record the loss.

How do you account for excess revenue when the trade-in price exceeds book value? Take the balance on the new equipment, sometimes called the "boot," and add it to the book value of the old asset. In other words, if you receive $1,000 credit on a trade-in of an old asset for a newer $5,000 one, the boot value of the new asset is $4,000. If your old asset has a depreciation value of $500, that would normally seem like $500 in additional revenue on your books. Instead, you must add the boot ($4,000) to the book ($500) and value the new asset at $4,500 rather than the actual $5,000 price. That way the *value* of the asset in question stays constant and your books don't fall out of line.

That may not seem fair at first, but the $500 difference will be reflected in a change in the depreciated value of the new asset. Rather than adding it to your books as $5,000, it's added as $4,500

# GENERAL LEDGER

When depreciating groups of assets, it's wise to create a subsidiary ledger to account for the elements in this group. A subsidiary ledger allows for the individual aging of assets as needed without overcomplicating the main ledger. Whatever form you choose, allow space for a description of the asset, as well as a space for acquisition, depreciation and disposal of the asset. This subsidiary ledger will come in handy in managing the depreciation of those assets and filing tax returns.

To make things even simpler, you may also consider using a composite rate depreciation that averages the assets within individual groups and computes a percentage composite rate for assets listed. This will clean up the process for assets of different ages and a variety of depreciable values.

and depreciated accordingly. Unless you do the same thing again with one more asset down the road, the difference zeros out at the end of the new asset's depreciation period.

## LEASING

Increasingly, companies are bypassing the purchase of fixed assets in favor of leasing. These days, that includes everything from real estate to fleet vehicles to aircraft to computers to workers. In addition to being an asset management strategy, leasing also can make sense from a financial and operational perspective, particularly in areas where equipment such as computers, copiers and other such goods quickly become outmoded.

Leasing has become an increasingly more appealing alternative to purchases, and industry statistics bear this out. According to a study by the Equipment Leasing Association, a trade group for leasing companies, 85 percent of business equipment today is financed, of which 33 percent is leased. In addition to that, 80 percent of the Fortune 500 companies use leasing as part of their management strategy. Leasing's annual volume rose from $100 billion in 1989 to more than $180 billion in 1998. Projections for year-end 1999 have that volume hitting the $190 billion mark.

Financial advantages top the list of reasons to lease, research shows. Specific advantages cited include:

- the availability of 100 percent financing with no downpayment required;

- little or no impact on bank lines of credit or key financial ratios by which companies' capital positions are judged;
- ability to deploy assets to items that appreciate in value;
- and tax advantages, including deduction of interest and an escalated depreciation schedule.

There are two types of leases, each of which must be treated differently on your books:

• A *capital lease* is similar to a purchase in the way it acts and is treated from an accounting perspective. Terms extend over the depreciable life of the asset. In addition, the lease requires payments equivalent to the fair market value of the asset. The four criteria that define a capital lease are:

- transfer of ownership of the leased item at the end of the lease;
- the lease often contains a bargain purchase option for the lessor;
- the base term is based on 75 percent or more of the economic life of the leased asset;
- the present value of the lease payment is equal to or exceeds 90 percent of the market value.

• An *operating lease* implies a much lower level of "ownership" and doesn't comply with any of the aforementioned criteria. There are no future obligations or ownership rights and rent expense is recognized as the asset is used. Many experts believe that financially healthy companies are better off with operating rather than capital leases because it is less like ownership than a capital lease. From a business standpoint, a lease has its advantages. As long as they are accounted for correctly, the choice of how to handle your company's fixed asset needs is up to you.

*We work not only to produce
but to give value to time.*

*—Eugene Delacroix, artist*


*I go on working for the same reason
that a hen goes on laying eggs.*

*—H.L. Mencken, satirist*

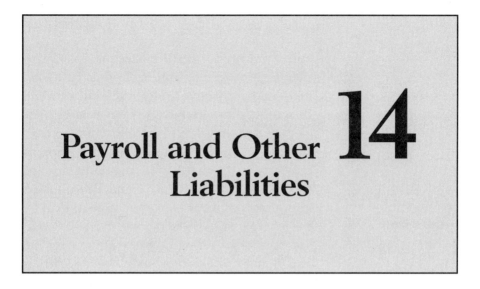

# Payroll and Other Liabilities 14

Liabilities, also known as *payables*—or "accounts payable," as we discussed in earlier chapters—are amounts your company owes as part of its cost of doing business. They're the opposite of receivables—amounts owed to your company—and, we hope, don't exceed the value of those receivables for any extended period of time. Payables tend to be recognizable expenses, such as invoices for goods or services that enable you to do business, loan payments due to banks or other lenders, rent and utility bills and even taxes.

One of the most critical liabilities and often one of the largest for any company is payroll. Those are the wages and salaries you owe workers and executives who drive the company, produce and distribute the goods and otherwise make it possible for you to deliver on your promises to customers and to stay in business. That's a liability not to be taken lightly and one, if not satisfied on a regular basis, that can close down a company's operations swiftly and painfully. Any employer will tell you that happy employees tend to be more productive than unhappy ones. A regular and reliable payroll function goes a long way toward engendering that enthusiasm.

Defining payroll is a little more complex, however, and requires a fairly comprehensive system to help you keep up with those complexities. There also are tax implications, which we'll cover in an upcoming chapter. As mentioned, payroll consists of salary for professional staff and wages for the hourly workers. But you also may have piece-work rates with which to deal, or sales commission

## DEFINITION

The word *payroll* refers to the total amount paid to all employees for a given period. This includes wages and salaries, as well as bonuses and commission paid out of this account. Taxes paid on amounts earned by employees are also part of your company's payroll profile, along with any other deductions taken. The term refers to the gross amount earned, not the net received on the actual paycheck.

and other pay-for-performance methodologies that requires greater effort on your part than merely identifying a salary level and dividing the number into 26 biweekly pay periods.

In addition, there's vacation time to consider, sick leave to compute, profit sharing to factor in . . . perhaps even customer tips for which you will have to account. Payroll is an important liability made even more critical by the complexity of its management. A good system will go a long way in making your life and that of your company's employees that much easier. Some companies use professional payroll services to manage these complexities and you may, too. But the principles are the same no matter who does them, so it's worth your while to understand the purpose behind the action.

## DEVELOPING A PAYROLL SYSTEM

Most companies find that developing a payroll system isn't terribly difficult, even though it can be time consuming to administrate with a need for great attention to detail. (Remember, both your employees and Uncle Sam will be watching, neither of whom will feel much generosity of spirit for any errors you may make.) Much of the preparation must be done up front, and careful attention during this step can save you from a world of woes during the system's administration.

What steps go into payroll system development? First and foremost, make sure all the proper documentation has been collected from new and existing hires so that proper withholding can be done. (That includes a signed W–4 statement.) Make sure your employees understand the length of pay period (intervals of a day, a week or a month between payments) and how that pay will be delivered (cash, check or direct deposit). There's a difference between wages, salaries, commissions and bonuses. Your system's success depends on staff clearly knowing when to expect what and how much of what they will receive.

Once you've done that, you're free to set up your pay dates and establish operational steps that may look something like the following:

- Have at hand all employee records of time put in, work performed and money earned. This includes but isn't limited to time cards, piecework record sheets, sales commission reports and salary records.

- Compute any changes to payroll, such as additions of new hires, salary increases, bonuses, vacation and sick time deductions, overtime and holiday pay. This is also the point where you deduct income taxes, union dues, charitable contributions, health plan copayments, retirement and 401(k) contributions and the like.

- Figure up the payroll amount for the period and cut checks or make the direct deposits to employee accounts. Apply deductions and credit the appropriate recipients. Electronic transactions and direct deposits have become almost universal for large employers, although some still give employees the choice of receiving a check. A surprising number of staff still like the idea of money in hand, even if it means an extra trip to the bank for them.

- Complete the payroll journal and make necessary changes in the general ledger to bring company records up to date.

Make sure that all internal ledgers, journals and accounts align and that payroll entries are updated wherever they need to be. Your accounts will quickly fall into disarray if you don't make sure all accounts agree, and that can affect future payrolls.

## GENERAL LEDGER

If the idea of an outside payroll service appeals to you due to the complexity of the payroll operation, remember that it's still a cost vs. benefit decision. If the ability to manage payroll internally taxes company resources beyond what is economically and physically feasible, then maybe an external firm is the better choice.

But before making that decision, map out the steps and their related costs of managing payroll internally and compare it to the cost an outside firm would charge. Remember that at least some of your controller's time must be spent preparing payroll prior to sending it out-of-house. If that time can be economically expanded to cover the rest of the steps in the payroll process, then it might be more economically feasible to do it yourself.

## WHAT EMPLOYEES EARN

Earnings computation is the most critical part of determining payroll, and often is the easiest factor to figure. No matter what function an employee fills—from president of the company right on down to mailroom clerk—there is a personnel file on that individual containing the necessary salary information. Aggregation of those records, as well as the payment scenario of each, is the heartbeat of any payroll system.

Determining payroll may be as simple as multiplying the employee's hourly rate by the number of hours the employee worked, then subtracting the appropriate deductions. For the arithmetically minded, that factors into the following equation:

Earnings (E) = Hours (H) $\times$ Rate of Pay (RP)

If the employee described by this payment scenario works more than his or her 40 hours and is entitled to time-and-a-half, the above equation can be altered to include a factor of 1.5 for hours beyond the normal 40.

For salaried employees, the equation is a little different. Their rate is computed based on annual gross amount divided into the number of pay periods in the fiscal year. If, like most businesses, you pay staff every other week, the salaried employee equation would look like this:

Earnings (E) = Gross salary (GS) $\div$ 26 pay periods

Thus, if a salaried employee paid every other week earns $52,000 per year, each period's pay check would begin with a gross amount of $2,000 from which deductions would be taken.

Bonuses come from a different point of view and may or may not be subject to arithmetical equations. Bonuses are almost always based on performance—either the company's or the individual's—and may be computed either as set amounts, a percentage of salary or a percentage of profits over a certain expected level of earnings.

In addition, bonuses can be determined before or after taxes have been taken out. They can be considered a part of the income from which the level for a bonus is derived, or they can be an amount extra to the base for which the bonus has been awarded. The rules governing bonuses are a great deal more variable than those governing salary. But they are still considered income and subject to withholding taxes. That's the one variable over which employers have no legal control.

## Deductions from Payroll

Employees' total earnings, the ones from which you deduct all the necessary amounts, are called *gross pay*. Once the deductions all have been taken, the remainder is net pay, also known as "take home pay" and "Is that all?" All gross pay—whether salary, wages, commissions or piecework pay—is subject to the following deductions:

- Federal Insurance Contributions Act tax, also known as FICA, is withheld from virtually all paychecks to fund federal health and disability programs, insurance benefits and Medicare programs for the aged. With few exceptions, FICA is assessed at a specified rate up to an amount paid for the calendar year. The program and its financial support requirements are revised by Congress now and again, but this does not change the payroll deduction requirement for employers or employees.

- Federal income tax, another mandatory withholding requirement, is dependent on gross pay, marital status, exemptions, deductions and other variables as well as the deductions listed by the employee on his or her W–4 form. Like FICA, employers are required to withhold federal income tax as the income is earned.

- State income tax functions much the same way federal income tax does for those states that assess it. Most state income tax models follow the federal income tax formula. Some municipalities also assess local taxes that need to be treated the same way.

**Other deductions:**   Noncompulsory deductions are numerous and generally are withheld at the behest of the employee and, sometimes, at the employer's direction.

- Some retirement plans require compulsory contributions by the employees as part of the employer vesting program. Even if the employee does not work for the employer long enough to be vested, employee contributions are always returned to the employee, no matter how small the amount, upon termination of employment.
- Health care or insurance co-pays are usually taken right out of the paycheck as a deduction from gross pay. How much is taken out depends on the comprehensiveness of the plan and the generosity of the employer.
- Voluntary deductions to employer-sponsored 401(k) retirement plans also are deducted prior to net. And so are automatic charitable contributions, social club memberships and health-care prepayment programs.
- In the event that an employee is allowed to borrow from his or her retirement fund for a major purchase, like the down payment on a house or to fund a child's college education, repayment of those funds to the account also are deducted from the gross amount.

## A Sample Pay Sheet

The best way to illustrate some of the aforementioned deductions and applications may be to show a sample time sheet with all possible deductions applied. Let's look at the pay stub for week 25 of the 26-week pay cycle for Max Waxman III, grandson of the owner of Waxman Waxworks, a manufacturer and distributor of candles and paraphernalia. Max III is a department manager in charge of scented tapers. Here is Max's statement:

| Gross earnings for the period | | 2,699.54 |
|---|---|---|
| Deductions: | | |
| FICA | 164.58 | |
| Fed. withholding | 334.70 | |
| State withholding | 170.11 | |
| Health care co-pay | 38.49 | |
| Health Flex pay | 12.50 | |
| Retirement—Elec. | 54.99 | |
| Retirement—Mand. | 83.49 | |
| 401(k) loan payback | 65.91 | |
| Total Deductions | | 924.77 |
| Net Pay for period 25 | | 1,774.77 |

Max III is a moderate to high earner, and he has a lot going on in his time sheet.

The FICA and federal and state withholding taxes are mandatory, and take the largest slice out of his gross pay. Health care co-pays and two retirement contributions comprise the next largest segment. One set speaks to the immediate needs of his family, including his wife, daughter and little Max IV, the other to the long-term benefit needs for himself and his spouse upon retirement. While this is still a deduction, it's also an investment in his own future.

Max even contributes a small amount—$12.50 per pay period—to a pretax health care deductible payment plan that allows him to pay for prescriptions and medical treatment co-pay charges in pretax dollars. This saves Max about $85 per year in income otherwise sapped by taxes. The final amount is the payback for the loan taken from his 401(k) plan to put the down payment on his house. Although not shown here, the rate at which Max is repaying the fund—and, ultimately, himself—will add an additional 60 percent on the amount which he borrowed from himself in the first place. His employer merely assesses a small maintenance fee.

Much of what seems like a long laundry list of activities on Max III's paycheck is required by state and federal authorities; with much of the balance a part of the standard employee benefits package. The small remaining portions represent a distinct benefit to the employee who knows how to take advantage of it and doesn't require a great deal more time and effort on the part of the employer.

That's one way to turn the payroll task into an employee benefit which, in turn, should result in more loyal and effective employees.

## EMPLOYER PAYROLL LIABILITIES

Employees are not the only ones obligated to pay taxes based on income. The employer also has financial obligation based on the salaries he or she pays. That's part of the cost of doing business and can add up over time.

Employers are required to contribute to FICA at the same rate as that of the employee, thus sharing the burden. The employer has the full burden of paying state and federal unemployment compensation taxes to help underwrite an income stream to those employees who have been terminated. All employers pay federal unemployment; some states also require it.

In addition, sick leave and vacation pay can also be counted as payroll expenses, since they generally come from a different fund and are not tied to a productive day's labor. As illustrated by Max III's time sheet summary, retirement contributions by the employer also may be counted as a cost against payroll. Funds most certainly have been reserved for such expenditures, but since they're considered expenses, this is the account against which they're measured.

## COMPONENTS OF YOUR PAYROLL
## ACCOUNTING SYSTEM

Payroll reflects your company's relationship with employees at its most intrinsic level. And a good payroll accounting system protects that relationship through accurate records of time and effort spent by the employee and compensation given by the employer. Safeguarding that system and the records it contains, as well as making sure it facilitates payment in a timely fashion, is critical to not only the financial well-being of both the firm and the employee, but also of the relationship between the two entities.

Payroll records come into play in many ways other than merely that of compensation. They're a requirement of many federal, state and local laws and, as we already have seen, facilitate the country's taxation efforts. Government agencies often require periodic reports to help determine the level of taxes due from the employer, and those records must be open for inspection by the proper legal authorities. In addition, payroll records have been used in union negotiations and to settle disputes involving sick leave, vacation rights, and retirement benefits and pensions.

All of these uses are built on three major components of the payroll system: the payroll register, employees' earnings records and payroll checks. Needless to say, all records must reflect the same transaction and amount levels in order to keep the books in balance; but each component plays a role unique to its purpose and critical to the effective operation of your payroll system.

## The Payroll Register

Often formatted as a spreadsheet, the payroll register illustrates all payroll information broken down by both employee and category of payment for all staff during each pay period. Remember Max Waxman's pay stub? The payroll register formulates a much larger document that cross-references payments to Max, his brother Ajax, his cousin Drax and all the other employees who work for Waxman Waxworks.

The cross-referenced spreadsheet, usually set up in columns, allows for several things. First, it provides complete payroll information for each employee; but it also provides critical categorical information—how much was doled out in employee-based FICA payments, for example—for all the different deductions listed on the time sheet. Such referential information is valuable when it comes time to report employee earnings, tax contributions, retirement account activity and other information that will have an impact on the company's financial profile.

In addition, the easy access of information allows comparisons from period to period as a way to measure trends and activities compared to budget and to look for unusual circumstances. The payroll register is no longer just a databank of information but a strategic tool that will allow for the necessary adjustments to individual columns.

The register also may be used as a posting medium to record employees' earnings, much the same way a voucher register and check register are used. It also may serve as a supporting record for a compound journal entry to make sure each debit and credit is properly assigned. The expenses incurred for hiring the services of employees are recorded as debits to salary expense accounts, but amounts withheld have no effect on these accounts. Taxes are treated as liabilities and their payment recorded as such.

In fact, all payroll taxes become liabilities against employers at the time the employees are paid the amounts against which those taxes are assessed, rather than at the time the employees completed the labor for which they're being paid. This will make it necessary to accrue wages to cover the periods when the work has been completed and the employee is paid. However, the only legal obligation is to make the necessary account adjustments when the new tax year starts in January. Whatever adjustment mechanism you apply should be applied consistently.

## Records of Employee Earnings

As part of an addendum to the payroll register, employee earnings records are also an important part of your payroll system. Much of this may be drawn from the aggregate totals of the payroll register, but it's important to remember that the amount an employee earns will determine the level of his or her federal and state tax and FICA contribution. The earnings record should also be sufficiently detailed, showing the amount of wages, overtime, commissions and other income sources so you can better track the financial relationship between the employee and the company.

## Payroll Checks/Direct Deposit Vouchers

The last and most evident portion of the payroll system is, of course, the distribution mechanisms. Some companies still distribute payroll checks, but the majority of larger firms make direct deposits into employee bank or credit union accounts, bypassing the need to generate and process paychecks. Direct deposits are credited that much sooner to the recipients' accounts, depriving the issuer of a minimal amount of float time for each check but saving processing-related costs. Admittedly, some employees still like the feel of having a check in their hands, but most are seeing the added benefit and convenience of direct deposit.

No matter whether your company issues checks or deposit statements, however, it's customary to itemize deductions and give employees a full accounting of where the money they earned is going. Max Waxman's pay stub does exactly that, itemizing deductions and contributions and giving a full and fully traceable record of that deposit.

In fact, there is a part to Max's pay stub that you haven't yet seen. That's the extension of deductions taken throughout the calendar year. By showing the aggregate deductions from all preceding pay periods, Max's pay stub acts like an individualized payroll register which, when combined with that of other employees, forms the composite document that becomes that company's payroll register.

Here's what Max Waxman's full pay stub and payroll record for pay period 25 looks like:

|  | *Current Period* | *Year to Date* |
| --- | --- | --- |
| Gross earnings | 2,699.54 | $61,551.11 |
| Deductions: |  |  |
| FICA | 164.58 | 3,673.05 |
| Fed. withholding | 334.70 | 6,652.76 |
| State withholding | 170.11 | 3,769.11 |
| Health care co-pay | 38.49 | 859.02 |
| Health Flex pay | 12.50 | 300.00 |
| Retirement—Elec. | 54.99 | 1,230.99 |
| Retirement—Mand. | 83.49 | 1,846.56 |
| 401(k) loan payback | 65.91 | 1,581.84 |
| Total Deductions | 924.77 | 19,913.33 |
| Net Pay for period 25 | 1,774.77 | 41,637.78 |

Max's payroll record offers a comprehensive picture of his relationship as employee to the company as well as painting a fairly clear picture of his retirement situation and status as a taxpayer. Imagine

## GENERAL LEDGER

As with any funds disbursement point within your company, payroll is an area especially susceptible to fraud and embezzlement activities. Good internal controls are critical to the protection not only of assets but also the integrity of payroll records and the process itself. First and foremost, all payroll disbursement should be supported by approved and signed documentation—time cards, payroll sheets, documented overtime hours, commission records—before disbursement of

the information at a company's disposal once all such information has been combined into a single document.

## OTHER EMPLOYER LIABILITIES

These days, salary is still important but sometimes runs secondary in potential employee appeal to fringe benefits. We're seeing all types of benefits, depending on how high a job candidate is to the executive firmament. However, there are several basics that apply to all parties:

- *Vacation pay* is a long-standing benefit, the cost to the employer of which is accrued as the employee earns such time. The value of that time needs to be computed relative to the employee's salary and the proper amount reserved. When the employee exercises vacation privileges, the cash value of the time taken—factored from like value of the employee's salary—will be classified on the balance sheet as a current liability. The vacation pay reserve or account will be debited and the salary account credited, along with the appropriate accounts for withholding taxes and other deductions.

- *Sick leave* is often treated in much the same way as vacation time. Some companies have no formal sick leave policy in hopes that by keeping the door open as needed, fewer employees will feel obligated to exercise that option.

- *Pension contributions* can be handled in a similar fashion, although the wide array of choices, along with the uncertainty in funding for benefits that will be exercised at different levels in the distant future, or perhaps not at all, make this a more complex area to handle and difficult to explain comprehensively.

Contributory plans require employee contributions, while noncontributory plans are entirely employer supported, which means they have their own set of accounting needs. Funded plans require the setting aside of all funds necessary to pay out retirement benefits and usually are run by an outside agency, such as an insurance company. A lot of companies have abandoned traditional defined benefit plans in favor of defined contribution plans, such as 401(k) plans. This is a more flexible type of plan and one that lifts the financial and tax burden from the employer and shares it with the employee.

Employees constitute the largest expense born by most businesses. Careful management of the payroll function, which is the record and disbursement mechanism for that expense, is vital to protect what is easily the largest investment your company makes on a daily basis.

### GENERAL LEDGER
*(Continued)*

funds is allowed. Payroll additions and deletions should be supported by the proper documentation from personnel. Remember that the proper checks and balances, along with a solid paper trail and the appropriate authorizations, are critical to protecting this highly vulnerable link in the funds chain.

*Men can do jointly what they cannot
do singly; and the union of minds and
hands, the concentration of power,
becomes almost omnipotent.*

—Daniel Webster

# From Proprietorship **15** to Partnership

Many an entrepreneur has dreamed about flying solo, of hurtling to the top of his or her game, unfettered by the restrictions and demands of others. What could be better than sailing past all the masses, proving your mettle against the competition by flying directly to the light and seizing the golden prize?

That's what Icarus attempted to do, and he paid a dear price. The young man from Greek mythology mounted to the heavens on wings made of feathers and wax. But he flew without counsel and, nearing the sun, saw his resources melt away, causing him to plummet from the sky.

Icarus would have made a bad businessperson because he was driven by vanity without concern for the challenges that lay before him. Many a successful business was built on the inspired efforts of solo practitioners, but the most successful of them knew when the enterprise had outgrown their abilities and looked for ways to preserve their endeavors that were in line with the means available to them.

Knowing when to fly solo and when to enter into partnership is what this chapter is about. Accounting for the exigencies of a partnership will round out the lesson. Each type of management has its season. The path you choose and the way you account for it will be significant determinants of your overall success.

## BASIC BUSINESS
## BUILDING BLOCKS

Business types come in all sizes and shapes, colors and tastes. Some are correctly matched to the individuals pursuing them and the industries in which they exist, while others are wildly out of step with the norm. No matter where your company starts or ends its existence, it likely will fall into one of the following three categories:

• *Sole proprietorships* form the largest segment of the smallest businesses in this world. The bold pioneer and independent thinker thrive in such environments, as do the corporate retiree and the hobbyist turned professional. You're your own boss and have no one to answer to other than the federal and state governments. But freedom has its price and the weight of the enterprise rests on your shoulders.

• *Partnerships* bring together like-minded individuals in pursuit of a common business goal and empower them to act as equals in pursuit of that goal. The law defines partnership as "the association of two or more persons to carry on as co-owners of a business for profit." All partners may be active, or the business may be driven by one visionary individual with the financial stake being shared equally among many. None of the partners enjoys total freedom, but they bring with them the combined resources of numerous individuals and from those strengths, presumably, the business will grow.

• *Corporations* are complex structures that offset the individual freedoms of their officers with an equal offset of financial responsibility. Incorporation offers those involved the least amount of freedom and certainly the greatest number of laws and restrictions governing operations and growth. If the corporation is publicly held, there are a board of directors and slate of stockholders who are also determined to exercise their influence.

On the other hand, corporations offer the greatest foundation for long-term growth, are seen as the most appealing type of company structure in the eyes of many lawmakers and lenders, and are the only structure for which stock can be sold. We'll talk more about the advantages and challenges of incorporation in the next chapter. For now, we'll concentrate on the difference between being a soul proprietor and a partner.

## Flying Solo

A sole proprietorship is the most rudimentary form of business and the basis for virtually all small businesses. It's also the structure of choice for those who like to go it alone and those that have a single marketable skill or interest they're willing to offer the public in exchange for a decent living. What makes it so prevalent, too, is the ease with which a sole proprietorship can be gotten up and running. All you need to do is secure the necessary permits—if any—and find the right space. Once it's furnished, you're ready to open the door of your dry cleaning business, dental office, baseball card shop or anything else that suits your needs and knowledge base.

In addition to ease of set-up and operations, sole proprietors immediately enjoy the fruits of their labors in that all profits belong to them. Accounting procedures often are simple and uncluttered. Paying taxes can be as easy as filling out the standard IRS 1040 form using Schedule C: Profit and Loss from a Business or Profession and making the necessary quarterly estimated payments.

If a neighboring business is undercutting your prices, you can immediately respond without seeking a change in corporate policy. The business is yours with which to succeed or fail. You gain all the benefits and shoulder all the liabilities. Provided that you 1) are able to commit the long hours and hard work, 2) don't mind never taking vacations and 3) have a personal health profile you know won't fail you and will allow you to be at work every day, then sole proprietorship may well be your best option.

Of course, growth opportunities will be limited—yours most likely are the only resources on which you have to draw—and you may have trouble raising money when business revenue cycles are off. If you do hit a major snag or someone decides to sue you for some reason, you have no one else to turn to other than the person looking back at you from the bathroom mirror.

There are individuals who enjoy the challenge and thrive in this kind of environment. If you're one of them, than this may be the route for your enterprise. However, there are other options that offer similar freedoms while pooling the resources of several (or even many) to accomplish a single goal. Partnership, even with its complexities, may be more to your liking.

## Pursuing a Partnership

As defined by the Uniform Partnership Act, a partnership is a relationship between two or more individuals with the purpose of pursuing a single business venture. It's an opportunity to combine operational and capital resources, along with the managerial talent and experience of the parties involved in hopes of reaching a higher level of success within the business framework. Partnerships of all types and sizes operate successfully within the framework of this definition and are ideally suited for some industries, especially the medical and legal professions.

Two cardinal rules define partnerships:

1. Any partner can legally bind the partnership into a contract or obligation because that person acts as a legal representative of the business entity. If one partner takes a bold step and signs a contract for a new building, that contract is binding to the partnership whether the other partners have signed an agreement or not. Such is the nature of partnerships.

2. Partners are liable jointly and singly for the debts of the business. If your partnership's debts exceed the resources within the partnership, each partner can be held liable for paying the debt out of his or her own pocket. There's no question, as co-owner of the business, your assets are considered fair game to debtors. This is similar to sole proprietorships. Corporate structures, on the other hand, have safeguards in place to protect principles from such obligations.

## THE NATURE OF PARTNERS
## AND PARTNERSHIPS

There are characteristics, as well as types of partners, with which you should be familiar if a partnership looms on your horizon:

• By its very nature, a partnership is considered to have a limited life. Whenever old partners leave the business or new partners join, the partnership is considered dissolved and a new partnership formed if the enterprise's operations are to continue. There is no limit or restriction on the number of times this can happen. The only requirement is that it must happen each time the players change for any reason, including changes due to bankruptcy, incapacity, withdrawal from activities, or death.

• Most partnerships are considered general partnerships in which all partners have unlimited liability for debts incurred by the business. More and more, professionals are forming limited liability partnerships, known as LLPs, that restrict partners' liability to the amount of their original capital investment into the business.

• In the same way all partners share in the debts and liabilities of the partnership, they also share co-ownership of the assets of the business, which means an equitable distribution of those assets should the partnership formally dissolve. They also participate in the distribution of income (and absorption of loss) enjoyed by the partnership. The partnership is not required to pay taxes as a business entity, but partnership earnings need to be reported on partners' personal income tax forms.

Despite an almost universal understanding of these principles, good business practice dictates that all such standard and nonstandard requirements be drafted in a partnership agreement, sometimes called the *articles of partnership*. Once written down, those principles will be less likely to be misunderstood.

There are also several different types of partners that can become involved in the business:

## GENERAL LEDGER

The articles of partnership, also known as the partnership agreement, will become the most critical document guiding the operation of any partnership. The content of the different documents will vary depending on the partnership's specific needs, but all should contain basics such as:

- The name of the company; its purpose for doing business; and the location of its headquarters or business domicile.

- The names and natures of each of the partners (active, silent, and so forth); the amount of their contribution and the scope of their ownership and operational involvement.

- Who has authority to execute the

- An *active partner* is one that participates operationally and financially, one for whom the partnership is the primary source of personal income.

- An *ostensible partner* may not be actively involved, but he or she is someone the public knows to have involvement in the business.

- A *silent partner* is inactive, but financially involved. In addition, he or she is known by the public as having a vested interest in the success of the business.

- A *secret partner* also is involved in the business, but that involvement is unknown to the public. Despite how it sounds, there's nothing wrong with secret partnerships as long as the company isn't violating any legal or ethical standard.

- A *dormant partner* is considered inactive at the time and may or may not be known to the public.

- *Subpartners* and *limited partners* participate as less than full partners in the venture.

- *Venture capitalists* also form a partner through their investment in your firm. We'll talk more about them in Chapter 17.

## Partnership Advantages and Disadvantages

Partnerships are relatively easy and inexpensive to form. All that's really required is a formal agreement between two or more people, who can then pool their talent and resources in pursuit of a joint business goal. Because partnerships aren't taxable business entities, overall personal income taxes of the individual partners may be less than what corporate business taxes would have been. The partnership's only limitation, as we explained before, is that its life is limited. New partnerships must be drawn up every time a partner enters or exits the scene.

Basic accounting for partnerships utilizes the same systems that we described for businesses in general earlier in this volume. However, there are several areas in which partnership accounting requires special treatment: formation and investment, income distribution, dissolution and liquidation.

## Investments in the Partnership

Each partner, no matter how active or how silent, makes a financial investment into the enterprise. That's what defines them as partners. In some cases, if two businesses join in partnership, that contribution will extend to liquid assets, receivables, inventory, fixed assets and any other items of value. An agreement also will be struck to satisfy the debts each business faces before the partnership agreement is signed.

A separate entry into the ledger will have to be made for each of these investible assets, debiting each to the proper asset account. Assuming there also may be liabilities to assume, those liabilities will also be credited to the appropriate accounts. The net amount contributed is credited to the partners' capital account. Receivables are recorded at face

## GENERAL LEDGER
*(Continued)*

needs of the partnership; the duration and extent of this authority.

• Financial obligations and advantages of each of the partners, including details on salary allowances and cash withdrawal privileges; division of ownership as well as profits and losses.

• The bylaws for the organization, if there are any.

• Steps to take in the event of the addition, withdrawal or death of a partner.

• Operating guidelines and division of financial liabilities.

The more comprehensive the partnership's articles are, the less likely there will be conflict and confusion. It's worth the effort not only to plan ahead, but to record those plans in detail.

value with provision given for any that appear uncollectable in the future. Other assets should be given due consideration and attention paid to market value with accommodation made for depreciated amounts on fixed assets.

## Sharing the Wealth—Or Lack Thereof

Contributions to the partnership by partners may be even among all partners. Or the financial investment of one partner and/or the contribution of expertise from another may be valued higher than that of the rest. In either case, the return on investment to the partners should be commensurate with their experience and/or involvement, and certainly within the guidelines of the articles of partnership we hope you drafted before the enterprise got under way.

Partners are owners, not employees, of the partnership and are entitled to earnings just as much as they are obligated to cover losses. They also have an obligation to nurture and grow the business through their investments and/or their efforts. It's important to note that their financial involvement is legally considered an investment, not a loan, which further supports this assertion.

Despite that, active partners often receive their net income in the form of salary allowances, since it is likely that their daily involvement keeps the enterprise afloat. There also may be instances of withdrawals of cash by the partners at certain times. Both of these provisos must be outlined in the articles of partnership.

Assuming there is agreement on both the salary draw and the cash advance, those amounts in aggregate will be subtracted from the partnership's net income prior to the division and distribution of the remaining funds. In these cases, the partners' true net incomes will be the salary allowance or cash advance, plus their portion of the remaining revenue. The division of that net income is recorded as a closing entry on the books.

If the partners so choose, that excess net after salaries can be retained and interest earned on the amount. The total interest earnings generally are divided in much the same way among recipients.

Needless to say, net losses are handled much the same as net income. The net loss is subtracted from the salary allowance and the latter amount adjusted accordingly to keep the partnership from slipping into red ink. As owners, the partners bear the brunt of the loss, just as a solo entrepreneur would have to cover his or her debts if sales totals did not exceed amounts due. It's usually at this point that the partners long for their days as employees.

## Reporting the Finances

The details of all financial activity—either positive or negative—should be disclosed in specially prepared financial statements at the end of each fiscal period. Those statements may be separate, or prepared as addenda to the income statement. The impact on owners' equity also should be measured and recorded.

# DISSOLVING
# THE RELATIONSHIP

Because of their limited life, dissolution of a partnership for either good or bad reasons is governed by distinct accounting steps partnerships are required to follow.

• New partners can be admitted to the financial interest side of the business for a number of reasons, but all partners must vote before that new person can be truly named a partner. There are only two ways that partnership status can be attained: by purchasing an interest from a current partner; or by contributing assets to the partnership. The purchase of interest from another partner doesn't affect either total assets or total owners' equity. Under the second scenario, both are increased due to the additional contribution. The appropriate ownership accounts will have to be adjusted to reflect this activity.

This activity may result in the revaluation of assets to make sure they are in line with market value. If this happens at the entry of a new partner, net increases or decreases of these assets are then applied to the old partners.

• If a partner chooses to withdraw from the company, perhaps due to retirement or illness, the other partners may purchase his or her interest. This is, in effect, an individual deal among participating partners. The only adjustments to the books are to credit and debit the capital accounts of the purchasing and withdrawing partners, respectively. If the settlement is made by the partnership itself, this then reduces the owners' equity in the firm by the amount paid to the withdrawing partner and in increments outlined by the articles of partnership.

• The death of a partner, however, dissolves the partnership. Accounts are closed on the date of the death and whatever net income or loss remains is transferred to the appropriate capital accounts. The balance of the deceased's capital account is transferred to the liability account of the deceased's estate. Articles of partnership may be written to allow the accounts to remain open until the end of the fiscal period. In either case, the remaining partners may continue doing business.

## Liquidating the Partnership

The process is simple. If the partnership is to be liquidated, assets are sold, creditors paid and the remaining cash or assets distributed among the partners. Net loss is handled in the same way. Assuming all or most active partners have a salary allowance, the amounts are added or subtracted from the allowances already owed, with proper crediting done to each partner's capital account. Follow the same guidelines that exist for other funds distribution steps in the articles of partnership.

In the worst case scenario, when the money owed exceeds the accumulated assets of the partners, the partnership itself has a deficiency claim against each of the individual partners. The partners, as principles in the partnership, are equally liable to creditors to make sure all debts have been paid and may be subject to legal action jointly and individually if the proper steps aren't taken to settle up.

***What to Watch For:*** The greatest error during the liquidation of a partnership is the improper disposal of assets among partners. Gains and losses represent changes in partnership equity. Both should be handled in the same way you've been handling increases in net income or net loss. Use the same income sharing ratio on which the partnership was founded and you should be able to finalize the venture in an equitable fashion.

*A corporation is an artificial being, invisible, intangible and existing only in contemplation of the law.*

*—Chief Justice John Marshall*

*Corporations can't commit treasons, nor be outlawed nor excommunicated for they have no souls.*

*—Sir Edward Coke*

# Understanding the Corporation **16**

Although there is no necessarily logical progression from sole proprietorship to partnership, many a company is thought to have come of age with its incorporation. The first two types of businesses can operate somewhat casually, almost informally, in terms of the agreements by which they create their business entities. Not so with a corporate structure, a clearly defined enterprise operating within its own set of guidelines and rules designed both to protect and profit the people it serves.

There can be large partnerships with upwards of 1,000 principles pursuing the same enterprise, usually in different environments or communities. But the vast majority of large companies—along with a growing number of smaller ones—are incorporated for the simple reason that, while they operate with significantly more guidelines and restrictions, corporate structure also does a much better job of both protecting its principles and building a foundation for growth.

In addition, as Chief Justice Marshall points out, the corporation is viewed as a legal entity separate from its principles and subject to its own requirements, criteria and sets of rules. Thus, in the eyes of the law, it often appears to have greater strength, legitimacy and stability. Partnerships and sole proprietorships, which rise and fall based on the taxable fortunes of their owners, aren't afforded such luxury. Incorporating may offer its own set of challenges, but it rewards with tangible business benefits that may signal a higher level of commitment on the part of those behind the corporation's formation.

## CORPORATE NATURE AND CHARACTERISTICS

Within the corporate structure there are several different kinds of corporations:

• Nonprofit corporations are business entities organized for educational, charitable, philanthropic or recreational purposes. The Corporation for Public Broadcasting, designed to raise funds for the continuation of public radio stations nationwide, is just such an organization. Nonprofit corporations are usually dependent on member dues, gifts or grants from public and private sources to do their work. Other nonprofits, such as utility cooperatives, provide services in exchange for fees, but offer those services at cost rather than with an eye toward creating a profit for owners and stockholders.

• For-profit corporations, such as General Motors, engage in business enterprise with the idea of maximizing wealth for stockholders. Among these are nonpublic corporations, the ownership of which is held by a small group of investors, and public corporations, shares of which are traded in public stock exchanges and available to anyone with the purchase price.

In either of these cases, it's important to once again emphasize that the corporation

*GENERAL LEDGER*

Corporations are defined by key characteristics that include a separate legal entity from the individuals who run it; limited liability for stockholders in the company; the availability of separate units of stock, the transference of which doesn't upset operations; a distinct organizational structure; and an obligation to pay corporate taxes.

exists as a legal entity and can conduct business in its own name. It can acquire, own and sell property, incur liabilities and enter into contracts according to the guidelines of its charter, also known as its *articles of incorporation*. Obviously, an officer of the corporation would be required to facilitate any and all such transactions, but resulting liability and earnings from those transactions would be listed in the corporation's name, not in the name of the officer. This is an intrinsic and critical difference from either the sole proprietorship or the partnership.

A nonpublic corporation's ownership rests in the hands of its primary investors who may operate much like partners without the liability or tax advantages of a partnership. Accounting requirements for this type of corporation are similar to those of partnerships without the legal trappings of a partnerships' limited life (see previous chapter).

In the case of a public corporation, ownership rests in the hands of whoever owns stock in the company. For the record, stock is defined as transferable units of ownership, known as shares, each of which comes with a certain level of rights and privileges. Owners of those shares—the company's stockholders—can buy or sell those shares as often as suits their fancy without interrupting the company's daily business. Once again, sale of ownership privileges in either a sole proprietorship or a partnership would change the company's entire nature, and likely grind daily operations to a halt.

These stockholders have limited liability for the debts incurred by the corporation, unlike partners and proprietors who are individually liable for financial shortfalls of their enterprise. In the case of bankruptcy, however, they're the last to be paid. If a corporation does run aground, in most cases the worst that will happen to stockholders is that they will lose the amount originally invested. That's because the corporation, as a legal entity, is responsible for its own acts and obligations, protecting the stockholders from liability beyond their investment.

Stockholders, as you probably know, are represented by a board of directors elected to oversee management of their investment. The board has obligations that include but aren't limited to the following actions:

# GENERAL LEDGER

Incorporation offers many advantages to for-profit businesses of all sizes, including better access to capital markets than partnerships or sole proprietorships. One advantage it doesn't offer is relief from taxes. In the case of sole proprietorships and partnerships, there is no corporate tax. Since the principles are intrinsically involved with—and personally liable for—the debts of the business, taxes owed on profits are paid on the income earned by the principles. In the case of a corporation, a business tax is assessed because a

- First and foremost, as representatives of the company and its stockholders, the board must abide by both the laws of the land and the bylaws of the corporation.

- The board is required to hold stockholder meetings regularly to report company progress and profit and loss to the stockholders. That's a legal obligation the board has to the owners of the company.

- The board, or its designated representatives, is required to operate in a manner responsible to the well-being of the company and protection of its assets. This also includes providing operational details as appropriate to stockholder needs. Things like meeting minutes constitute legal documents and can be used in a court of law to prove whether boards or individual directors have been negligent in their representation of stockholder interest.

- The board is usually responsible for policy development and often takes part in strategic planning with company executives.

- The board must take active steps to advise stockholders of board elections and actions that affect their investment in the firm. Stockholders have the right to vote for corporate officers and must be notified of procedural changes that will affect the value of their stock beyond normal market fluctuations.

- The board and its members must act in manners befitting their positions as corporate representatives and especially within the moral and ethical confines of the law. This includes regularly paying income taxes, especially those based on corporate earnings.

## FILING FOR INCORPORATION

Some businesses file for incorporation without the aid of legal counsel, a precarious step at best but one that's permissible within the laws of most states. In most cases, incorporation filing forms require the following information:

- The *company name,* usually something simple and evocative of either the business or industry, followed by the word "Incorporated," "Limited," or their recognized derivatives. Check with the various state and/or federal authorities to make sure some other business hasn't incorporated under that name. Legal counsel can conduct an effective search and provide you with advice in the event that your proposed name or something similar has been found.

- *Identification as a standard C corporation or S corporation,* with its tax advantages, needs to be spelled out in the incorporation papers.

- The company's *mailing address* must be included. In some states, a street address is required and a post office box insufficient.

## GENERAL LEDGER
*(Continued)*

corporation is considered a separate entity in the eyes of the law. In addition, personal income tax is owed on earnings of the officers and management of the corporation as well. In effect, the corporation is paying taxes twice. In return, however, officers and management are insulated to a much greater degree from creditors and corporate debts.

- In addition to its location, the *market* in which it will be operating also is critical.

- The *period of duration* for most corporations is often considered in perpetuity. Few companies form with their principles thinking they will be out of business after a certain period of time. If there is a limitation on the time in which the business will be incorporated, however, it should be noted here.

- Your company's *reason for existence and lawful purpose* should be listed here as well. The statement need not be operationally specific, but descriptive enough to explain the company's line of enterprise.

- If your company is a public company, you'll need to include *the number and type of shares* to be issued and their par value. Any privileges that accompany the different classes of shares issued also should be noted. Additionally, if the board authorizes a certain number of shares, the articles may also restrict authorization of increases or decreases in those shares to the board.

- Speaking of the board, *the number and nature of that board* should be clearly described. Many states require no more than one director who, in turn, can serve various officer roles at the same time. Identify all involved, including their full names and addresses. In that same vein, the incorporator founding the enterprise must also be identified by name, identity and address.

- Identify the *date* at which the corporation's legal identity will become effective. This usually coincides with the day the business starts its operations.

- Finally, check to see whether the articles of incorporation need to be *notarized*. If so, the proper seal is required. So is the name and address of the corporation's legal agent, the one who will be the primary contact for officials from the state in which the business has been incorporated.

Once incorporation has been approved, it behooves the company to hold a meeting to elect officers and directors in accordance with its articles of incorporation. This group is obligated to draft and approve operating bylaws and establish all the professional relationships necessary to formally operate the business. These include establishing a banking relationship and obtaining a corporate ID number from the Internal Revenue Service. There's also a need to identify a fiscal year and make sure all regulations and restrictions governing corporations and businesses in the specific industry in that state and municipality are understood and complied with.

After that, the board is free to do what it wants, as long as what the board wants to do operates in the best interest of the company and its stockholders, and as long as those interests can be served in a legal and ethical fashion.

## RECOGNIZING STOCKHOLDER EQUITY

Stockholder investment in a company, also known as shareholders' equity or capital, comprises the owners' equity in that company and must be recognized as such. There are two types of these funds that must be accounted for:

- Stock purchases by stockholders constitute investments made in the firm. These are known as contributed capital or paid-in capital.
- Net income retained by the corporation is known as net earnings.

From an accounting standpoint, those amounts look like this:

| | |
|---|---|
| Capital | |
| Common stock | $500,000 |
| Retained earnings | 45,000 |
| Total Equity | $545,000 |

Each type of stock—common and preferred—should have its own account in which amounts are recorded. The retained earnings amount noted above is the result of the balance in the net income account being transferred to the retained earnings account at the end of the fiscal year. If there is a net loss in retained earnings, however, it's shown as a deficit, deducted from paid-in capital in the stockholders' equity section of the balance sheet.

## Know Your Shares

The stock market and the idea of corporate ownership can sometimes mystify the uninitiated, and it's true that even veteran traders are sometimes at a loss to explain activities within the market. But the particulars surrounding the nature and issuance of corporate stock aren't all that challenging to understand.

Capital stock is the term often applied to ownership shares in a corporation, the number and nature of which are authorized by the corporation's charter, developed and approved by the board of directors. The corporation itself owns shares of the stock, to be sure; shares remaining in the hands of stockholders is known as *stock outstanding* and it is well within the legal right of the corporation to reacquire that stock if it is put on the market. The value of that stock is assigned a certain arbitrary amount, known as *par,* although some stock is issued without a stated value, known as *no-par stock.*

Corporations often issue two types of stock. *Common stock* offers owners equal rights and equal values for all shares. *Preferred stock,* designed to appeal to owners with more to invest, comes with certain advantages and generally returns a more consistent yield. Dividends—a distribution of earnings declared by the board—must first be paid to preferred stockholders before it can be shared with those owning common stock. No matter what the type of stock, however, all offer stock owners certain rights: the right to vote on issues concerning the company; a share in the distribution of earnings; the right to purchase the same amount of stock should another issuing be offered, also known as preemptive rights; and a share of assets upon corporate liquidation.

Preferred stock has other characteristics that distinguish it from common stock. In most cases, preferred stock is limited to a certain yield, making it nonparticipating stock. That which offers dividends in excess of that amount is called participating stock. Preferential stock may be said to be cumulative if it returns a dividend even in those times when no dividend is returned on common stock. Of course, there is also noncumulative preferred stock which does not have this right. Preferred stockholders also will have first claim to assets upon liquidation of the corporation.

## Issuing Shares

The accounting procedure for recording stockholder purchases—quite literally, investments in the corporation—are like those for any other type of owner investment in any other business. Assets received are debited and liabilities assumed are credited. The primary difference is that different accounts must be set up for each of the different classes of stock. Preferred stock, which always has a higher par value, is not lumped together with common stock, since the two account for different levels of investment. This account information is kept in the stockholders' sub ledger.

Par, no matter where it is set, is the benchmark price of a specific stock. But par isn't always the price at which the stock is traded. Shares sold at more than par are said to be sold at a premium; those traded at less than par are sold at a discount. The company's financial condition, the stock's earnings and dividend record, its potential earning power and the availability of money

# CHIT

A corporation has the right to repurchase stock it has issued to stockholders should it become available on the market. This repurchased stock is known as *treasury stock* and does not come with all the same rights as stock outstanding. From an accounting standpoint, it must be deducted from paid-in capital and retained earnings at the end of the accounting period. Differences between the price paid and the selling price shows up in a paid-in capital account designed specifically for treasury stock transactions.

## *GENERAL LEDGER*

The purchase of stock is becoming more commonplace and is easily in reach of most people with an interest in becoming involved in the market. Stock sales usually require payment in full upon purchase, or may allow installment payments over a reasonable period of time. The issuer should debit the amount to a specifically defined asset account and then credit it to a capital stock account. Any premiums or discounts above or below the stock's par value will be debited or credited to the appropriate account.

for investment purposes all control the price at which stock is sold. Most newly issued stock is sold at par.

Premiums and discounts on par should be listed separately on the balance sheet. Premiums are considered stockholder investments, thus are part of paid-in capital, but not part of the company's legal capital, the amount retained to run the corporation, and often serve as the basis for dividends. That explains the need to list it separately from the par value of the shares. Discounts are considered contra accounts and must be offset against the value of the stock. The discount is not an asset, nor should it be amortized against revenues as if it were an expense. Various states have different laws governing issuance of discount stocks.

In the event that your company issues stock in exchange for nonliquid assets such as real estate or equipment, those assets should be assessed at fair market price. If this proves too difficult, then fair market price may be determined as the par value of the stock, if that amount is more easily arrived at objectively. Thus, an investor willing to trade a plot of undeveloped land for $25,000 in stock has agreed that land is worth $25,000. That's the amount that should be entered on your books.

## Where There are Stocks, There Also May Be Bonds

In addition to issuing stock, the company also may sell bonds as a way to raise funds. Bonds are interest-bearing notes that serve as loans and are sold to corporate investors, such as banks or insurance companies. Unlike stock, which is relatively permanent, even long-term bonds eventually have to be repaid. Bondholders are creditors of the corporation and their claims for repayment rank ahead of those of stockholders.

## THE COST OF INCORPORATING

Setting up a corporation, especially with its complex rules and regulations involving stock issuance, is not without its costs. Such things as legal fees, taxes, fees paid to governing bodies, administrative charges and even the printing of stock certificates all fall under the heading of *organizational costs*. Thus, they must be charged to an account labeled as such. They are as essential as the plant and equipment it takes to manufacture and distribute whatever it is you make, yet have no value upon liquidation. They still must be considered; however, the Internal Revenue Service allows them to be amortized over a period of 60 months, a period most companies would find acceptable, given the amount in question.

*If you would know the value of money,
go and try to borrow some.*

—Benjamin Franklin

# Sources of Business Finance 17

Many businesses start on the proverbial shoestring, but most of them have someone to help them tie the knot. That someone is usually a commercial lender, an individual and/or an institution that makes sure your business has ready capital with which to launch and grow the enterprise. There is almost always need for the principles within the business to have a financial stake in the operation, but few can go it alone without the help of financial backing, either in the form of venture capital or commercial loans that offer the necessary resources to make the company a success. This chapter will focus specifically on those two sources, each of which is very different in its uses and in the role it will play in your company.

We'll focus first on commercial lenders, many but not all of whom are bankers, because they are the more common of the two with which you likely will deal. A cardinal rule to keep in mind is that lending is a business, not philanthropy. A good lender who wants to stay in that business will approach commercial lending at a high level with an eye for a good return. That's true even if this person is a friend, neighbor or relative. Sound business judgment, plus strict oversight from regulatory agencies, will keep the best lenders on the straight and narrow, even if they want to do you a favor. Those are the types of individuals with whom your company should deal.

Do you qualify as a good loan candidate? Polished wingtips and a spanking new headquarters may or may not make you a good risk. But if your company has a positive cash flow to support its claims of stability, valuable collateral—including real estate, equipment and a list of reliable accounts receivable—and a strong management team with a clearly articulated business plan well into the process of its execution, then you're a very good candidate for a business lending relationship.

A good business lending relationship is usually what both parties try to find. Financial institutions can be valuable allies in the pursuit of your enterprise, offering services as well as ready cash to finance and support your business ventures. Entrepreneurs who make good business decisions generally make money. Lenders who make good business loan decisions make money right along with them. As lenders are evaluating you for reliability and credit worthiness, you should be evaluating them for their scope of services and how well they appear to truly understand your industry and its needs. The relationship is very much like a marriage. Once you find the right lender with the qualifications necessary, it's worth the effort to make it work.

## TYPES OF LOANS

Securing a commercial loan is like making most other business decisions. You'll be presented with some options and from those options you'll make a decision on the loan that's best for you. There are different types of loans available for different purposes. Here are a few of the standard loan types you'll find during your search:

• Basic commercial loans generally are granted to help nurture and grow businesses and are usually written for about a year before collection is due. They can be as large as the borrower needs them to be and can qualify for, assuming the lender has the resources to cover such loans. Smaller lenders may need help underwriting the loan from a correspondent institution, or they may need approval from their loan committee. Assuming that you're dealing with a federal or state regulated and insured institution and not Louie the Loanshark, that's perfectly fine. Your loan can be used to cover whatever expenses may be necessary to run your company.

Commercial loans, like consumer loans, can be secured or unsecured, depending on the size of the loan and the rate you desire. A secured loan is protected by collateral—real estate, equipment or even accounts receivable—and, in the event of default, the lender is legally empowered to seize the collateral. All but the largest companies or the smallest borrowers are granted secured loans. Unsecured loans have no collateral pledged and the borrowers are trading only on their past record and/or good name. Unsecured loans usually are offered at a higher interest rate because the lender assumes more risk.

• Term loans stretch the life of the loan over a longer period of time—say three to five years—and are often part of a company's business-building strategy. Term loans can either be secured or unsecured and often are drafted to meet a company's specialized needs. Corporate expansion strategies that have high up-front costs and a longer payback time may require specialized term loans with minimal periodic payments and a balloon payment for the balance due at the end of the loan. Smarter lenders will work with corporate officers to make sure the terms of the loan and availability of cash facilitate the company's success, and won't stand as a roadblock to its progress.

On the other hand, since term loans usually run over a period of years, they're always approached with care. Even the best laid plans of corporations and principles may run up against an unexpected or insurmountable hurdle. When the business succeeds, the lender is assured payback. But when it doesn't succeed, even the most heavily collateralized loans are sometimes hard to collect.

• Lines of credit are becoming increasingly common options, not only on the commercial side, but among consumer loans as well. A line of credit is an open source of cash a business may draw on as needed for the duration of the loan, usually about a year. Companies are limited to borrowing within preset terms and amounts, but then may use the loan for any good business purpose. This may include purchasing equipment, supporting operations and cash flow during slack periods and other similar expenses.

Lines of credit generally are limited to companies that already have established relationships with the lender, who also provides other financial services to the company, such as corporate checking accounts. There may be limits on how long the line of credit, most of which are executed through renewable 90-day notes, can run and whether or not there needs to be a cooling off period between successive lines. Lines of credit are designed to support the company's other sources of revenue, not be the sole source of that revenue. The rate of the loan is dependent on the company's size, stability and relationship with the lender, with interest rates tending to be lower for better clients.

• Some companies also have the structure in place to offer time/sales financing in which the purchase is sold to the financial institution as a receivable. If you've ever purchased an appliance with no money down and 90 days to pay, you've participated in such a plan. The lender usually buys a package of such contracts at a discount, with the loan's collateral consisting of the lender's interest in the sales contract. As the lender receives payment, it pays the company after withholding several percentage points of the loan value for handling the collection aspect. The relationship continues until the customer pays off the full amount.

## Choosing the Right Lender

We spoke earlier about what constitutes a good lender, and there are many who could meet your business borrowing needs. Not every marriage works out, however, so exercise good business judgment before pledging to the relationship. (You can bet that's what the lender is doing.) Here are some suggestions for choosing the right lender:

• Find a lender that fits your company's size and scope. The large national bank holding companies have all the resources you'll ever need and more, but if you're just a small fly-fishing rod company in western Idaho, you may represent a mere flyspeck of business to them. Find a lender that views your business as significant to its portfolio. That's how you'll be sure to get the level of treatment and the professionalism that you want.

• Make sure the lender understands your business. A Christmas tree grower has much different and more seasonal needs than a canning company that can work year-round and around the clock. A lender that understands what your company does and the industry in which it operates can be a much better strategic partner as well as a good source of funds for your firm.

• The right lender will also be one that takes a proactive approach to helping manage your company's finances. These may be fee-based services, or they simply may be advice on how much to borrow and how to use it. A lender who is proactive in this vein will be a better investment of your company's time and money.

• The right lender also will have a good personal working relationship with your staff. You can call it positive chemistry if you want, and we all know that people will work more effectively with people with whom they like to work. Those are critical points when it comes to working with your lender. The lender needs to have the right professional criteria and be an excellent practitioner of the discipline. That person also should work well with your executives, because together they will be making decisions critical to the future of your company.

• Base at least some of your decisions on references from reliable professionals—attorneys, accountants and others who know your

## GENERAL LEDGER

If you've filled out loan papers—and who among us hasn't?—you know the lender often requests personal information you generally don't give out to a complete stranger. With commercial loans, this process is heightened, but the information needed is less personal and more related to the business to which the loan is being granted. Why you want the loan, how much you need (as opposed to how much you want) and when you plan to pay it back, are all legitimate questions that the business lender may ask. Refusal to answer any of these may raise suspicions and you may walk away without the needed funding.

company and its business. Then check the references the lender provides thoroughly and carefully. That's the best way to uncover the lender's style, acumen and other characteristics that will become critical over time. Bring your accountant, attorney and any other consultants you work with regularly in on this process.

## Preparing for the Loan Request

Thorough planning is an important strategy before meeting up with your business lender. Remember that his or her concern over your well-being and business success is secondary to the payback with interest of the amount you'd like to borrow in the time on which both of you agree. The lender is working with you, not for you, and your ability to meet the lending institution's need are the most critical thing to them. Arriving prepared and explaining thoroughly what it is you want and why will impress the lender that you are the person who can make sure the money is paid back. Here are some other considerations before stepping into the lending officer's office:

• Know how much you want to borrow, what you're going to use it for and how you're going to pay it back. Loan requests built around strategy are granted much more often than vague, unexplainable requests. Outline all necessary conditions of the loan and be prepared to defend your needs.

• Make sure all corporate documentation and strategic plans are up to date, viable and easily explained. Again, strategy-based borrowing shows a much higher level of expertise, which means greater safety for the lender. Lending officers will review plans closely in direct proportion to the size of the loan you're requesting.

• Have the company CFO or accountant prepare a projection that clearly demonstrates the payback scenario you plan to follow assuming your plans work. Have a short but effective contingency plan in the event something unforeseen interrupts the process. That way, the lender will be assured that you will pay back the loan one way or the other.

• Write down your loan request and rehearse the key points with the executives in your company who need to know the reason for the loan and who may be part of the team requesting the funds. Incorporate these individuals into strategy development and make sure they are prepared to talk intelligently to the issue if called upon. If all key personnel understand and are involved in strategic development and use of the loan, then the lender will be more likely to grant your request.

Even in today's more sophisticated and faster-paced times, lending boils down to a process known as "The 5 Cs of Credit," measuring sticks used by the lender to help determine whether you should be granted the loan. These are:

- *Character.* Since the lending officer has an obligation to his or her institution to make good loans, your character and that of your company comes significantly into play in helping that person make the right decision. Lenders want to lend only to those companies that will repay the loan on time and according to terms. Your character helps them make what at best will be an educated guess.

- *Capacity.* Will your company actually be able to repay the loan when it's due?

- *Capital.* How much have the officers and principles invested in the firm? If it's little or nothing, chances are they won't work as hard to protect or repay the lender's investment should things start to go awry.

- *Collateral.* What has your company pledged to secure the loan and will its value be enough if the loan defaults? Often, this is one of the most important criteria.

- *Conditions.* How will market conditions affect your ability to repay the loan? No one can predict the future, so there's always some level of risk involved in making loans. Are current and pending conditions likely to increase or decrease the risk?

## Final Steps

The loan process usually starts with a query call made to a commercial lender or sometimes by the lender to a prospective borrower and

## GENERAL LEDGER

No matter how thorough the preparation or how reasonable the request, some loans simply aren't granted. If you find yourself in that position, review what you have been through before simply stomping off in a huff. In addition, ask yourself the following questions:

• Is my loan request reasonable and appropriate? Or is there something in there that is keeping this loan from being granted?

• Did the loan form I filled out do a good job of representing my request? Is there something missing that could have helped or something included that tripped me up?

doesn't conclude until extensive paperwork has been completed and the company's request evaluated for both risk and reliability. That's where an underwriter steps in and evaluates things as they appear in black and white on the loan application against a series of criteria and steps designed to measure how desirable you are as a borrower.

Since the lender generates the paperwork, most of the covenants will be designed to protect the lender and obligate the borrower. Review the documentation carefully before signing. While much of the document will be based on underwriting standards dictated by the institution, the industry or its regulatory body, some terms may be negotiable. Have your CFO and attorney review the loan documentation, too. Up to this point, it's all been talk. Your signature on the document will decide what your future will look like. Make sure as much of it as possible is working in your favor.

## ENTER THE VENTURE CAPITALIST

Commercial loans for your business aren't the only source of funds. In fact, if you're a startup company looking for seed capital to launch your enterprise, they may not be an option at all. Commercial lenders are in the business of making money for their institutions by loaning businesses funds at market rates. Although the limitations have loosened somewhat over the past decade, loan underwriting standards are still fairly stiff and lenders quite conservative. If you're a new enterprise or one without a proven track record, you may have trouble finding someone to finance your dream.

That's where venture capitalists come in. It's their job to help fund startup firms with seed capital and help get their enterprise underway. Venture capitalists tend to be successful business people with excess funds to invest who are looking for something that will offer a greater return than the stock market. The right idea in the right managerial hands often will have venture capitalists banging on their door to become financially involved in the enterprise.

As true as that statement could be, however, it isn't often the case. Other than the sunrise and taxes, there are few sure things in the world. Venture investors have even more stringent requirements than many lenders. It's up to the business that's out seeking funding to impress upon these investors why their product or firm will be the next Microsoft. And that's not an easy task.

Notice the continuous reference to venture capitalists as investors? That's the most important distinction between them and commercial lenders. Venture capitalists don't lend money, they invest in the company. Unlike commercial lenders, who merely expect loan payback plus interest based on a prearranged schedule, venture capitalists will take a greater risk, but they will expect greater reward in return. They will do everything in their power to make sure their investment doesn't go sour on them, even if it means offering management expertise, something a lender would never do.

## GENERAL LEDGER

*(Continued)*

• Are there financial aspects to our company about which we should be more concerned? Were we honest with the lender and are we being honest with ourselves about our credit worthiness?

If you are denied, find out why and in as much detail as possible. It may be something that's easily remedied before you write your next loan request. Or it may be something that runs much deeper and poses a serious threat to your company. If that's the case, the sooner you find out, the better.

## GENERAL LEDGER

No company is too small to succeed, but some are too small to attract the attention of venture capitalists, who usually look for financial need at a minimum level of $250,000 and preferably much, much more than that. Venture capitalists spend a lot of time researching the firm and its marketing before pledging funds. Smaller investments mean smaller returns, and anything smaller than a quarter-million usually isn't worth their time and effort. For needs less than that, contact your local office of the Small Business Administration and find out about an SBA loan.

That shouldn't discourage any startup firm, however, from seeking venture capital. Many a successful product has been launched because the right person with the right amount of money met someone with a great idea and no way to fund it. While lenders deal in money, venture capitalists share the element of vision, which allows them to see beyond potential short-term risk and into the future of an exciting new product or enterprise. Quite often they're known as "angels" because they arrive almost magically with the necessary capital at a time when an entrepreneur needs them the most. And that's not a moniker bandied lightly about, especially in the business world.

### Types of Venture Capital

The discipline of venture capital is much more than a businessperson with money looking to make a savvy investment. Venture capital is in and of itself an industry with a wide variety of types, sources, uses and descriptions. For new companies with little operating history, smaller firms looking for personal and expert involvement, and companies just not yet ready or able to go public, venture capitalists may be the only option. The cost isn't cheap. Depending on the nature of the investment and its demands, the venture capitalist could end up owning as much as 60 percent of the company. But sometimes it's the only option, and sometimes it's the best option.

Venture capital isn't just for new firms, either. Companies in turnaround situations or in need of expansion capital may find venture capital deals to their liking. It also may be an option for leveraged or management buy-outs of firms. In fact, wherever there is a need for capital in a situation that commercial lenders would find unappealing, the venture capitalist may be willing to step in—but only if the stakes are high enough and the returns turn out to be worth the investment.

The typical venture capitalist deals in numerous types and levels of financing. In fact there are three stages of early financing alone:

- Seed financing is just that, funds that are committed to help a new idea germinate and grow. The funds—generally less than $50,000—go into product and market research and development.

- Startup funding is provided to firms that have been operational for less than a year and have yet to offer products to market. Capital is used to enable both product production and market penetration.

- First stage financing follows, with funds earmarked to initiate commercial manufacture and sales.

For the venture capitalist, that's just the start. Seed financing and startup funding play only a part. Funds are also available to companies at the following levels:

- Second-stage financing comes into play when the company already has launched its product and made its initial moves in the marketplace. Financing at this level helps small or young companies grow and expand.

- Third-stage financing goes even further and constitutes a much higher level of expansion. This may include construction of a new manufacturing facility or expansion efforts into a foreign market.

- Bridge or mezzanine financing is offered to those companies planning to go public in a short time that need funds to tide it over until its initial offering.

The type and level of financing will depend on just where the company is at the time of the request. Venture capitalists receive hundreds of legitimate proposals each year, but only invest in a handful. Just as it is critical to find the right lender, a good match between venture capitalist and firm it invests in is also important to success.

## Finding the Right Angel

Like commercial lenders, venture capitalists come in many sizes and shapes. Some operate individually, finding opportunities that suit their interests before getting involved. Others operate in concert with other like-minded investors, who band together with or without a mediator or agent to consider possibilities. They're always hungry for the right opportunity, but that doesn't mean they don't entertain hundreds of proposals each year before picking out the select few they choose to support. Generally, those choices result from months of painstaking research and may involve several thousand dollars of the investors' own money before they're satisfied that your firm is the right one. Finding the right firm before starting the process will save both sides time and money.

First and foremost, find a firm that can provide both the capital and expertise necessary to get your enterprise off the ground. A big advantage of venture capitalists is that most of them are seasoned business professionals who take special interest in your firm once it becomes one of their investments. Many entrepreneurs are simply specialists who have come up with a marketable idea but don't necessarily have the business expertise to turn it into a commercial enterprise. That's where the venture capitalist can step in and offer the help you need. But make sure the venture capitalist has enough capital to make that dream a reality. Otherwise, both of you may find yourselves in search of a third investor. That's not a position in which you'll want to find yourself.

Your best choice of venture capital firm will be one that understands and is experienced in your industry. Remember, you're trying to tap their expertise as well as their purse. The very best choice will be someone who has experience in your industry and contributes both a financial and professional advantage. The very worst is some-one who has no idea what you're doing and may pull the plug on funding at a time when you need it most.

The firm you choose should be ethical and legitimate with a proven track record. The venture capital firms you approach will expect significant demonstration of your skills, abilities and knowledge. Since you will be pledging significant return for their invested dollar, you have the right to similar information about them. Ask for and follow up on references and contact other companies with which they've dealt to see what kind of partner they will make.

Once again, the right chemistry between principles of both groups is critical to success. You may be embarking on the unknown using a lot of money provided by a relative stranger. Things may get tense enough without the usual human relations issues that come up. Individuals that trust each other and perhaps even like working with each other will find the going much smoother when they reach the inevitable bumps in the road.

## Setting the Stage

Venture capitalists are not retail outfits that you simply walk into and make your pitch. Most of them keep very low profiles simply because, if their interest in investment became known, there would be no end to the people trying to pitch them their latest and greatest idea. Many work through a variety of agents—accountants, attorneys, brokers and other professionals they trust to act as middlemen to keep the crowds at bay and only let the most worthy candidates through the door. The first step to setting the stage, then, is to build a network of such individuals so that, when the time comes, these middlemen trust you enough to deliver your ideas to the venture capitalists.

The ultimate goal, of course, is to set up a meeting to make the pitch. But good prior preparation is vital to making this meeting successful. A comprehensive business plan is absolutely vital to providing the necessary information to allow the investor to make a wise decision. Here are some things you need to include:

- Start with an executive summary that offers a concise analysis of your ideas and the concept behind your company and its goals. You need to interest the investor by mounting a compelling argument for your idea and your company's existence within the context of the industry in which it operates.

- Include a comprehensive customer analysis, showing where the company's products stand in terms of competition and client desires. That also means a discussion of the market and audience segment you serve. Again, context is critical because you're educating the investor to your point of view.

- Discuss your competition in terms of your strengths in relation to theirs. A positioning statement can show how you stand apart from that competition and why your firm is the best investment for someone presumably interested in this marketplace.

- Sales and marketing strategies are critical in helping define not only your company's positioning, but also how you plan to support the financial growth of the firm, plumping the venture capitalist's invested amount in the process. You may include in this analysis future or additional product or service developments that strengthen your firm's ability to compete. That may be critical to help you not only survive but thrive.

- Provide an outline of the company's key operations and individuals. The management team, especially, will be of significant interest to investors because it is they who will be leading the activities that will have direct impact on their return on investment. They will want to know who these individuals are and what they can do before making a financial commitment.

- Include current financial information, and an up-to-date financial statement. This should go without saying. If they're investing in your enterprise, your financial well-being is of paramount importance to them.

- Finally, how do you plan on returning their investment to them? For many such investments, the payback comes either when the company goes public or is sold to a larger firm. Generally, it's at that point that the investor withdraws his earnings and looks for other places to invest it. If you have something else in mind, disclosing it up front could save you a lot of time and misunderstanding.

## Making the Pitch

If you have done all your prep work, you have a pretty solid proposal outlined in writing and a go-between who believes in the legitimacy of your vision and the approach you want to take. Perhaps that person has introduced you to several likely venture capital firms, or perhaps only one. In any event, you are ready to present. Keep the following things in mind:

• It should go without saying, but it sometimes bears repeating that your presentation must be complete, professional and to the point in its research and delivery. Unprepared presentations will immediately raise a red flag among professional investors. In many ways, this may be the most critical moment in your business's life. If you can't handle this well, they may think, there's no guarantee you'll be able to handle the rest of the job you need to do, either.

• Despite what we just said, emphasize content over style. Your audience will be comprised of sophisticated and accomplished business executives. Perhaps they've even been standing where you now stand. Show recognition of that experience and ability by neither wasting their time nor insulting their intelligence.

## GENERAL LEDGER

Venture capitalists will look for red flags before giving any money to your firm. You need to perform the same due diligence on them. As you check references, ask the following questions:

• Did your executives find it hard to reach the investor when they needed him? If so, it may get worse once the two groups are linked.

• Have past venture capital relationships been successful for the firm? How is its overall track record?

• Has the flow of capital been steady and available when needed? Interruptions in that flow could cause big problems.

• If you understand your company and its products inside and out—and you should before you meet with this group or individual—you should be able to anticipate and be ready to answer at least some of the questions that will be asked. Having ready knowledge about the industry, competitive challenges and marketplace issues will communicate your expertise and make the potential investors more confident in your abilities. Be ready, too, to explain those unique characters and properties of your company that may not be self-evident to the investor.

• Remember that management ability is one of the key factors the investors will judge, so make sure all the right members of your executive team present all the right information in ways that are both informational and compelling. The potential investor will be concerned as much with what is not said as what is said, and with who hasn't spoken as much as with who has.

• Have ALL the necessary supporting documentation in the investors' portfolios that are distributed as part of your presentation. One can forgive the occasional omission of unusual information needed to respond to unexpected questions. Too many omissions, however, will raise suspicions regarding the thoroughness of both your research and your ability to execute tasks.

## THE BOTTOM LINE

No matter how exciting your enterprise and how compelling your proposal may have been, it ultimately boils down to two things:

1. *Your company's finances.* How strong are you fiscally, have you shown good financial management skills or are you saddled with debt? Venture capitalists invest to help companies grow, not to dig them out of their debt.

2. *The terms of the deal.* You'll pay more dearly to venture capitalists than to commercial lenders, and how much more dearly may make or break the deal. That's the purpose of their investment and the answer to this question will likely be what helps them decide whether they're going to be your angel, or someone else's.

*Let me tell you how it will be.*
*There's one for you, 19 for me.*
*'Cause I'm the taxman. Yeah, the taxman.*
*And you're working for no one but me.*

*—George Harrison*

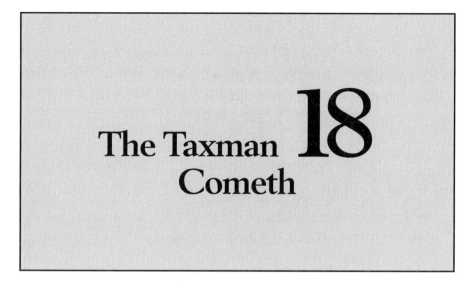

# The Taxman 18 Cometh

About the only time a businessperson regrets his or her success is when taxes are due. Sales growth, increased revenue flow and raises in pay look pretty good right up until the time that Uncle Sam comes knocking at the door, his hand out and his palm itching. Suddenly those boosts in earnings aren't quite so sweet, particularly if they've thrust you into a higher tax bracket.

But taxes are really a measure of success. The more money you owe, the more successful you've been. If you let that be your economic mantra, you may even come to believe it. Add another zero to that tax payment check and feel proud about the work you've done, the market share you've gained and the sales you've closed. You can never fully escape from those taxes, but knowing they're the result of your success may minimize the sting.

As a businessperson there are things you need to know about taxes and things you need to leave for your tax preparer. That may be your accountant or it may be some outside expert. Frankly, there's a lot of information and implications that you have to fathom and much of it changes on a somewhat regular basis. The purpose of this chapter is not to provide a comprehensive resource. Instead, the goal here is merely to familiarize you with taxing issues involved in the business world and give you some context in which to place those issues. Particular details will be left for more timely resources and their utilization for professional tax accountants and form preparers.

## GENERAL LEDGER

The IRS allows cash accounting for businesses that meet certain requirements: if they have gross receipts of less than $5 million; if they are a professional firm, such as a medical or legal partnership whose stock is owned entirely by the employees or partners; and, in certain cases, if they are C or S corporations. If you're interested in cash accounting, check with your tax preparer to see if your firm qualifies.

Let us stress the value of a CPA trained specifically in corporate tax preparation. Most companies have financial professionals capable of mastering the tax question. However, whether that's the best use of that person's time in light of all the other issues with which he or she has to deal is a decision that needs to be made from a resource management level. If so, then that person needs to remain current on all changes in tax law. If not, spend the money for outside assistance and let your financial professional concentrate on helping run the company. After all, it's tax deductible.

## BUSINESS INCOME ACCOUNTING

From the point of view of both federal and state governments, the corporate tax equation is a simple one:

- Businesses operating under accrual accounting principles owe taxes on income when it is received and may take deductions when expenses are incurred.

- Businesses operating on a cash accounting basis owe taxes on income when it is received and may take deductions on expenses when they are paid.

Simple as that may seem, there may be myriad complexities in the operations side of making this happen. And even though the IRS allows you the choice based on your structure, please know that companies that operate with inventory must account for it on an accrual basis.

Similarly, it's important to know that tax payments are due when cash is received, even if it isn't processed during that time frame. Since your company pays estimated taxes on a quarterly basis, the tax owed on a big sale is due when the sale is made and funds received, even if those funds may not be processed until the next quarter. Failure to follow this protocol not only will irritate the IRS—something you never want to do—but also will unbalance your books. Be careful of both in your tax accounting and payment schedule.

In the end, from a taxation standpoint, accrual accounting offers the greatest flexibility in meeting needs and requirements. In addition, it will give your firm greater ability when it comes to matching revenues and expenses, which means a more accurate and useful financial statement.

The IRS is very clear on when corporate taxes are due. Without fail, they must be paid by the 15th day of the third month after the close of your fiscal year. If your fiscal year ends on June 30, your corporate taxes are due September 15. When it comes time to pay those corporate taxes, however, there are several options:

• C corporations pay the income tax themselves as a corporate entity. It's considered an operating expense on the financial statement.

• S corporations, which are rapidly growing in popularity, pass profits and losses directly on to shareholders, who in turn pay the appropriate income taxes similar to those taxes paid by sole proprietors and partners in partnerships. There is no formal corporate tax to list as an operating expense. What's more, during a corporation's early years, this eases the blow on operating expenses. Stockholders gain the benefit of the revenue, but must pay estimated taxes on projected earnings or losses.

Similar in structure and intent to a partnership, in an S corporation stockholders share the company's financial burden. That means pass-through responsibility for revenue, expenses and tax deductions relative to the level of stock being held. On the benefits side, this includes tax-exempt interest, which increases the stock's value but stays tax-exempt, and first year expense deductions and tax preference items. Interest and dividends on corporate investments and losses in other areas also fall into this category.

Keep in mind that S corporations have no earnings and no profits. All the financial activity and obligations pass through to the stockholders. Profits and losses may deeply affect the stockholder's role within the company, but will have no effect on the welfare of the company itself. In addition, as a corporation, it will continue to operate no matter what the ebb and flow of stockholders may be. Profit and loss are allocated for each tax period and ownership changes are adjusted accordingly.

There are requirements that define the nature of the S corporation for which interested parties are responsible in addition to filling out the necessary forms:

- S company stockholders must be U.S. citizens or residents. They also may represent an estate or trust that is a designated stockholder.

- S corporations may offer common or preferred stock, but not both. They are limited to offering one type of stock only.

- S corporations formed before 1996 may have only 35 stockholders; those formed after may have as many as 75. Husband-and-wife investors count as one stockholder, but consent from both is required before investment.

IRS Form 2553 is the form that needs completion in order to apply for S corporation status. The form must contain the signatures of all stockholders of the corporation. Forms filed after the start of the year for which they are effective need consent forms filed from those who held ownership during the previous year, even if they have sold their shares. If the majority of stockholders change their mind and no longer want to be an S corporation, they can file a revocation form effective on the date they specify. Failure to specify a date will mean automatic default to the 15th day of the third month after the end of the company's tax year.

## FORMING A LIMITED LIABILITY PARTNERSHIP

If a group of stockholders find the rigors of the S Corporation, as they say, too taxing, they may consider forming a Limited Liability company, also known as LLC. As a partnership, it allows more owner involvement than an S corporation does, but still offers the same profit and loss pass-through feature to its owners. In addition, there are greater advantages with fewer restrictions, including the proviso that the LLC may allocate those profits and losses in whatever way may seem reasonable regardless of how stockholders are invested in the company. Some state laws differ when it comes to LLC requirements, but the quasi-corporate structure has increased in popularity, whereas the number of S corporations are in slow decline by comparison.

### Other Partnership Structure Obligations

As we previously mentioned, partnerships aren't subject to corporate taxes, passing that obligation on just like S corporations and LLCs to the individual partner. Partnerships need to file Form 1065 with the IRS to alert the agency of its taxable status.

Partners must report their share of the group's profit and loss on their income tax as they would income from any other source. If they also draw a salary from the organization, that is reported as ordinary income despite the ownership relationship. Self-employment tax is due on whatever the partners collect on the firm. As you might expect, if no income of any kind is drawn, no tax is due. Changes in partnership status must be reported to the IRS within 30 days of the change. However, adjustments for changes in the distribution of income, loss deductions or credits among partners will be approved or not approved by the agency only after the change has occurred. You may find the need for adjustment after the fact.

## GENERAL LEDGER

Few words strike greater fear into the hearts of business owners than "tax audit." Your best strategy in dealing with auditors is to choose a representative to work with the auditors who is articulate and intelligent in answering their questions and representing your needs. If you don't choose someone, the IRS may choose for you and you may not like their choice. However, in the case of partnerships and LLCs, all owners are held liable and may be in the dock with the representative to face the music and

In terms of limitations and loss, under IRS rules, a partner isn't liable for a loss that exceeds his or her financial interest in the company. If and when such an event does occur, partners may not deduct the loss until the partnership has sufficient capital to cover the loss. The IRS defines the partners' financial interest as the amount of the original investment minus withdrawals taken over time plus accumulated taxable earnings that haven't yet been realized.

## OTHER TAX AREAS OF INTEREST

Tax accounting for the corporation—and remember once again that it's only the corporation, not the partnership or sole proprietorship that pays business taxes—is a complex process worthy of its own volume. However, there are a few things you may find it helpful to know:

• During the past two decades financial institutions have seen a big increase in cash deposits, thanks primarily to illegal activities such as drug transactions. To combat this problem as well as collect taxes on these amounts, which the IRS feels are due, laws were passed requiring that any cash transaction of more than $10,000 needed to be reported to the IRS on Form 8300.

The form isn't that difficult to complete, but must be done within 15 days of the transaction. Please note that it is illegal to split the amount into smaller deposits, no matter what its source, to avoid reporting it. Doing that will signal the IRS that your firm may have something to hide. Even if you don't, you probably don't want the inevitable agency visit that will follow. Failure to file the form will result in a $50 penalty for each instance, which may be rescinded at the judge's discretion. Maximum penalty amounts can't exceed $100,000 in a calendar year for businesses with less than $5 million in revenue, or $250,000 for those with more.

Please note that those fines are for unintentional violations. If a judge determines that you intentionally sidestepped the law, the penalty for each instance is the amount in question or $25,000, whichever is greater. And that will be just the beginning of your problems.

• If you're a very small business with less than $2,500 in expenses per year, filing tax form C-EZ may be an option for you. However, you may claim no home office deduction, have no employees, no prior year suspended activity losses, no depreciation and must be a sole proprietor. Check with your tax preparer before assuming you qualify.

• Professional deductions are an area you will want to consider to help lower your tax burden. The IRS keeps a pretty close eye on such things, but there are still legitimate expenses that contribute to the cost of your business's success. The following costs qualify:

   • professional dues, staff development costs and subscriptions to professional

## GENERAL LEDGER
*(Continued)*

pay the piper. If you don't like the price of the tune, however, you can appeal the decision within 90 days of assessment. If the designee fails to do that within this period, individual partners have an additional 60 days to file their own appeals.

# *CHIT*

Investments in new business development is one area entrepreneurs frequently miss when tallying up deductions at the end of the year. Site visits, consulting fees, research, legal fees and other costs can be deducted as investments in new business development, whether the business has been acquired from someone else or developed from the ground up. Many of those costs can be amortized for up to 60 months, too. If, in the end, the new business investment doesn't work out, you can still deduct those expenses as a capital loss.

publications or journals that will improve staff performance and raise company revenues;

- supplies and resources, including such mundane items as paper clips and the paper to which they are attached;

- rent, utility and telephone costs for office or plant space;

- staff salaries, wages and commissions;

- fixed asset depreciation costs, which we talked about earlier;

- and costs of fleet and personal vehicles used in the execution of commerce.

There are also professional costs that appear to be reasonable deductions, but don't qualify according to IRS rules. These include:

- daily business lunches, even if you spend the entire time talking shop;

- expenses paid on behalf of clients, such as licensing fees paid by an attorney for an associate. Those may not be deducted by the payer even though the associate for which they were paid could deduct them if he or she paid those same fees;

- professional development and preparation, which include tuition and expenses should you decide to go back to school;

- personal professional expenses if you are an employee rather than a sole proprietor.

## Employment Tax Accounting

Whether your business has one or 100,000 employees, you are liable for payroll taxes. Indeed, they may constitute some of the highest taxes your company will have to pay. In this case, correct tax computation is not only of interest to your company and the IRS, but also to the employees from whom you withhold those taxes. We talked a little about payroll accounting requirements in Chapter 14, so you may want to refer back to that discussion. But there are still more criteria to consider when computing and paying these taxes.

The first step is to make sure you have been using W–4 withholding forms completed by employees to withhold the proper amount from each paycheck. From the information listed on those forms and utilizing state and federal income tax tables, you should have withheld the correct tax amount from the gross pay listed before arriving at the employees' net earnings for each pay period in the calendar year. It's a fairly straightforward procedure, and not difficult to follow.

Once you've withheld payroll taxes, you must determine when to pay them. Many firms submit them on the same day in which they withhold them in order to keep their books in line and make sure they are delivered in a timely, efficient manner. Some companies hold onto payroll taxes a little longer, however, to earn interest on the monies before distribution. Electronic tax filing is making it increasingly more difficult to play this float, but it is an available option if you determine that interest on the amount in question is worth the effort.

Be careful not to violate the statutory limits by which you can withhold those funds. Those limits are based on frequency of payroll and can be found in the tax tables.

Keeping internal paperwork current offers a similar challenge and is absolutely critical to maintaining the integrity of your accounting system. Quarterly reports must contain all necessary payroll and withholding information, which in turn are used to verify payments and compute unemployment taxes, social security and FICA payments. Employment tax obligations change as companies

## CHIT

Depreciation is another strategy by which you can save tax dollars. Business equipment, including computers, have a measurable life, the value of which can be depreciated over time. You can't depreciate land, which lasts in perpetuity, but you can depreciate the facility on it. Check with your tax professional about using depreciation to reduce costs.

increase in size, so keep current with the needs generated by your firm's progress.

### The Rest of Your Tax Burden

Corporate, payroll and miscellaneous tax issues comprise a great deal of your company's tax awareness. Here are a few more, just to close the circle:

• Sales tax, something all of us face every day, must be withheld on nearly every item sold at the time of the sale. There are a few exceptions, such as sales to schools, libraries and other government agencies that are tax-exempt. Items sold for resale to another firm also are tax-exempt if the original seller has a valid reseller's license. Check carefully. Some states require sales taxes on goods only, while others require it on goods and services. Other items, such as food or periodicals, also may not be subject to taxation.

• There are also such things as usage taxes, which apply to businesses that purchase from sources that don't withhold sales tax, such as out-of-state mail order houses. Under these scenarios, the buyer pays sales tax directly to the government, since the seller did not charge the tax.

• Property tax on the real estate your company owns functions much like the property tax on the home in which you live. Taxes may be due on leased property, too, depending on how the lease has been written. If you own a business out of state, make sure your taxes are in line with other comparable parcels.

Some municipalities have skewed the scale in the past to make taxes more affordable for home-grown businesses.

Depending on your industry or geographic location, there may be all kinds of other taxes as well. It behooves your tax specialist—either internal or external—to stay abreast of those taxes affecting your firm. What you save in taxes may more than pay this person's salary or fee.

*When a fellow says, "It ain't the money
but the principle of the thing,"
it's the money.*

—*Frank McKinney*

# Protecting the 19
# Bottom Line

Being successful in business and making money is a very fine thing indeed. All businesses strive toward that goal. Couple that with efforts to minimize expenses used to make that money, and you have the operating scenario for almost any business, for-profit or otherwise, in the world.

Some companies who talk the talk don't always walk the walk though. Some firms grow too fast for their own good and find that they have set the stage for putting themselves out of business by being unable to commit the resources to sustain that growth. Other companies find themselves overspending on expenses both elaborate and mundane. They still make progress, but not at the pace they had hoped to keep. Instead, they find themselves flush with cash and no particular plan for how to spend it. Those companies wind up with low returns due to poor investment strategies or significant and unchecked expenses until, like the U.S. government some years back, they are the proud possessors of $600 toilet seats.

To this point we've discussed good accounting techniques and sound financial practices. This chapter will focus on ways to preserve the company's bottom line through good cash management strategies and effective cash forecasting and money management policies. One addresses expenditures, the other revenues; both interact to make your firm's financial position safe and sound within the resources you have at your disposal.

## ENTER THE CASH MANAGER

In business, as in many other things, size matters. The larger the business, the more critical the need for close attention to the bottom line because the greater the risk of loss. That's where the cash manager comes in. Whether this person is the company's chief financial officer, chief executive officer or someone hired specifically for the purpose, the cash manager's job is to protect and develop the company's liquid assets—specifically cash—to better maximize their use and return to the firm.

The responsibility of the cash manager, a term that's more operationally specific than descriptive of a title, has little to do with building the bottom line. A cash manager does not supervise the sales force or monitor manufacturing. A cash manager is usually part of, but may not be head of, the executive team. Quite simply, the cash manager's job is to make the most out of the money that's available to the company. The cash manager does this through two primary methods:

• In consultation with department heads and others, the cash manager makes sure that operating expenses have been trimmed down to the minimum level reasonable to still accomplish the organization's strategic goals. Perhaps the executive team would like to travel across country for some expensive leadership training when the local university offers perfectly acceptable and much more economical alternatives. Maybe manufacturing has its eye on some expensive foreign-made sub assembly for the product you produce when research has shown that a more generic domestic sub assembly can do the same job for one-third the cost. It's the cash manager's job to raise issue with these expenditures to make sure the company is getting maximum value for its investment.

• The cash manager is also often the one who takes excess funds earned on sales and expense savings and invests them in stocks, bonds and other vehicles, again with an eye toward increasing the company's return. This means the cash manager must be up to date and conversant with the company's strategic goals and know which investment vehicles will help achieve those goals. Perhaps long-term bond investments that preserve the cash but gain reasonable returns in a safe environment are what's called for. Or maybe it's a matter of maximizing capital return with overnight investments that gain earnings each and every day while keeping the capital liquid. That's the cash manager's responsibility based on the company's strategic goals.

Quite simply, the cash manager manages the money, just like the job says. That's a task easily described, but one that requires both a practical and strategic thinker who has the financial background and understands both how money works and how the company works. This person then must combine the two in an effective synergy that will result in a stronger bottom line.

This is a not an easy position to be in for many corporate cash managers. The training and knowledge required are quite extensive. In addition, the cash manager must have the ability to stand back regularly from daily operations to look at the operational effects those decisions have on the safety and soundness of the bottom line. Part of this distance has to do with keeping activities in perspective. The other part relates specifically to department heads and other decisionmakers who may not understand the broad implications of what to them seem to be perfectly reasonable actions. In some companies, the cash manager is forced to make unpopular recommendations or take difficult stances on a regular basis. These are not shoes that everyone is able to fill.

In some companies, this job is the responsibility of the chief financial officer; in others, it may be split among several responsible parties on both the "treasury" side of the house and the cost-accounting function. Whoever does it—and however many do it—will need the proper training and strategic sensibility in order to make this function effective.

## Cash Manager Qualifications

In most cases, the best person to protect a company's assets is the one with the greatest to lose should the company fail. This immediately suggests that the owner, the largest stockholder or the chief executive officer may be the best candidate for the job. In some companies, that may be true. But in many others, the role each of those individuals plays quite often would conflict with the cash manager's goal. Can the CEO execute grand schemes if he or she must worry about pinching pennies on daily operations? Can the major stockholder gain major market share if it also means a significant drain on that person's assets to achieve that goal?

The best person to act as cash manager is someone with significant training in finance and a better than average sense of corporate strategy. It also requires someone who isn't afraid to take a risk when it's necessary and hold back when it's not. The cash manager must have a vested interest in the outcome of the company's activities, but also exercise a tight enough grip on funds control to provide more steam when necessary and to cut it off when it's not required.

A good cash manager candidate, especially if you're shopping outside the firm for such an individual, should come with the following credentials and experience:

• The proper background and references are as important here, if not more so, as they are for any position. Look for comparative performances in a similar role and with similar responsibilities for another company. The ability to keep a close eye on expenses is critical, but investment expertise is a whole new ball game. One of the things you'll want is a capable and facile investor who can move with the market, maximize its up swings and avoid its downturns as often as humanly possible. Look for a candidate with significant background in this area from an environment that most closely matches your own.

Be careful, however, to match that individual not only to the skill set required but also to your corporate culture. This is a very influential position. If your company is conservative by nature, a high flyer will not be successful in your environment, may alienate the board and executive staff, and likely won't generate the returns you're seeking. In addition, make sure that person's track record balances against the research you do to back up his or her claims. An average 10 percent growth in an overall 7 percent growth environment is more impressive than an average 12 percent growth in a 15 percent growth environment. Just as it's the cash manager's responsibility to create similar margins for your firm, it's your responsibility to understand what this person's past activity for other employers really means.

Don't forget to adjust those claims and your future expectations to the inflation rate. That, too, is a perspective into which this role is cast.

• Capital preservation strategies should be a central skill in your cash manager's portfolio. This is not just a matter of numbers. Look for the thought behind those actions about which the cash manager boasts. Cast it in the context of both time and place and try to understand the reasoning power of the individual and the strategy he or she employed to achieve those goals. Such thought processes say a lot about a person's skill under fire and perhaps in the very situations faced by your company. The secret to money management, of course, is to maximize growth—especially cash—while minimizing threats to the company's bottom line. At the same time, the cash manager should know when to put those funds to work and when to let them alone.

• Money management should become part of your company's strategic goal. As such, it's worth the effort to check out the corporate environment for potential candidates for the position. Make sure there are the type of similarities in the environments that would allow this person to be successful for your firm. Moreover, find out whether this person was a good match in his or her previous slot. That's a critical step in knowing whether or not he or she would be a good match for you, too. Once you're reasonably sure you understand that, measure as best you can how the cash manager's skills and abilities match the needs of your firm. In some cases the effort will be unnecessary; in others, however, it just may be your company's salvation.

• When in doubt, sound the cash manager out. If you're in the hiring mode, the best way might be to show that person the company financials, allow time for analysis, and then let that person cut loose with the observations and recommendations. An astute cash manager should be able to tell within a short period of time what it takes to keep your company running and what he or she might be able to do to improve its capital return. The nature, tone and strategy behind those recommendations will tell you a lot about the way the cash manager thinks and what you might expect from that person.

Once you do have a cash manager on board, give that person sufficient latitude to do the job he or she was hired to do. A clear understanding of the company's operating philosophy is necessary, of course. But be careful not to micro-manage the individual. Loose guidelines and a clear charge to maximize the company's bottom line are probably the best support you can give the person.

Once all are agreed to the philosophy and the cash manager's authority, stand back and let the professional take over. Make sure the entire company abides by the philosophy and you'll have a much better chance at corporate success than before. Chances are, your bottom line will thank you for it.

## COUNTING ON CASH FORECASTING

At least half of the cash manager's role will focus on liquidity management—investing excess cash in revenue-generating stocks, bonds and other vehicles. A savvy cash manager—let's call him or her an investment or treasury manager at this point—understands that the goal of such activities is to invest funds in ways that will enhance the company's financial foundation and growth by adding significantly to the bottom line. What's the best strategy by which to accomplish this goal? That all depends on your company, its age and position within the marketplace, the nature of its management team, its need for liquidity versus security, and 101 other little aspects that characterize your company's investment plan.

In today's market, there is a different investment strategy for every company. Fast-growing startup firms may be more risk-tolerant and willing to take the chance on high yield, fast-running vehicles that may or may not return big dividends because they need the cash. On the other hand, old-line blue chip firms with established products and market positions may not need ready cash and may be looking for a safe investment with a solid yield, something that won't bring gray hairs to the head of the investment manager but will result in a steady strengthening of the firm's financial foundation. Neither strategy is wrong if it's appropriate to the strategic goals of the company. It is beyond the scope of this volume, however, to go into great detail on any particular growth strategy. That's a discipline in and of itself and falls under the authority of your investment manager. Let that person stick his or her neck out this time. That's what you're paying for.

What we can do is talk a little bit about cash forecasting techniques as a way to support the process. Cash forecasting is a part of any cash management system and is critical to estimating revenues, expenses, profits and losses in order to develop investible cash flow estimates. This is more than an academic exercise. It's a way for the cash manager to estimate the amount and timing of cash surpluses, which is critical for selecting the right investment vehicle.

There are a number of methods by which cash managers construct such a plan. Here are three of the more common ones:

1. In the first method, cash receipts and disbursements are analyzed and a picture of each cost element of cash-based function is created so that forecasts may be developed. Essentially a cash forecasting method, this technique also provides a fairly comprehensive picture of variances in receipts and disbursement. That aids in developing a clearer understanding of cash flow and support control mechanisms by establishing patterns between forecasted activities and estimates. Assuming the net result offers enough excess liquidity at predictable intervals, this can mean more effective and lucrative short-term investment activity.

2. The adjusted net income plan is most applicable where receipts are somewhat predictable and expenses are stable entities. As its name implies, this strategy begins with the company's income and expense statement. Noncash transactions are subtracted from the net income to arrive at a cash

# *GENERAL LEDGER*

Your company's investment strategy has numerous variables, but three primary reasons for investment stand out from the rest:

• Companies invest for safety purposes to prevent capital loss.

• Some firms utilize liquidity growth strategies to convert investments back to cash.

• Return, in order to maximize investment dollars, often is the most critical and common reason.

The best strategy? Take a balanced approach that employs a little of each of these strategies for a well-rounded investment policy.

income or loss and then further adjusted for nonoperating balance sheet changes. In this strategy, which relies only on adjusted net income, the true extent of gross cash receipts or disbursements isn't really known or understood. Stable companies may find this useful, but those with tight cash margins may be hard put to have the latitude this strategy requires.

3. The differential between capital as it appears at different times during the pay period is also sometimes used. Known as capital differentials, this strategy takes the net working capital at the beginning of each accounting period, adjusts it by the net income and other receipts or disbursements due, and arrives at an estimated working capital figure for the period. From this amount, the necessary working capital is deducted to arrive at an amount of cash available for investment.

No matter which strategy is used, the cash manager should establish a well-defined work plan before proceeding. Fundamental steps to such a work plan include defining the purpose of the forecast and what the cash is to be used for; gathering and evaluating necessary data; preparing the forecast, following the performance of your effort and adjusting for future changes in the strategy. It also helps to isolate cash flow from operations (CFO), cash flow from financing activities (CFF) and cash flow from investment activities (CFI). The more you can refine the cash management tools you use, the better off you'll be both in controls and results.

Of all the steps, defining the forecast's purpose is likely the most critical because it sets the stage for all other activity to follow. The more clearly the assumptions behind this definition can be articulated, the better results you're likely to have. Following through on the steps should result in a clear forecast of very achievable activities and actions.

## TRACKING THE MARKET

Earlier we mentioned liquidity management, not only in preserving but enhancing the bottom line. It's true the cash manager's role is to help monitor expenditures, but it's also to make solid investments with excess cash to help shore up and even enhance profitability for the company. Investing is a discipline in and of itself that deserves its own volume. The best we can hope for here is to offer as few basics to familiarize you with the world of stocks and bonds.

Good strategies rely on sound data, and there are some excellent sources of information your cash manager should consult when making investment decisions. Understand, of course, that none of these sources offers fool-proof approaches to investments. But keeping track of market fluctuations and the stock performance of some preferred companies allows a better sense of activity and a more profound level of knowledge when it comes time to invest company funds. It also aids in the understanding of basic business trends. In fact, when it comes to investing, every little bit of information helps.

In terms of resources, investment managers religiously consult the *Wall Street Journal.* Other indicators include *Standard & Poor's 500 Composite Stock Price Index,* which tracks performance trends of 500 companies listed on the New York Stock Exchange. On-line sources like Bloomberg.com and CNBC.com also offer up-to-the-minute investment information. Computers linked directly to the market receive updates every two minutes of the 400 industrials, 40 financial institutions, 40 public utilities and 20 transportation firms that make up the 500 companies. The close watch allows investors to make trading decisions throughout the day. The Dow Jones Industrial Average, which averages 30 stocks, is another indicator worth watching.

## Learning the Language

In order to invest successfully these days, you need significant background and special training in the ins and outs of the stock market. If you don't have that already, we can't provide it for you here. What we can do is give you 11 important terms you will need to recognize if you want to understand what your investment manager is doing. They're listed in alphabetical order for easy reference:

- The *asking price* is the current cost-per-share of the stock or investment, usually computed by adding the net asset value per share and the sales price, if one exists. It's also called the offering price.

- The *bidding price* is different from the asking price because it's the amount that purchasers bid to own the stock. It's the net asset value per share and also the price at which the company will buy back the stock.

- *Capital growth* describes the shares' increase in net value over time.

- *Diversification* refers to the activity of spreading investments over a variety of mutual funds, usually to reduce risk. By not putting all the eggs in one basket, the investment manager protects both the investments and the investors.

- A *dividend* is the distribution of assets resulting from earnings on investments or increases in value among stockholders. Dividends are awarded at the board of directors' discretion.

- The *net asset value per share* is arrived at by subtracting liabilities from assets, and usually translates into the market price of the stock.

- A *no-load fund* is one whose shares can be purchased at the net asset value without the add-on of either fees or commission.

- Your company's *portfolio* is the sum total of its investment activity and usually includes stocks, bonds, mutual funds and other investment vehicles.

- If you *redeem* an investment, that means you sell it.

- Of course, the *redemption price* is the price you receive when redeeming (selling) the shares.

- The *seller's fee* is the amount earned by the broker for handling your transaction. It's added to the net value per share and paid by the buyer. By law, it may not exceed 8.5 percent of the transaction amount.

This is just a small start. What you've seen will not make you a killing in the stock market, but it will set you on the road to understanding what cash and investment managers can do for your company and why having a good one is critical to protecting the bottom line.

*The road of progress is,*
*inevitably, under construction.*
*Be careful which detour you choose.*

*—Anonymous*

# Understanding 20
# Growth Cycles

From a finance and accounting standpoint—or any standpoint, for that matter—funds management is critical to your company's success. But there's another aspect to a healthy bottom line that needs consideration. It has to do with understanding and managing your company's growth cycles. Success is a wonderful thing but, frankly, if you're not careful, you quite literally could "grow broke."

Growth is what most businesses strive for, but growth without planning could wind up harming the company's bottom line—as well as its reserves, its operating ratios, its credit rating and a host of other critical factors. Companies that grow too fast strain their resources, putting themselves in a position of being unable to satisfy demands. Once you've extended yourself beyond your ability to meet demands, service gaps develop and revenue begins trailing off just as expenses begin to grow out of control. If you're not careful, having too much business could quite literally drive you out of business.

That's why it's critical to manage your firm with an eye toward sustainable growth, evolving at a rate that not only makes sense for your company but also allows you to sidestep the pot holes and pitfalls on the road to progress. Too much growth, like too much of anything, isn't necessarily a good thing.

Knowing how to manage growth starts with understanding the nature of growth, both of your company and the products it produces. During certain steps in a product's or firm's evolution, growth is good. In fact, it's critical. At other times, the better strategy is to pull back. Managing growth means knowing when to follow which course. Once you reached that level of understanding, it's time to define a strategy for sustainable growth. If you choose the right strategy, then you should be able to continue until your company reaches the next phase of development.

We'll cover each step in turn, but let's start with the basics. That's always the best place to begin.

## DEFINING PRODUCT LIFE CYCLES

All products, like all companies, have life cycles, individual phases of development and market awareness that coincide with the product's introduction, growth, maturity and decline. Each stage of that cycle has its own identifying marks and its own processes. Some stages make money for the company, other stages cost money. Knowing what phase your product(s) may be in can make all the difference between success and failure. More importantly, it can help you identify how company growth may be affected and whether you need to turn up or turn down the heat.

All products go through four distinct phases in their product life cycle:

### Stage One: Product Introduction

Every journey begins with a first step, as Confucius was fond of saying. So, too, every product begins with an introductory phase during which you attempt to enter the marketplace and introduce an otherwise preoccupied public to what you have to offer. As ubiquitous as it now seems, Coca-Cola was once a medicinal beverage that needed to be introduced to a turn-of-the-century public that was not only unfamiliar with the brand, but with the entire concept of soft drinks. Coke has come a long way from the pharmacy shelves to becoming the cultural icon it is today.

Depending on your industry, the introductory phase is a period of moderate to high costs, with high costs being the more likely of the two scenarios. Chances are, you will have research and development costs to pay down, along with a major investment in marketing support in order to make your product well-known. There are merchant incentives and product giveaways and introductory events as well, along with the possibility of a below-market price (if that is your introductory strategy) to stimulate sales. Couple that with moderate to low revenue from a public new to your idea and you can see you're in a stage in which profits may be small while costs may be large.

## Stage Two: Product Growth

Once you've successfully completed the introduction phase and the public is familiar with and has accepted your product, you enter a growth phase in which you can plan on making up for lost financial time. Profits may soar while expenses decrease. With your R&D likely paid off and customers familiar with your offering, development and marketing expenses begin to tail off as sales grow. By the early 1990s, Microsoft had become a household word in terms of software marketing. Sales began to ramp up without the need for a media campaign and R&D needs tapered to a lower level—some would say too low—while profits soared.

But the growth stage isn't all roses and sunshine. Once you've proven the market exists and defined successful strategies for tapping it, competitors likely will enter the picture to trade on the spade work you've already done, with similar products designed to fill similar needs. Some may attempt to undercut your prices as part of their own introductory strategy. Although marketing expenses will be less than the major push you launched during startup, a certain level will need to be maintained to keep your name foremost among providers. Rest assured, your increasing revenue and decreasing costs will cross each other on the growth chart, but you can't afford to let your guard down during this stage.

## Stage Three: Product Maturity

Every growth arc eventually levels off, and it's at this point that your product will reach maturity. That's when your competitors, who also now may be firmly entrenched in the marketplace, begin to pose a serious threat. Your product strategy will change and costs may

## CHIT

Your company may do better if there is a specific executive designated to oversee growth. That doesn't mean that all decision-makers can stop being involved in achieving the company's goals. Far from it. What it does mean is that one person—and maybe that's the CEO, the CFO, the product manager or someone else who has the expertise to understand what he or she is looking for—needs to watch for danger signs specific to the firm and the industry and then sound the alarm when the signs appear. Such an early warning system may help prevent more serious situations from occurring.

increase as you reposition yourself through increased marketing and attempt to hold your industry leader status.

This also may be a phase where price discounting becomes part of your battle plan. With R&D costs far, far behind you and the only thing drawing on resources other than basic production and distribution is a slight increase in marketing, you may be able to afford to offer price advantage as one of your more attractive features. Assuming your product continues with some level of success in the marketplace, those limited losses due to discounting likely will more than be made up for with the increase in volume.

But take care: Too much discounting without the requisite growth in volume could result in significant losses. Some maturity phases last a long time, so be careful how deep you dig with your discount and monitor customer response to the strategy closely. On the other hand, some mature phases come and go quickly, so you need to be flexible and reactive in whatever strategy you pursue.

### Stage Four: Product Decline

No matter how popular the product you produce was at launch, it eventually will succumb to the wheels of progress and go into decline. Depending on how the company may choose to handle this stage, it may not require high costs in terms of expenses. The possible exception is for companies attempting to breathe new life into old products through repackaging, repositioning and increased marketing. As the product's flame begins to flicker, however, it will have an impact on revenues. What once was a top shelf item could become a bottom shelf product or cease to exist altogether.

The lesson from all these steps, of course, is that different product phases require different strategies which, in turn, will result in different financial activities and impacts. How you go about defining a sustainable growth rate will vary with the phases of your major product. Awareness of which stage you're in is critical to the success of those efforts.

## BUSINESS LIFE CYCLES

Businesses go through phases very similar to those of product life cycles. That is, they embrace the same opportunities and run the same risks as those found in the product life stages. The same level of care must be taken in order for the business to avoid those same types of traps.

• Every business has an entry stage, a time when it's new to the world of commerce and its principles are eager to gain marketplace recognition. Resources often are limited, the revenue stream may be no more than a trickle, and its needs are great. This is a very dangerous time for new businesses and the time during which most of them fail. At this point, all growth is perceived as good growth because the need levels tend to run very high. Good resource management becomes vital to survival, as does adequate capitalization to produce what's known as straight-line growth.

• The growth phase, which naturally follows, can be an exhilarating time for a company. The name is known, the products introduced and the customer base defined. Startup costs are declining and profits tend to run high. It's an exhilarating time that requires significant energy with which to keep pace, along with sufficient financial support.

• As a firm enters maturity, it's usually entering a period of smooth sailing. But those calm economic seas can be misleading. Costs may be level and profits sufficient for the time being, but nothing exists in stasis. Eventually the firm will enter a period of decline, so the strategy here is to maintain the mature phase—and the profits it generates—for as long a period as possible. Companies aware of the rigors of maturity can do very well. Those not paying attention may find themselves facing rough waters ahead without the necessary skills to navigate the currents.

• Corporate decline, the final phase, is a hard course correction to make. A company prepared for the inevitable may be able to maintain its decline for a long period of time with appropriate plans in place to exit the market gracefully. Those that have created an exit strategy may find a graceful way out. However, many firms stumble around attempting to breathe life into the corpse without luck. Whether there's reason to stay or it's time to go, financial planning should reflect this phase accurately and offer plans accordingly.

## Good Growth/Bad Growth

Growth for its own sake is not an effective strategy for most businesses, even during its entry stage. Growth in revenues almost invariably means a growth in expenses. Depending on the ratio of that growth to capacity, a company can easily drown in its own excess without even realizing what happens. The secret is a control plan that will result in sustainable growth for the company and the products it sells with a clear idea of the potential profit margin and what that means to the bottom line.

Believe it or not, excessive growth can be bad for a company because of the undue pressures it can put on resources. For instance:

• More orders mean more products, which can lead to more workers to support increased production and distribution. However, the revenue from those increased sales may not be sufficient or consistent enough to support the added staff, negating the value of those sales with a corresponding increase in expenses. If the majority of those revenues are in accounts receivable, the situation can become downright desperate.

• The company's management structure may need to grow and develop to support new initiatives, creating an unwieldy, top-heavy environment that again may increase costs beyond the relative economic value such an increase was designed to support. The resulting environment of too many chiefs may do long-term damage to the company's growth and productivity.

• Increases in production capabilities and/or facilities not financially supported by increases in sales can result in unnecessary and under-utilized capacity that will turn into a detriment rather than an asset as the company moves through its growth cycles.

Such scenarios show that not all growth is good growth and plans must be carefully monitored so the effect of that growth doesn't go south.

## A SUSTAINABLE GROWTH STRATEGY

In terms of definition, sustainable growth can best be summed up in the adage, "It takes money to make money." How much money it takes depends on how much growth you plan to accommodate. But as long as growth is the result of planning, and your expenses coupled with your desired growth margin balance against revenues—in much the same way as your books must balance, as a matter of fact—then your growth level likely will be sustained and progress made.

The growth stage of a product or company is one of the hot spots in terms of maintaining sustainable growth because it's the phase during which the company sees its most rapid change and real-izes some of its greatest growth needs. Increased sales mean increased costs. Some companies borrow to sustain production or operations needs, which can be the kiss of death if done indiscriminately. With-out a strategy for revenue growth, such as the sale of common stock, serious problems could occur for the company overstepping its bounds. Sometimes sustainable growth occurs by default.

Understanding the ratios for sustainable growth isn't compli-cated if we understand how the balances of revenue and expense works within company operations. For the purpose of discussion, we'll assume your company is seeking as rapid a growth rate as pos-sible, has an existing capital and dividend policy it needs to maintain and is unable or unwilling to sell shares of stock, one of the strongest ways to raise operating capital. The scenario is common for most firms in the growth stage of the life cycle.

The balance sheet model becomes the key to sustainable growth during this stage. In order to increase sales, the company must increase assets such as inventory, accounts receivable and the production capacity to meet the increased need. The cash required to pay for these assets may come from commercial lenders or, better yet, revenues due to increased sales. As equity grows, liabilities increase proportionately. Taken together, these determine the rate at which assets expand. This limits the growth rate in sales. In the end, it appears that the sustainable growth rate is determined by expansions in owner equity. Equity levels define sustainable growth.

Put another way, sustainable growth in sales is impacted directly by the profit margin and asset turnover ratio measured against both corporate growth policies and the asset-to-equity ratio. There are algebraic equations to prove this theory, but from a practical standpoint, it's enough to know that companies exceeding their sustainable growth rates need to improve operations or be prepared to alter financial policies to accommodate growth. Otherwise, the imbalance may knock them financially off-kilter.

*The alternative to too much growth?*

- Reduce or reverse your revenue growth rate so sales slow down and you have a chance to make good on orders using current assets. In most cases you'll have a chance to recoup those sales as the cycle begins to flatten out. But if you plunge yourself into an expense ditch that's too deep for your firm, you may have a much harder time climbing out.

- Modify company policies to reduce capital and put more cash into circulation. This could have the same effect as wandering too heavily into debt, leaving you without adequate resources for future efforts. In this case, however, the assets you're using are yours. If and when you do trip up, you still may be able to turn to commercial lenders as a resource. Review your dividend policy and consider how much you should plow back into the firm to underwrite new production or retire operational debt.

- Look for ways to better use existing resources to meet growing needs. By making sure all plants are running at capacity and all employees have incentive to perform at higher levels, you may be able to meet demands without making significant investments for which you'll have to answer later. In that same vein, you may disincent sales staff to moderate growth cycles. In addition, rely on just-in-time inventory and labor to moderate costs and reduce the amount of asset investments in stockpiled goods and materials.

Your best option likely will be a combination of all three elements used in varying degrees. Again, the key to sustainable growth is good planning and effective management follow-through. It's as critical here as it is anywhere else in your operation.

## Turning the Tide of Growth

Good planning, as we have repeatedly said, is critical for creating sustainable growth. Much of it involves a good management team up to the task. In fact, management is the key to this whole issue. If your company is having trouble with growth, review the management structure first. There may be inefficiencies in production and distribution systems, to be sure, but chances are that inadequate management is more likely at fault. Your management team should have the following characteristics:

• Experience in managing growth for your company or another company is a critical skill. The more they understand about what lies ahead for the firm based on their past experience, the more successful they will be in countering the negatives and capitalizing on the positives. Their ability to raise capital may be paramount to success.

## DEBIT

Smaller companies tend to struggle more with sustainable growth because they have smaller margins to begin with, higher startup costs and a greater appetite for growth overall. Depending on the safety net provided by owners' equity, they may survive quite nicely as their business catches fire. But those operating on a shoestring with a heavy debt load may find their fund resources drying up just when they need them most. Remember, forewarned is forearmed.

• Flexibility to move from an aggressive growth mode when called for to a more tranquil maintenance environment that pulls back the reins when necessary is among the most important skills the team needs. Not all groups can travel effectively between the two extremes and those that can't become a detriment in the area in which their skills fail.

• In addition to skills and abilities, the management team also needs empowerment and accountability. Their success is determined by the company's success. And vice versa.

***Unsustainable growth:*** What happens if, despite the best laid plans, unsustainable growth occurs? There are ways to turn the tide on this situation:

• Selling equity in the company in the form of stock may be the quickest way to raise the necessary capital. But unless the company is already public or able to take the steps to go public, this is not an option. In addition, many companies choose not to do another stock issuance because of its cost or the fact that it doesn't match their current financial strategies. A company too highly leveraged in the market can run into problems all its own, and short-term gain may result in long-term loss of earnings and ownership. In addition, too much extension will result in a loss in earnings per share, which could harm the firm's financial position and its image in the marketplace. Without proper planning, increasing equity could have a negative rather than a positive effect.

• The company also can take steps to reduce its dividend payout ratio on existing shares. This may be a more practical alternative than it may at first seem. Rather than miss their dividends, shareholders may view the reinvestment in company growth as a very good thing and more valuable to their long-term investment than having cash in hand. A reduced or eliminated dividend now likely means a higher one in the future, given that management's growth strategy is effective. But, communicating that strategy is critical. A dividend cut without the promise of attractive returns will have the opposite effect on shareholders and drive the market price down.

• Increasing leverage through more borrowing may also be a reversal strategy providing that there are adequate safeguards in place. Commercial lenders will not loan money without the promise of adequate payback. But it does create future financial obligations for the firm and may severely affect the firm's cash flow, not to mention its sustainable growth pattern.

• Pruning away excess enterprise is another strategy to consider. Companies that are over-diversified may be able to eliminate unprofitable operations and plough those resources back into core businesses. In some cases, diversification may allow the freeing up of funds from operations not affected by those issues having an impact on the core business; in other cases, complete elimination may be the answer. In addition to generating capital through the sales of marginal businesses, it may also eliminate some sales streams and reduce pressure on the company.

• Changes can be made in the sourcing of operations from more expensive in-house operations to out-of-house providers who work on a contract basis. This not only reduces overhead, usually one of the most costly expenses to any company, but also may help refocus the company on its core competencies, which may lead to further refinements, cost reductions and revenue stream eliminations.

• When all else fails, reprice your product to the higher end of the market. Capacity will be reduced and revenue will increase on those units you sell. Your market position will be secure, your revenue strong and you'll have time to regroup and rethink your overall strategy. Plus, you can always discount your price again in the future if you need to recapture the volume you lost.

## Falling Behind

Companies that out pace their sustainable growth rate face problems that can, if left unchecked, put an end to their operation. An equally vexing and no less critical situation occurs when a company's sustainable growth rate outpaces its actual growth. Growing beyond your ability to perform can stretch limited resources to the breaking point. But having those resources in place and not being able to grow to match the capability of those resources can also put your operation behind the eight ball. Idle staff and quiet production facilities are cost items rather than investments in growth. Both can have negative effects on growth margins, which can decrease the company's value for all involved.

Once you recognize that this is a problem for your company, decide if it's a long-term condition or something that is either short-term or seasonal. The remedies you choose for one will be very different from the ones you choose for the other. You also need to understand whether this is an issue specifically affecting your firm or an industry-wide phenomenon. If it's the latter, there may be nothing you can do.

In any case, it's critical for management to examine its own performance to decide whether or not their action—or, perhaps, inaction—may be the factor driving the slowdown. Honest self-examination often is a painful process, but it's critical whenever a crisis affects vital operations. It may be an issue of repositioning the firm, changing strategies or even changing management teams. Only after you're certain the problem isn't within your own house can you afford to look to outside sources.

If you're facing this challenge, there are several common responses:

• Some companies find themselves doing nothing about the situation, happy to continue running the business despite the lack of significant returns. They sit quietly on an ever-increasing pile of idle resources that should be deployed in growth and development. Underutilized resources can have several negative impacts on a business, not the least of which is depressing the value of the stock, a situation about which stockholders will have quite a bit to say. Savvy corporate raiders with ideas about growth could move in and change everything, including the management that sat idly and watched their company's slow decline.

• Another option may be to return the funds to stockholders as dividends or use the refunds to repurchase shares. Corporate psyches and tax laws don't seem to favor this approach, however, and Uncle Sam imposes taxes on earnings both at the corporate and dividend level. Besides, earnings reinvested often bring greater returns, which seems to better feed the corporate mind set.

• A third strategy is diversification, which is another way of saying that the company is buying growth options by investing in or starting businesses. For business leaders, this strategy definitely has appeal, particularly for firms that have a keen eye toward either vertical or horizontal growth integration strategies. Moreover, in cases where the core business is beginning to fade in the marketplace, this is a way to explore new options. Since fast growth firms have mirror-image problems of slow-growth firms, it may be possible that reinvestment by one firm into another may solve both companies' problems. And that, more than most other alternatives, would be a constructive use of funds.

One word of caution: Never confuse growth—either fast or slow—with the effects of inflation. The gross amount may change, but the relativity between expenses and revenue won't. The main difference is the time delay between the increases in revenues and that of expenses. That can provide a false sense of prosperity to firms that are soon crushed under the realities of the marketplace. Companies that mistake inflation for growth often find themselves in hot water. And, additional inflation is not the way to cool things off.

*The future ain't what it used to be.*

*—Ascribed to various authors*

# Forecasting 21 the Future

Accounting for past financial activity and analyzing present trends are just part of the overall financial management picture. One of the most critical functions any financial professional performs has to do with future projections, casting one's line into the unknown for the sole purpose of snagging the best possible future scenario for growth and opportunity. Many of us would like to see the future; financial professionals are not only obligated to see it, but also to interpret it correctly. A tall order? That's why they get paid the big bucks.

In some ways, financial forecasting is more important than accounting for the present because of what it means for corporate growth. The entire stock market ebbs and flows based on bets, hunches and projections about future financial activity of public companies. People generally don't invest in a stock, bond or any other type of vehicle if they don't think it has the likelihood for a solid financial future. Financial forecasting is often an art, occasionally a science and something every financial professional has to do, even if it's only during budget time. There are forecasting techniques that are as simple as they are accurate. This chapter looks at a few of the more common strategies.

## DEVELOPING A PRO FORMA STATEMENT

Every organization and many individuals plan for the future. They develop specific goals and strategies for future growth and development. The vast majority of this planning, whether on the personal or professional side, revolves around finances. That's because most plans need benchmarks and in the world of business, money is that benchmark. That makes the financial professional, if not the key planner, then certainly one who is near the top of the planning pile.

Everybody in business plans something, even if it's just the guys in the mailroom planning when to go on their next delivery route. At the higher level, however, those plans take on a financial cast. The tool that's usually used is a *pro forma statement*. A pro forma statement is simply a prediction of what the company's finances will look like at the end of the accounting period. This may be the quarterly financial report or the year-end wrap-up. In any case, the part that extrapolates from current trends and offers a best guess at where the company will wind up financially is some type of pro forma statement.

And, despite its very official sounding name, pro forma statements can be as formal or as informal as they need to be. Pro forma statements usually are part of the accounting system electronically linked to the general ledger, spreadsheets that can change the entire system with the stroke of a key. On the other hand, pro forma statements can be written on the back of a lunch bag and still do their job. As long as the statement displays the necessary information in a logical, rational and consistent manner that is useful to the user, it qualifies as a pro forma statement.

Before moving forward, however, make sure your pro forma makes sense. If you've created a comprehensive, consistent and accurate document, then chances are you're ready to execute plans. But realize the pro forma is the most critical piece of the puzzle in making financial projections. If yours is inaccurate, sloppy or doesn't pass the smell test, stop where you are and start again. It doesn't pay to take any chances with this important step in the process.

## METHODS OF FORECASTING

The pro forma statement may not be enough in and of itself. The data should be linked by an analysis methodology that will spin the information in a certain way to get the required point of view. One such methodology is to tie the income statement and balance sheet figures to projected future sales. That's called *percent-of-sales analysis* and there is a distinct rationale for its usage. In most cases, variable costs, current assets and current liabilities vary directly with company sales. Percent-of-sales takes these variables into account when arriving at its conclusions, providing simply derived, logical estimates of the variables that it measures.

The first step in using percent-of-sales? Perform a historical audit to see which financial statement items have varied in relation to sales figures. Those items that have varied in the past can be estimated as a percentage of sales in the future. From that basis, it is then necessary to forecast sales and to do so as accurately as possible. Sales forecasts are no longer merely a number designed to motivate sales staff. Under percent-of-sales estimates, those projections now are a critical part of forecasting the entire organization's future financial well-being. That means greater care needs to be taken. Once the appropriate pro formas have been completed, remember to test the sensitivity of the appropriate variables in the sales forecast for consistency.

The final step in percent-of-sales forecasting is to estimate the individual items based on trends that have been uncovered and make the necessary and, most likely, accurate projections. If your inventory has traditionally been 5 percent of sales and sales is estimated to be $2 million, then it's safe to say that inventory likely will be $100,000.

One easy method is an industry trend survey designed to reveal how your percent of sales stacks up against that of the competition. Consider it a "top-down" approach that's based on four steps: a) identify industry sales figures; b) recognize your firm's market share of that industry; c) forecast total industry sales; and d) tabulate that forecast times your percent of the market. If you're

## GENERAL LEDGER

When it comes to estimating the need for external funding, operating executives find that the company's income statement has more to share than the balance sheet because the income statement merely measures profitability. The financial executive, however, finds the reverse true. When estimating future financial trends and needs, the income statement has value only so far as it affects the balance sheet, which measures the company's true financial position and net worth. Because the balance sheet offers a comprehensive snapshot in time of a company's full financial position, it becomes the key indicator for the financial executive.

using reliable numbers, your figures should be accurate within a few percentage points.

Percent-of-sales approaches have been used to successfully borrow money from lenders because of the logical, real-world way in which they analyze trends. A well-prepared pro forma, coupled with this type of analysis, may be able to overcome standard objections and stretch loan limits and criteria, if need be, to prove the worth of a more ambitious growth and development plan that may require greater capitalization than the lender would normally provide. Such a strategy would be affected by a variety of elements, including liquidity, cost increases or decreases and earnings trends. However, a detailed forecast that incorporates financial trends from previous years may be enough to change the thinking of the lender.

Sensitivity analysis is another method of forecasting. Those are the "what if?" questions so popular in corporate planning retreats. What if sales increased by 15 percent? What if it decreased by 15 percent? What if we shaved operating costs by 10 percent and forced workers to take a pay cut? What if management team members were all transported far beyond the Northern Sea?

Kidding aside, the sensitivity analysis is a useful tool to get the creative juices flowing. More importantly, it provides model information about the range of possible outcomes. If sales did, indeed, decrease by 15 percent, cutting operating costs by 10 percent might be just the start of the concessions necessary to keep the company on a financial even keel. By running a sensitivity analysis, you can easily see the measurable effect of major and minor changes in financial activity and what it could do to short-and long-term growth scenarios as well as measure potential volatility in relation to the market. If done properly, sensitivity analyses can be a good motivator and an excellent call to arms.

Sensitivity analyses also allow for management by exception. Running what-if scenarios will demonstrate clearly those variables that have the greatest impact on your company's financial forecast and those that have only a secondary or negligible impact. If time, money or other resources are limited, management can concentrate efforts on these primary indicators and most critical assumptions. That knowledge carries over from the planning to the implementation phase, allowing operations executives to work most effectively on those variables that appear the weakest or ploughing resources into those areas that promise the greatest return.

But be cautious in how you proceed with sensitivity analyses. They are simple in concept, but affect a vastly complex organization—your company. Care needs to be taken to do such analyses in the most comprehensive and complete sense possible.

If you truly do want to explore the effect a 15 percent drop in sales will have on your financial picture, it requires more than merely slashing 15 percent off revenue. Loss of that revenue also will mean a reduction in commissions paid to sales staff and managers, as well as a rise in inventory to account for the unsold goods. Loss of that revenue may indicate a need for increased outside financing, which will increase loan presence on your books. Depending on your business, it may truly mean reducing pay or cutting staff which, in turn, brings an entirely new set of financial what-ifs, as well as impacting operations for other lines of business.

The old carpenter's axiom, "Measure twice, cut once," has special application here. Make sure you've run the scenario from all angles before deciding on it as a course of action.

Sensitivity analyses have been run ever since the first businesses traded grain for goods in ancient Babylon. The advent of computer spreadsheet programs increased the use of simulation methodologies that function as an extension of sensitivity analyses. It differs from the basic what-if scenario, however, by virtue of the fact that it can measure a wide variety of probabilities at once and predict the likelihood of each scenario occurring based on the variables with which the program is fed.

At first pass, this sounds like an exciting approach that has extreme merit and, by capitalizing on the speed of computer technology, is something most companies otherwise couldn't do. The technology is fed variables, but it also can pick random values for those variables for which there really is no good projection available. This creates what are called trial scenarios at different percentages that can be run, along with the likelihood of occurrence. That 15 percent sales decline we talked about may be a real threat, or there may only be a 20 percent likelihood that it may occur given the other market and financial variables in place. On the other hand, the trial may reveal the strong likelihood or near certainty of a 10 percent sales decrease due to issues that otherwise would have gone unmeasured.

Unfortunately, simulation results aren't always that clear-cut. The big advantage is the program's ability to run all variables at once. The big disadvantage is the complexity and sometimes obscurity of the results. That's because simulations are mathematical programs that score probabilities based on mathematical sequences rather than business scenarios. A 10 percent decrease in sales certainly can be threatening to a company's financial well-being, but what other factors may mute its effects? How does this compare to what the rest of the industry is doing? Is this perhaps the desired outcome for a company experiencing a growth rate that is too rapid when measured against its ability to sustain it?

Simulation can provide excellent data, but if too much of the planning takes place inside the computer and not in the boardroom, planners who are not careful will lose the depth of insight the planning process provides. Left unchecked, over-reliance on simulation scenarios can rob them of their ability to make contributions to the long-term fate of the company and turn them into a reactive rather than proactive body.

## Impacts on Your Projections

Those who create pro forma projections know that everything the business does during its accounting cycle can have an impact on the outcome of those projections. In addition to the sales increases and decreases we already discussed, operating costs can make a huge difference; so can the cost of raw materials, especially if they increase unexpectedly, potential labor problems and entry of a new competitor in the field. The greatest benefit of all this forecasting is that it provides scenarios that allow you to measure the impact of those variables and produce very reliable outcomes. That is, indeed, why we do such things in the first place.

But there are variables that, by their very nature can cause even seasoned planners a little heartburn, variables that depend on one another or even the outcome of the process itself for their relative accuracy. Let's take a look at a few of these and also solutions to their challenge.


• Interest expense is one area that can cause novice planners problems because of the way it interacts with indebtedness and the need of accurate projections for both. As a rule, interest can't be accurately estimated until all external funding is accounted for. But since that external funding can depend on the amount of that expense, it would appear neither can be accurately estimated without knowing the full amount of the other which, in turn, is dependent on the accuracy of the other. When you add the impact changes in rates may have, things get even more complex.

There are several ways around this conundrum. The first is to define a set of simultaneously run equations and load them into your computer spreadsheet. As the spreadsheet runs the equations repeatedly, the resulting answers get closer and closer to a simultaneous solution. Another is to establish two funding accounts on both sides of the balance sheet—short-term securities and notes payable—to balance each other out. The final way is to forget the whole problem and assume that your best estimate will be good enough for forecasting purposes. Given the fact that no variable becomes absolute before the amount has been posted to the general ledger (after the deed is done), this most likely will be adequate for your needs.

• A more profound problem revolves around the seasonality of the pro forma statements and the fact that their projections are snap-shots in time. Annual pro formas may indicate either a very good or very bad financial picture based on where the company is at that point in time. A Christmas tree farm may have a December 31 pro forma that indicates a very strong financial picture. However, it will be at least another nine months before the grower begins to realize revenues again, a period during which he is also experiencing signif-icant operational costs. The best answer is to run pro formas at least on a quarterly, if not a monthly, basis.

## Other Types of Forecasts

Despite their applicability, pro formas aren't the only way to do a fi-nancial forecast. There are other methods appropriate for other companies, other purposes and other applications. Here are a few more for you to consider when it comes time to look into the crystal ball at the future of your firm.

***Cash flow forecasts:*** These are probably among the simplest to understand and, therefore, to use. A cash flow forecast lists all the anticipated sources and uses of cash for the period in which the fore-cast applies. That would include all revenue and expense from and to all sources. This does not measure profit and loss, of course, just the flow of funds through the organization.

In a cash flow statement, there are three ways to measure that flow about which you need to know:

1. Basic cash flow simply measures income and outflow of cash regardless of how large or small the amount and no matter how significant or irrelevant either the source or destination

may be. It does not analyze how any of that plays into the company's strategic plans. It's just the transfer of cash through the company. That's all.

2. Operating cash flow is based entirely on measuring operating revenue and expense. This method does not take reserves into account. Operating cash flow is perhaps the truest measure of a healthy business. A strong flow representing daily business means a strong company because reliance on reserves isn't a factor.

3. Discretionary cash flow refers to cash that's segmented into specific areas. By isolating cash flows for both widget sales and gadget sales, you can examine how each line of business is doing without losing the individual perspective to the overall whole. Discretionary cash flow is a good way to analyze business for any segmentable section of your company.

If you have to choose one, operating cash flow is likely the most useful overall as a financial barometer of your business's health. It gives you the most information with the least amount of effort.

***Cash budget:*** A cash budget also serves as a forecasting tool if used correctly. A cash budget is no more than a list of receipts and disbursements over a specific period of time. Because these are actual rather than anticipated revenues and expenses, the cash budget almost functions as a detailed cash flow without the element of accrual accounting.

## YOUR COMPANY'S PLANNING CYCLE

Financial forecasting and pro forma statements are primarily used as tools in your company's planning process. And planning should be a company-wide exercise in which all principles participate, from the president of the firm right on down to the line workers. Everyone is involved in managing some aspect of his or her day, even if it's personal time usage in relation to expectations. The first step in any plan is the broad gathering of those components for the purpose of setting goals, outlining strategies and assigning tasks.

From that point many companies use the three-tier approach to planning as part of their annual development exercise. In most cases, those planning stages represent a progressive narrowing of influence with an ever-tightening focus on the strategies needed to help the company accomplish its goals. Stage one occurs among the top executives, who take a creative and largely qualitative approach to the project. They amass market data, as well as trends from their own company's performance as well as the performances of competitors. From that they draft a broad, far-reaching plan with the role of financial outlines relegated to defining the parameters and structures under which the firm operates.

The next level of planning occurs at the operational level. The grand schemes describe what the goal is; the second tier planners outline strategies for achieving that goal. If the grand plan is to recover last year's 15 percent drop in sales and add 3 percent on top of that, it will be up to the second-tier planners to strategize how that is going to be done. At this stage, rough financial forecasts based on overall parameters outlined by upper management will need to be created.

Third-tier planners—those responsible more or less for the plan's execution—are the ones who really put the price tag on the process. They do that by creating both operating budgets and capital necessary to execute the goals and measure both short- and long-term expenses and assets. Once this level of planning has been completed, all three levels are rolled together and that becomes a company's financial forecast. If done right, there should be few or no surprises when the final results pop up. If all planning tiers have been honest in their assessments, then the resulting combined effort should work very nicely.

Taken altogether, it's clear that a company's strategic plan comes from a central source, of which financial planning and budget development are but a part. The resulting equation should be an adequate and accurate measure of your firm's future.

*Big shots are just little shots*
*who keep shooting.*

—*Christopher Morley*

# Troubleshooting 22
# Your Financial System

Architect Ludwig Mies van der Rohe noted some time ago that, "God is in the details." And it's the details and your attention to them that can make or break your company's day-to-day operation and financial well-being. When those details go awry—or simply in anticipation that those details eventually will fall from center someday—you and your company's management team need to be prepared to take the steps to troubleshoot your system whenever and wherever you see cracks and faultlines appearing.

Some of the signs are obvious. Production quotas fall short or shipments aren't made. Staff is reporting irregularly for work. Management fails in some key decisions and market position stumbles. Something just isn't right.

If the fall off is specifically financial, the problem may come under the heading of theft or fraud. We talked about that at length in Chapter 10, and identified some visible and not so visible warning signs along with ways to control and rectify the situation. But sometimes there's more to it than that, and the cause is less pronounced nor as easily identified. It's at that point, obscured by uncertainty over what's ailing your company, that you have to be ready to go in and troubleshoot your system.

## FIRST STEPS

Strong internal controls are the most important aspect of any system, another item we talked about in Chapter 10. Without them, all the troubleshooting in the world won't save you or your firm. After that, you need a sound strategic plan.

Most companies have a written strategic plan and most plans have action steps outlined to help the firm accomplish the plan's goals. If you are such a company, the first question to ask is whether those action steps are being followed. That may seem painfully obvious, but that's often a place that's easily overlooked. And since, as discussed in the previous chapter, the steps in the planning process are intrinsically linked, a missed step in one area could have an impact on an area entirely different from the place where the shortfall occurs. If you find such an oversight, fix it. Then see if it makes a difference with the problem you're having with your system.

Not all solutions are that easy, however. Modern business is extraordinarily complex and in many cases, the problems are harder to uncover than the solutions are to implement. Overall internal control systems, much like the ones described in Chapter 10, are critical for operational preservation. The best kind of control systems are flexible and easily managed. They tend to be simple rather than bureaucratic and aren't costly to develop or maintain. Within that framework, a well-designed system will measure cause and effect and be able to point you to the source of the problem.

You may already have such a system in place. But if you need to establish one, remember the following:

- All good control systems are based on performance standards for the operations or functions they control. It doesn't matter if we're talking about a manufacturing operation or your company's sales performance. No control measures can be effective if they don't have standards to measure against. That's a management function and should be part of the planning process. Effective planning is the first step toward effective controls.

- Once you have those standards in place, use them. If you don't, then there's no reason to have them; moreover, they will not help you troubleshoot your system should things start to go awry. If you don't make budget, for example, there's a problem. It may be in the motivation of your sales force or the ability of your manufacturing operation to keep pace with demand. Perhaps the management effort tying them all together is letting both sides down. In any case, without implementation, the standards you have established will do little good in rectifying the situation.

- Be prepared for deviations, both positive and negative, from the norm and know when those deviations have exceeded the limit of acceptability as defined by your policy limits. Nothing is static and everything is subject to the winds of change. Sometimes that wind blows in your favor, sometimes not. Know what your pain threshold is and act accordingly. You want your company to move forward with the prevailing winds, but you don't want those winds to blow you over. Understanding the level of deviation you can and will accept is a step toward control.

- When you deviate too much, take prompt corrective action based on previously understood goals and standards. Be sure your system can bend, but don't allow it to break. Acceptable standards of deviation exist for every business and every industry. Know yours and use them as part of your strategic plan.

## MANAGING ACCOUNTABILITY

Accountability for the company's well-being and profitability is the responsibility of all employees, but it helps if you have one person in each department as the designated troubleshooter. Someone tuned in to the operational rhythms of the department might be able to spot malfunctions more quickly than anyone else, and might be able to turn on the resources necessary to reverse whatever negative flow may develop.

One of the most important things for that operative to remember, however, is that data is what drives production and should be used to determine when the system starts to crack. We mentioned types of data earlier in the chapter, indices that something is amiss. That same data should form the basis of any analysis focused on company shortfalls, after which opinion can be weighed as to the possible causes of the fall-off. Once again, previously established internal controls go a long way in setting the stage for success and providing the mechanism for troubleshooting. Additional data, sifted through operational knowledge and experience, can help augment those standards and allow the troubleshooter to arrive at his or her conclusion earlier and with more precision.

## Conducting a Business Audit

In the worst cases—or even for those who merely want to keep things on course—periodic audits may be necessary. Realize we're not talking about financial audits. Those are ongoing exercises, with outside agencies auditing most companies on an annual basis to help keep them on track and in good standing with their stockholders. The audit we're talking about is a systematic and formal evaluation of operations from start to finish, with measures taken at each turn in the road to make sure production is on track.

Audits take different forms for different industries and even different functions within that industry. The one thing all have in common is that those being audited tend to fear them. An audit, by definition, is a formal examination, usually of the financial books. Its purpose is to measure the accuracy at which the function under audit is being performed. Since no one is perfect, possibilities for errors exist, and no one likes to make mistakes.

However, audits also are examinations, the result of which can lead to operational improvement. That's a goal toward which your company should aim its operational audits. In a very real sense, it's a growth and development strategy, not a punitive exercise. Much like a physical checkup, audits can uncover problems when they're still at a manageable stage. An audit isn't likely to ruin anyone's career. In fact, it may do a lot to extend that career's life.

Some of the more obvious problems uncovered in an audit include production problems, sales slowdowns, staff turnover and other operational woes. Less obvious targets of an audit may include bad decisions made at any level within the company. Unlike operational problems, which may have some immediate impact, the effect of bad decisions may take weeks, months or even years to surface. And then it may be too late.

Good business, the old adage says, results from good decision-making. It's that simple. Here are some ways to look at the decisions within your company.

- Do the decisions make sense in light of corporate objectives? There needs to be either a direct or indirect connection to your strategic goals and results of the decisions you make. When things go awry, it's often the result of bad decisionmaking. And bad decisionmaking is often the byproduct of not linking those decisions back to the company's objectives.

- Identify the problem, articulate the issues affecting that problem, and proceed toward a solution. The old marketing adage of, "Ready, Fire, Aim!" does not work well under these circumstances. Knowing what you have to do needs to be balanced with a time line for the solution, access to the necessary resources, the budget with which you have to work and any other data critical to implementing this solution. Once again, the solution needs to be data- rather than instinct-driven for the best results. It helps to have a contingency plan in place just in case.

- Create and execute an implementation plan to solve the issue at hand. In addition to using the data you've collected, cast the plan in light of corporate goals and objectives and operating philosophy. Then take the steps necessary to execute the plan. Fail to take that last, critical step, and the plan has no more value than if it weren't created at all.

- When all is said and done, review the effect of your efforts and follow up with any additional action you need. Sew up all loose ends and make sure that resolutions you thought you effected were, indeed, in place and operational. Check and recheck the impact of your efforts, especially in light of any conditional changes that occur as a result of your efforts.

## SEVEN KEYS TO CREATIVE RESOLUTION

When it comes to troubleshooting your system, remember that insight comes from knowledge and knowledge starts with good information. That's the bedrock for any resolution effort. But at the same time, a good system by which you can maneuver through the mire sometimes created within your company to address the needs and effect solutions is just as critical as that insight. You will have to customize that system to your needs and that of your company. Once you do, however, it should serve your firm in most situations.

The following is a set of considerations—standards really—for you to use or adapt in troubleshooting your own system. They are more personal than corporate in nature, but all have application across the board and throughout your operation.

1. Have you set for yourself and your company a high standard and do you hold yourself accountable for all your actions both inside and outside the firm? You'd be surprised at the number of professionals who behave irresponsibly and then complain about the effect of their behavior. Maintaining high standards for yourself and those who report to you will have a lasting positive impact on your firm and reduce the incidents that lead to problems.

2. Are your goals and those of your firm put into writing and embraced as critical to personal and professional success? Research has shown that Harvard Business School graduates who commit their goals to writing are at least 10 times more likely to achieve them than those who have only a vague idea of what they want. Your personal performance standards and your company's operational goals should be treated the same way.

3. Do you perform periodic self-examinations and "reality checks" on your goals and those of your company? Since the only constant is change, the only thing you can count on is that things will be different tomorrow than they were yesterday. Goals that were set two years ago likely have little bearing today. If you're not reevaluating on a regular basis, then your strategies are going out of date without anyone lifting a finger to do anything to them. This could cause serious problems within your system, not to mention what it could do to your career.

4. In addition to the above, are policies and procedures reviewed on a regular basis by your management team and those responsible for upholding them? How strong are your company's

internal controls and how well do you know their specific criteria? Chances are the line workers have a distinct insight into the situation and may have more to contribute when it comes to operations than management. Don't ignore or misuse this valuable resource. They work under the light of such policies and procedures every day and have a good idea which rules are productive and which need to change.

5. Do you operate in a way that protects your firm and the business it does? Staff loyalty is critical, but that loyalty comes as more than just an oath. It also relies on having smart operations that maximize company strengths and aims toward enhancing the firm's role in the marketplace. Team effort and shared knowledge are critical components of the right environment. Use them to your best advantage possible.

6. Do you and other firm executives seek appropriate council, both internally and externally? Chances are you're smart enough to know that you can't possibly know everything. That's where consultants come in. But those consultants aren't merely highly paid professionals. They're co-workers, fellow Rotary Club members, peers, friends, spouses or anyone with a line on whatever aspect of your business you're struggling with. Generous executives learn how to share the wealth; smart ones take their share of knowledge in return.

7. Do you regularly make the effort to communicate with the people whom your actions and those of the company affect? Most problems stem from poor communication, but that doesn't mean just talking. Communication is the proverbial two-way street that requires as much or more listening than it does talking. You can speak and not be heard and you can listen and not understand. Communication takes effort and it's worth that effort to make sure all parties are heard before the right decision can be reached. God gave us one mouth to speak with, but He gave us two ears so we could listen and better understand.

He also gave us ten fingers on which to count. And that's a good start for anyone interested in mastering accounting and finance. Have you started?

*Those who can, do.*
*Those who can't, teach.*
*Those who can't teach, teach gym.*

*—Woody Allen*

# Appendix:
# Quarter-Hour Classroom

Knowledge is critical, but unless you can put it to work in a practical setting, what you've learned will do you little good. Prentice Hall has designed this Quarter-Hour Classroom to give you practical applications and snapshot analyses of situations about which you've read, all within the time you take for a coffee break.

The following scenarios have been created to mirror actual business settings. By using them in conjunction with the related chapters within the text, you'll be able to test both theory and application. Good luck!

## 1. Putting Your Business Plan into Action

*The Situation:* Jensen-Maddox Industries, manufacturers and distributors of canvases and coverings for furniture, appliances and specialty products, is primed for expansion. The Midwestern manufacturer, which started as a producer of camp and stadium chairs, has narrowed its focus to concentrate on just the fabric portion of the furniture. However, the firm also has widened its horizon to the provision of canvas and fabric-based coverings for a wide variety of products, both consumer and industrial. Partners Jensen and Maddox have set out on a formidable task and they need money to fuel this expansion.

***The Analysis:*** Both partners have reasonable levels of capital in the company and are not in a position to invest more for an expansion scenario. The company's coffers and current sales have enough to fund the firm for current operations, with only a little left over to finance expansion. J-M Industries is going to need about $250,000 from an outside source to cover the cost of retooling existing technologies and expanding sales efforts.

Although its need constitutes a sizable amount, the partners know there is not enough required to consider an initial public offering. Nor is their need great enough to attract a venture capitalist. That means J-M Industries needs to secure a commercial loan for a quarter-million dollars. And that means the lender is going to want to see a business plan before parting with the cash.

***The Application:*** Partners Jensen and Maddox create a business plan that includes the following components:

## JENSEN-MADDOX INDUSTRIES
## BUSINESS PLAN

*Executive Summary and Situational Analysis*
Jensen-Maddox Industries manufactures and distributes canvases and cloth coverings for furniture, appliances and other uses. Originally started by George Jensen and Marvin Maddox in 1986 as a manufacturer of camp and stadium chairs, the firm has concentrated on the manufacture of the fabric part of the product, with purchase of the chair frames and structures. J-M Industries wants to capitalize on their strength and expand their horizon beyond chair manufacture and distribution to encompass a complete range of product uses.

*Market and Segmentation Strategy*
The market for canvas and fabric-based products and materials is vast and growing every day as the demand for lighter weight durable goods finds more and greater uses for the types of fabric J-M Industries manufactures and distributes. Increasing domestic and leisure activities, along with increasing consumer affluence, has increased the market for traditional fabric goods, such as backyard hammocks,

as well as new, more utilitarian products, including everything from boat to barbecue grill covers.

With a modest capital infusion, J-M Industries can capitalize on that growing market. From a production standpoint, the company has a successful history of manufacturing and favorable relations with suppliers. Cost effective manufacturing and distribution methods tested over time can give J-M Industries a competitive edge from a cost standpoint. Knowledge of the applications of the product, along with an awareness of and entry into new and expanding markets, will give the firm the necessary strategic edge.

*Customer Analysis*

The customers for the increased use of J-M-Industries' produced canvases and fabrics initially will be the leisure and outdoor industries, a market well-known to the company from its experience with camp and stadium seats. The standard customer is looking for an attractive material that is durable, versatile and uniform. By producing appliance and vehicle coverings, camp gear and supplies and tents in a limited but attractive variety of weights and colors, J-M Industries will be able to attract the attention of wholesalers and consumers in a market in which they already are vastly familiar.

*Competitive Analysis*

While there already are an average number of producers of similar goods, few have the key competitive advantage of manufacturing their own fabric. Most purchase the fabric from companies like J-M Industries and carry that overhead into their product price. Because we purchase the raw materials and manufacture the goods in-house, our overhead is contained with little additional charges to be tacked on to the products' prices. This gives us a market advantage in terms of price, which leads to greater flexibility and profitability.

*Positioning Statement*

J-M Industries' new Pinnacle line of canvas and fabric-based products captures the height of style and durability at a price that consumers not only can afford but will appreciate. Based on our production capability and product durability, Pinnacle represents the top choice in canvas and fabric-based outdoor products.

*Advertising, Promotion and Public Relations Strategies*
Extensive product advertising within wholesale and consumer specialty publications that focus on outdoor activities is central to J-M Industries' strategic marketing plans. Due to the competitive cost by which Pinnacle products can be produced, dealer incentives also are part of the plan, with a broadcast strategy of the entire United States.

One of the plan's most exciting components is the widely publicized field testing of the camping gear with the country's foremost outdoor couple, "Bouncing" Ben Belsen and his wife, Beulah, who will trek the length of the Rocky Mountains from southern Montana to northern Arizona using Pinnacle gear. Their travels will be recorded for a National Geographic television special.

*Sales Strategy*
As previously mentioned, dealer incentives will become a focal point of the sales strategy, which will be supported by the marketing and public relations efforts. The incentive plan will encourage dealers to offer one or more Pinnacle products as a loss leader while providing significant margin to encourage sales of full Pinnacle "suites" of merchandise. Sales incentives will include prizes to top sales associates. The top five winners will join "Bouncing" Ben and Beulah Belsen on the last week of their Rocky Mountain trek.

*Next Steps*
Once the Pinnacle line has proven successful, J-M Industries is planning the "Wet Wrap" line of waterproof coverings for appliances, boats, automobiles and trucks. Potential development plans include field testing by the United States military of Wet Wraps' durability and strength for use on tanks and amphibious assault vehicles.

*Operating Scenario*
From plants in Waupaca, Wisconsin, and Muncie, Indiana, J-M Industries plans to produce all its own fabrics and assemble all its own goods. Aging manufacturing and assembly technologies will be updated and retooled to accommodate the company's new needs. No new capital investment in equipment or machinery is required to accomplish the strategic goals. Adaptation costs for existing plant operations are limited. Much of the funding will go to market development and sales strategies to widen the customer base that already exists.

*Key Staff*
Company founders George Jensen and Marvin Maddox will capitalize on their Harvard Business School training and spearhead the efforts they used to begin the firm in 1986. Wally "Webfoot"
Simmons will continue as head of manufacturing. Suzanne Sizemore
and Chick Hernandez will continue their tag-team approach to
heading the marketing and sales functions.

*Financial Statement*

**Jensen-Maddox Industries**
**Period Ending 12/31/20XX**
**(Thousands)**

| | *Budget* | *Actual* | *+/–* |
|---|---|---|---|
| **Revenue** | | | |
| Camp Products | $165,000 | $158,750 | ($6,250) |
| Pinnacle Tents | 16,550 | 18,750 | 2,200 |
| Chairs | 95,500 | 118,000 | 22,500 |
| Other Products | 235,000 | 278,000 | 43,000 |
| *Total revenue* | $512,050 | $573,500 | $61,450 |
| **Expenses** | | | |
| Manufacturing | 155,750 | 164,900 | 9,150 |
| Salaries/Benefits | 210,775 | 231,010 | 20,235 |
| Marketing/Sales | 58,800 | 46,900 | (11,900) |
| Other costs | 36,000 | 41,550 | 5,550 |
| *Total expenses* | 461,325 | 484,360 | $23,035 |
| *Net Margin* | $50,725 | $89,140 | $38,415 |

*Payback and Exit Strategy*
Financial projections anticipate that the Pinnacle outdoor line will
be able to return its portion of the investment within two to three
years barring a major shift in the recreation market. Wet Wraps will
evolve over a longer period of time, estimated to be five to seven
years, depending on the continued interest of the U.S. military.

***The Results:*** By using the business plan as a financial development tool, partners Jensen and Maddox were able to secure the necessary financing.to grow their business.

## 2. Probing for a Security Leak

***The Situation:*** State National Bank has come to the conclusion that someone has been siphoning funds. There's been little outside indication that anything is amiss except for the questions raised from occasional customers that small amounts of money have been deleted from their accounts over time. Because of the ridiculously small size of the deletion, standard error was blamed and the bank made good in most cases. However, the situations raised the suspicions of management, who brought in a forensic accountant to review procedures and make recommendations.

***The Analysis:*** Forensic accounting, a relatively new discipline, proceeds on the premise that something is wrong and performs an audit of whatever aspect of the company it suspects might be the source of the problem. Records are scanned, employees interviewed and procedures reviewed in order to determine where the problem, if any, might be. In this case, the small amounts lost on a consistent basis indicated that something was amiss. There were no teller drawer inaccuracies, which is one of the few places in which an embezzler might have ready access to small amounts of cash. In addition, the company also had done away with petty cash for internal expenses, another source of temptation. Since the accounts for the most part balanced, any embezzlement going on was hidden neatly from prying eyes. And that could have meant that those amounts showing up were really just the tip of the iceberg.

***The Application:*** If small amounts were disappearing and there was no damage to ready cash, that could only mean someone had diverted funds through the electronic data system that accounts for entries. The accountants first checked the firewall protecting incoming and outgoing electronic transactions and found no security breach there. That meant the violation was coming from someone inside the facility.

Running trial balances of the accounts, a sure way to detect errors in operations, yielded little information. Funds transactions were checked and monitored. Overhead operational costs were reviewed and vendor transactions checked, all of which appeared clean. The forensic accountant also monitored transaction activity on the part of employees, not looking for illegal diversion of funds so much as an unusual level of activity. Reviewing the amount of activity, financial or otherwise, by staff or through operations for deviations from the norm often can help point to inequities that lead to resolutions of problems and issues in the workplace. That's how National State Bank solved its dilemma and captured a pair of felons.

***The Results:*** A cash transaction processor had designed a program that rounded each partial cent of each transaction down to the nearest whole cent. But rather than adding those partial cents to the institution's central fund, the program diverted them into an account held by the friend of the operator. Since the books balanced, the institution was never suspicious. Those depositors who did closely monitor their account activity and complained usually were even less concerned than the bank, which eagerly made good on such small amounts. However, over time those small amounts added up to tens of thousands of dollars, which the employee and her friend divided equally between themselves. Once the pattern of the activity was uncovered, however, the employee was caught red-handed in the process and both were turned over to authorities.

## 3. How Much is Enough to Operate?

***The Situation:*** Bob's Balloons and Bagels had been operating successfully for a number of years, building itself a tidy portfolio of retail trade as well as corporate clients who order both signature products for routine and special occasions. Whenever anyone needed bagels for daily consumption or balloons for holidays, anniversaries and special occasions, Bob was the entrepreneur to which they always turned. Because Bob was an entrepreneur, however, he saw a much larger empire than currently loomed before him. He longed to develop a plan to expand and become Bob's Balloons, Bagels and Baskets.

*The Analysis:*   Bob knew that adding a line of decorative baskets
to his current business would require some excess capital, but not
enough at this point to warrant seeking additional funding from outside sources. He was holding that card until the day he was ready to
launch Bob's Basket Warehouse, at which time he would use his
bagel and balloon earnings to finance his first love, decorative baskets. Right now he needed to phase in the new line of merchandise
and that would mean extra, unbudgeted expenditures.

Consulting the company's budget would do little good, since it
measured past financial activities. No matter how good that budget
looked today, Bob knew that it couldn't give him the information he
needed because tomorrow could be another story entirely. A review
of accounts receivable could shed some light on the financial situation, but there are few guarantees when it comes to payments and it
only shows one side of the balance sheet. Accounts payable offers a
similar one-sided scenario.

---

**Bob's Balloons and Bagels, Inc.**
**Operating Cash Flow Statement**
**Period Ending December 31**

**Cash Flow from Sales**

| | | |
|---|---|---|
| Bagel Sales | | $68,366 |
| Balloon Sales | | 39,110 |
| Other (Delivery charges, etc.) | | 6,600 |
| *Total Sales* | | $114,076 |

Add:

| | | |
|---|---|---|
| Equipment Depreciation | $7,500 | |
| Inventory Decreases | 5,400 | |
| Accounts Payable Increase | 6,750 | |

Deduct:

| | | |
|---|---|---|
| Increased receivables | 4,300 | |
| Increase in prepaid expenses | 8,880 | |
| *Net Cash Flow* | | $120,548 |

***The Application:*** In this case, Bob's best bet is to study his cash flow statement and try to determine a pattern for excess funds. Cash flow statements are not budgets, nor do they measure profitability. Cash flow statements simply measure the income and outflow of cash. By using the cash flow statement, Bob will know if he has the capital to make it financially feasible to purchase his first stock of baskets and try this new line of work.

***The Result:*** By examining his cash flow statement, shown on page 300, Bob determined that he had ample funds to launch the basketry side of his business, as well as offer two new flavors of bagels: herb and mustard seed, and blackberry jam.

## 4. Knowing Which Costs to Manage

***The Situation:*** Costs are on the rise and no one knows that better than you. As head of the educational section of a major publisher, you've seen costs increase over the years, but never to the point where they imperiled profits. These days, however, that margin has become perilously thin and your counterparts on both the senior management team and the finance and accounting function are taking notice of the net income performance levels of your department. You make the case that the cost of good editorial services is increasing as the marketplace becomes more competitive. No one disagrees with your assessment. However, they task you with reducing those costs to increase that margin. You have no choice because that's your job.

***The Analysis:*** Expenses incurred by your department come from several sources, easily categorized as part of each volume's per unit price. First there's the initial cost of the creative process itself, classified as the percentage shared with the author and characterized by the advance that the company must forward to commission the work. Your budget also supports a half-dozen copy editors and a near equal number of layout and design people, all of whom are intrinsic to the volumes you produce. There are overhead expenses—heat, light, floor space—and equipment, most notably computers. There are also additional supplies, cover-art commissions and stock photo purchases and other miscellaneous costs. Producing educational volumes these days is a big job.

***The Application:***   As manager, you know there are only two ways to improve net margins: increase revenues or reduce expenses. The market is highly competitive right now and the idea of either increasing the cover price or counting on significant additional sales is both out of your control and too uncertain to be a viable solution, at least in the short term, which is the time period with which you're dealing. Something must be done within the next six months or your operation will be in financial trouble and you will be looking for new opportunities elsewhere.

There are two other opportunities available to you. Both involve identifying the value of fixed and variable costs. Remember that fixed costs refer to overhead that would exist regardless of the number of products or units you produce. Variable costs increase or decrease with the number of those products. The first and best strategy is to maximize the value of fixed costs because variable costs tend to take care of themselves.

Individual authors and their financial requirements vary based on the number of projects you do, but staff and overhead costs remain constant no matter how many books you produce. One method is to increase productivity, increasing the number of volumes and requiring more from each of your editorial and design staff. This increases the value of your fixed assets, which better maximizes fixed costs. More product on the market means more sales which, if produced with the same base of fixed costs, can increase the net margin. If this is not viable, you can follow a reduction strategy and lay off one or more staff. This can reduce overhead significantly, thus improving the net margin which, of course, is your overall goal. In either case, understanding the relative effect of fixed and variable costs can make all the difference in maximizing assets and increasing the net margin.

***The Result:***   Knowing that long-term success comes more often from growth than reduction, you choose to follow a maximization strategy. You explain to your staff the importance of increasing the net margin and what it will mean to their efforts. After some initial grumbling they realize that the company's welfare reflects directly on their continued well-being and enthusiastically support the acquisition of more manuscripts in order to both compete more effectively and improve the department's financial performance. And the staff unanimously support paying authors a greater percentage and large advances as part of the new talent acquisition strategy you've just launched to maintain your lead in the market.

## 5. Aging Gracefully

***The Situation:*** As a partner in the law firm of Tinker, Evers & Chance, you know that the management of the accounts receivable function of the firm can mean the difference between the new BMW you coveted when you passed the dealership yesterday and another six months with the Ford Fiesta (and with winter coming, too). Accounts payable is the money the firm owes to creditors. Accounts receivable is the money owed to the firm by clients. While both determine your income as one of the firm's partners, you know that accounts payable are more within the control of the firm. For accounts receivable, that's another story entirely.

***The Analysis:*** Ms. Puckwacket, the law firm's chief financial officer, has brought to the attention of all partners the current situation involving several well-known clients. Despite their level of activity, they have stopped paying their bills and the loss of those funds is having an alarming impact on the firm's cash flows. Ms. Puckwacket suggests a close review of the company's aging buckets to determine at what point those clients are turned over to collections.

An aging bucket, Ms. Puckwacket says, is the time period by which the account is overdue. Your accounts receivable have 30-day, 60-day, 90-day and even 120-day aging buckets. The amount of money falling into those longer-term buckets is increasing at an alarming speed. It's time, the CFO says, to do something about it. Yes, you agree, but where should we start?

***The Application:***   The first thing to do is to see where the largest amounts, as well as those owed to the firm the longest, fall. This is done by examining the firm's accounts receivable chart and its aging buckets. They look something like this:

| Acct # | Customer | 30 Days | 60 Days | 90 Days | 120 Days | Balance |
|---|---|---|---|---|---|---|
| 2261 | Ned's Ice Arena | $7,500 | $3,000 | $1,000 | 0 | $11,500 |
| 3131 | Wiseguy's Rest. | $9,000 | $6,900 | $5,400 | $3,000 | $24,300 |
| 0063 | Rose's Flowers | $3,500 | $2,000 | 0 | 0 | $5,500 |
| 1123 | Pop's Cycles | $1,500 | $1,000 | $500 | 0 | $3,000 |
| | *Totals* | $21,500 | $12,900 | $6,900 | $3,000 | $44,300 |

Clearly, Ms. Puckwacket has reason to be concerned.

The largest bucket is the 30-day bucket, but that's not at all surprising, since most businesses operate on the 30-days-net-due principle. The most troubling buckets are each of the ones that follow. From a collections standpoint, the older the debt, the harder it is to collect. The $3,000 in the 120-day bucket owed by Wiseguy's Restaurant should be the first and most easily collected. However, you know the owners and . . . well, perhaps you should work on clearing up the other debts first.

***The Results:***   By pursuing systematic elimination of debt starting with the oldest, you decide the firm from which there is the best chance of collecting its accounts receivable. The natural reduction over time in each of the aging buckets for each of the accounts shows that at least a portion of the payments due come in without having to be chased. That natural tendency, coupled with pressure from the back end, will reduce both the age and amount of the receivables over the shortest period of time. That will improve the firm's cash flow and put you that much closer to that new BMW.

As far as Wiseguy's Restaurant goes, the firm decides to mark it off to pro bono work and hope that they don't need any more legal services.

## 6. Living Large Inventory-wise

*The Situation:*   Megawide Industries produces furniture and utilities for large people. They're the equivalent of big-and-tall shops for appliances and home and office goods. Although manufactured in quantity, the assembly-line runs for Megawide products are not nearly the scale and scope of those for standard-sized chairs and other goods. Because of that, the retail sale price, by necessity, is higher in order to cover the necessary margins. Recently, Megawide executives learned that Snapdragon, Inc., the nationally known supplier of maternity clothing, has entered the appliance field with goods that will compete with some of Megawide's lines. Snapdragon's larger and more diversified product base may enable them to compete at a lower price. That means a retooling of Megawide Industries operations and strategies if the firm wants to compete.

*The Analysis:*   Megawide executives meet and decide that an upgrade to the company's production facility will mean lower product prices in the long run, allowing the company to compete more effectively with Snapdragon. That most likely will mean the borrowing of additional funds from a commercial lender to underwrite the improvement costs. Those steps are taken and the lender agrees pending his review of the current inventory and the inventory valuation process, a method by which the true inventory cost is determined. Since much of that inventory is being used for collateral on the loan, a true-cost valuation is deemed critical to the success of obtaining the loan. This valuation will be different from the sales price and will more accurately reflect the company's investment in its products.

*The Application:*   Proper inventory valuation includes both the fixed and variable costs of producing products. At each stage of subassembly the value of those products changes because of the additional applications that have been performed on the merchandise and the value those applications bring to the product. That means the distinct value for each subassembly step must be determined in terms of both fixed and variable costs. It's a complex equation, but from an accounting standpoint, it's critical to determining the products' true worth. Since that value affects the size of the loan for which the company qualifies, those are steps worth taking.

Using Megawide office chairs as an example, Jimmie "Crack" Korn, the head of production, first computes the value of the raw materials: the leather covering, wood and plastic elements of the frame, and the hardware and heavy duty casters. Jimmie also includes the cost of shipping and warehousing in the valuation of those materials. The materials then go through 12 distinct subassemblies to create the durable, nonstandard width chairs. The value of the labor and overhead, both direct and indirect, is computed based on actual costs and added based on the amount of time spent on each subassembly for each chair. The aggregate value of those subassembly steps, along with the raw materials cost for each chair, are added together to determine the true valuation of inventory.

*The Results:*  Jimmie's comprehensive process proves that he really does care about his business and that the reported inventory valuation for Megawide Industries is an accurate portrayal of its true worth. The lender guarantees the loan for the amount of the inventory collateral computed by Jimmie and the firm is off and running with new equipment and strategies for maintaining their market lead.


## 7. Planning by the Numbers

*The Situation:*  On-line Edibles, a new all-purpose food and cooking paraphernalia web site, has been in business for a little more than a year. It started as a hobby for Edna and Francis Wellstone and quickly grew into a sizable culinary business. The Wellstones began offering cookbooks and recipe cards and quickly advanced into the sale of cooking paraphernalia, such as high cost pots, pans, utensils and other kitchen gear. Based on their continued and growing success (Edna has her own television program, "CyberChef"), the Wellstones are seriously considering branching out in two other directions: providing fresh and preserved foodstuffs for use in their recipes, and offering an on-line cooking school, "Feed U," that capitalizes on Edna's program.

*The Analysis:* Despite the fame and growing fortune, the Wellstones are novices to business in general and to on-line enterprise in particular. In spite of some past debt from the couple's studies at various culinary institutes and traveling around the world to familiarize themselves with various cuisines, the Wellstones have managed to put some money aside. But they haven't the expertise to understand (a) if they have enough money to expand, or (b) what the first step is in addressing their situation. They know they have to budget, but they're not sure that is anything other than a list of liquid assets, which they know off the top of their heads. But even though they have that information, what do they do with it?

*The Application:* The Wellstones fail to understand that a budget is more than a mere accounting of funds. When well crafted, the budget serves as a strategic planning tool that evaluates the company's situation from a financial point of view. When combined with the operating statement, it does provide a snapshot in time. The progression from budgeted figures to their actual realization and then on to the next year's budget says a lot about the company's mind set toward growth and development.

The stage must be set prior to setting the budget. That's done by answering the following questions:

*What goals will my budget reflect?* Profitability is a key component and may be the single driving factor. But instead of short-term capital gain, profitability also may be defined as future market share growth, new product development or customer acquisition. Such higher goals may affect short-term income, but it may be more in line with company goals in the long run.

*Will company objectives be plainly visible in my budget?* Remember that a well-articulated budget contains clear representation of goals and methodologies that describe your sense of success. If your budget objectives match your corporate goals, then your budget becomes more of a strategic tool and less of a mere recitation of numbers.

***Does my budget identify tactics to achieve its objectives?*** Well-articulated budgets include a financial reflection of the tactics to reach identified goals. Evidence of such tactics contributes to the budget's strategic nature while enhancing its role as the tool to accomplish stated objectives.

***Has my budget outlined the procedures necessary to achieve the goal?*** Remember that procedures are to tactics what objectives are to goals. Tactics must focus on ways to penetrate and ultimately dominate those niches, as well as ways to knit them together for the full market presence you seek. And procedures will be the steps by which those tactics are executed.

***The Results:*** By utilizing the strategic elements of their budget, the Wellstones were able to determine that, while about 38 percent of income came from kitchen durables, the majority came from culinary education efforts. Entry into the foods business proper would use more than 78 percent of the available capital and drive the pair toward a commodities business at the expense of the education side of their endeavor. The Wellstones chose to abandon the thought of selling foodstuffs and limit their sale of kitchen durable goods. Instead, they revised their strategy and dumped the majority of excess capital into the development of Feed U. Not only could they afford it, but a financial analysis of past activities showed that they were in keeping with their core competency.

## 8. A Cash Stream Flows Through It

***The Situation:*** Tip Top Roofing Company provides services to many of the major residential and commercial builders in a large metropolitan area. The company's owner, Rick Tallman, has proven his skill and acumen as a small businessman and developer. Now that his business has hit the big time, however, he's finding that things aren't going so smoothly. There seems to be an endless flow of cash through his books, more so than in his early days, but he seems unable to stop the flow. It would appear a cash management strategy—and perhaps even hiring a cash manager—are in order.

***The Analysis:*** Cash managers come in many different shapes and titles, but all are there to preserve the bottom line, something that will be critical to Rick's business. At least half of the cash manager's role will focus on liquidity management, that is, investing excess cash in revenue generating stocks, bonds and other vehicles. A savvy cash manager—let's call him an investment or treasury manager at this point—understands that the goal of such activities is to invest funds in ways that will enhance the company's financial foundation and growth by adding significantly to the bottom line.

That was Mr. Stanke's job as the company's new cash manager. For Mr. Stanke, an old hand at keeping entrepreneur spending in line, there was no real trick to it. By using the budget like a tourniquet—the wily old money manager's own personal strategy—he was able to stop the flow of blood . . . er, funds, from going south. He was able to build up a nice well of reserves in the bargain. But now what should Tip Top Roofing do with those funds? Why, invest them of course. But that requires a little more technique than just stopping spending in order to be successful.

Specifically, Mr. Stanke began to think about cash forecasting to help him plan his investment strategy. Cash forecasting is a part of any cash management system and is critical to estimating revenues, expenses, profits and losses in order to develop investible cash flow estimates. This is more than an academic exercise. It's a way for the cash manager to estimate the amount and timing of cash surpluses, which is critical for selecting the right investment vehicle.

But how to go about successfully forecasting Tip Top Roofing's cash flow?

***The Application:*** Mr. Stanke discovered that there are a number of methods by which cash managers construct such a plan:

• In the first method, cash receipts and disbursements are analyzed and a picture of each cost element of cash-based functions is created so that forecasts may be developed. Essentially a cash forecasting method, this technique also provides a fairly comprehensive picture of variances in receipts and disbursement. That aids in developing a clearer understanding of cash flow and support control mechanisms by establishing patterns between forecasted activities and estimates. Assuming the net result offers enough excess liquidity at predictable intervals, this can mean more effective and lucrative short-term investment activity.

• The adjusted net income plan is most applicable where receipts are somewhat predictable and expenses are stable entities. As its name implies, this strategy begins with the company's income and expense statement. Noncash transactions are subtracted from the net income to arrive at a cash income or loss and then further adjusted for nonoperating balance sheet changes. In this strategy, which relies only on adjusted net income, the true extent of gross cash receipts or disbursement isn't really known or understood. Stable companies may find this useful, but those with tight cash margins may be hard put to have the latitude this strategy requires.

• The differential between capital as it appears at different times during the pay period is also sometimes used. Known as capital differentials, this strategy takes the net working capital at the beginning of each accounting period, adjusts it by the net income and other receipts or disbursements due, and arrives at an estimated working capital figure for the period. From this amount, the necessary working capital is deducted to arrive at an amount of cash available for investment.

***The Results:*** Since Mr. Stanke had gotten expenses under control, he was able to better chart the income and outflow of funds into the company. After the excesses were eradicated, cash flow was surprisingly consistent and even predictable from month to month. After experimenting with several of the methodologies, Mr. Stanke eventually settled on the adjusted net income plan because of the business' relative stability. By developing an investment program built from excess funds around that strategy, the cash manager was able to increase company revenues by a full 22 percent based on investment earnings, and earn himself a nice bonus in the process.

## 9. Growing Broke

***The Situation:*** The years had been good to Hatzen Horns, a novelty manufacturing and distribution company specializing in rubber wear and latex joke merchandise under the Snappy Tongue line of goods. The firm made its mark in the industry with the introduction of rubber vomit with the patented AromaCore® scent treatment that added extra realism to the product, sparking numerous spontaneous imitations wherever the product was unveiled. The company's fortune was made.

Several years ago the firm entered the rubber facial novelty arena with the introduction of the Pegleg series, which featured, among other things, rubber scars, moles, warts and wounds, as well as the usual lips, false teeth, nose enhancements and tumorous growths. Marketing helped introduce the products strongly, but sales efforts have stagnated from there.

***The Analysis:*** Executives at Hatzen Horns decided they needed to perform a life cycle study on the Pegleg series to determine where the product line was in its growth and development and how to market it from here on out. As a rule, all products go through four distinct phases in their product life cycle:

• The product's introductory phase, during which marketplace entry is attempted, requires extra efforts to introduce an otherwise preoccupied public to what you have to offer. Depending on your industry, the introductory phase can be a period of moderate to high costs, including research and development and marketing. There are merchant incentives, product giveaways and introductory events as well, along with the possibility of a below-market price. Couple that with moderate to low revenue from a public new to your idea and you can see you're in a stage in which profits may be small while costs may be large.

• After introduction comes a growth phase in which you can plan on making up for lost financial time. Profits may soar while expenses decrease. At the same time, competitors likely will enter the picture to trade on the spade work you've already done on their behalf with similar products designed to fill similar needs. Some may attempt to undercut your prices as part of their own introductory strategy. But rest assured your increasing revenue and decreasing costs will cross each other on the growth chart.

• When the product ages, the growth arc eventually levels off, and it reaches maturity. That's when competitors pose a serious threat. Product strategies will change and costs may increase as you reposition yourself through increased marketing and attempt to hold your industry leader status. With R&D costs far, far behind, price discounting becomes part of the battle plan. The result often is a slight increase in marketing or price advantage in the market.

• No matter how popular the product was at launch, it eventually goes into decline. Depending on how the company may choose to handle this stage, it may not require high costs in terms of expenses. The possible exception is for companies attempting to breath new life into old products through repackaging, repositioning and increased marketing. As the product's flame begins to flicker, however, it will have an impact on revenues. What once was top shelf could become a back shelf product or cease to exist altogether.

*The Application:*   Analysis revealed that the market for Pegleg products had begun to slip shortly after the company introduced its line. As the public became more sophisticated, there became less of a market for rubber noses and assorted other facial novelties. The Pegleg line was still considered the best of the breed, but there was less and less need for the merchandise.

This wasn't an assumption, but based on analysis by Hatzen Horns executives. Development costs for the merchandise had long ago been retired, so there was flexibility in pricing. There were several similar lines on the market, which kept profits in check by keeping the trial value artificially low. The company didn't suffer in terms of covering marketing and production costs, and even posted a modest net margin. But growth potential was severely curtailed and traditional efforts such as discounting, dealer incentives and frequent sales did not have the effect for which company officials had hoped. It was clear that Pegleg products had moved through the introduction and growth phases rather quickly and that maturity soon would be a memory as well.

**The Results:** With its products in decline, Hatzen Horns set about to retire the least profitable members of the line and provide only those that still showed some life. There was a brief resurgence of interest in rubber noses, which caused the company to launch a small but effective campaign around that product. But eventually the interest died out and the Pegleg line was formally retired in favor of more lucrative products for more sophisticated audiences, including some with batteries.

## 10. Brewing Up Good Acquisition Candidates

**The Situation:** Beer City Brands, a mid-sized Midwestern brewing company, has had a banner year. Its major line of lagers and ales have increased 14 percent in sales overall and 22 percent within the immediate (250 mile radius) market. The first figure means the company's name is spreading and the firm is on its way from being a former microbrewery to someday being able to enter the big leagues. The second figure means the reduced costs of local distribution, compared to higher-cost national distribution, along with marketing and media expenses, puts Beer City Brands in the position of having significant excess capital. It's time, company officials decided, to look into acquisition of additional breweries both to offset liquidity and increase capacity.

**The Analysis:** Buying a company is like buying anything else. Each opportunity comes with related challenges. Acquiring a privately held firm currently not on the block generally means paying a premium-plus price. The purchaser must carefully scrutinize the target firm to make sure appearances haven't inflated the company's true economic worth. On the other hand, companies that are on the block are usually there for one of two reasons: they were originally founded to be sold once they meet certain growth levels, or they are in financial trouble. Neither case automatically indicates problems, but research should be equally diligent before decisions are made.

For Beer City Brands, there was a plethora of small breweries to choose from. Executives who made up the acquisition team first were concerned about product knowledge and recognition of the breweries' existing brand. They paid close attention to candidate brewers' geographic locations. Production capacity was an issue, as were current product distribution systems. Access to raw materials always is key and so is the physical plant, particularly the condition, capacity and number of brew kettles and the age and operational efficiency of the bottling line.

One brewery in particular, Leiderhosen Lagers LLP, seemed particularly attractive. The brewery was located in a city in the northeast—Beer City Brand's second largest market—with easy access to major markets. In fact, the main brands, including the lager itself as well as the new Bismarck Bavarian Stout and Dresden Fire-brewed Beer, had established a beachhead as the more popular boutique brews in New York, Boston and Philadelphia. The capacity was about 40 percent less than Beer City's main brewery, but the facilities were relatively new and in good working order. Moreover, as far as the acquisition team members could see, the physical plant was currently only being run at about 70 percent capacity. That meant ample room for growth even within the current lines. An adjacent open parcel of real estate zoned for industrial meant even greater growth potential in the future.

***The Application:*** What the team wasn't privy too in its initial analysis was Leiderhosen Lager's financial picture. For that, they would need more information. The company's budget may tell them something about where the firm wants to go, but it does little to measure actual performance. For that they needed a different economic tool, and there were several from which they could choose. Two reports in particular are critical to any firm's financial progress:

- The *balance sheet* is a financial snapshot in time. At any given point, it can accurately measure the company's financial progress and alert company officials to perils and pitfalls, along with growth and positive trends.

- The *income statement* is a report with longer-term implications and one that reflects operating results for a certain period of time. Quarterly financial statements are not uncommon, but the document must be produced at least yearly to coincide with the budgeting cycle.

What the acquisition team needed to do first was look at the balance sheet to see what kind of progress, ownership and other financial issues might be critical to the current operation of the business they may be buying. Principles at Leiderhosen Lagers, once they understood Beer City's intent, were only too happy to comply.

The balance sheet looked something like this:

---

### LEIDERHOSEN LAGERS LLP
**Balance Sheet**
**December 31, 20XX**

**Assets**

| | |
|---|---|
| Cash | $84,000 |
| Accounts Receivable | $34,500 |
| Inventory | $42,500 |
| Land | $36,600 |
| Building | $100,000 |
| (Less Depreciation) | $48,125 |
| Equipment | $175,000 |
| (Less Depreciation) | $45,650 |
| *Total Assets* | $378,825 |

**Liabilities**

| | |
|---|---|
| Accounts Payable | $56,725 |
| Mortgage Payable | $41,500 |
| *Total Liabilities* | $98,225 |

**Owners' Equity**

| | |
|---|---|
| Uwe Werner | $151,892 |
| Christian Werner | $128,708 |
| *Total Liabilities and Owners' Equity* | $378,825 |

A quick overview shows that Leiderhosen Lagers LLP has $378,825 in resources and that these assets are being financed from two sources: creditors ($98,225) and owners' equity ($280,600). The right side of the balance sheet also can be referred to in total as *Equities* and subdivided into *Creditors' Equity* and *Owners' Equity.*

The balance sheet is a very informative tool, but a review of the company's income statement also was necessary to round out the financial information profile. The income statement is a tool that shows revenue and expense for a certain period of time without using the cross-functional transaction of the balance sheet. For those more interested in the result of financial transaction than the relation of financial transactions themselves, the income statement is the plainer, more accessible of the two tools.

Here's what Leiderhosen Lager's income statement looked like:

---

### LEIDERHOSEN LAGERS LLP
#### Income Statement
#### for June, 20XX

| | | |
|---|---|---|
| **Revenue** | | |
| Sales | | $325,000 |
| | | |
| **Expenses** | | |
| Mortgage payable | $1,458 | |
| Utilities and insurance | $1,668 | |
| Cost of goods sold | | |
| Labor | $145,175 | |
| Sales expense | $22,700 | |
| *Total Expenses* | | $171,001 |
| *Net Income* | | $153,999 |

---

The income statement purposely leaves out both contributions and withdrawals made by the firm's owners, Uwe Werner and Christian Werner. Those need to be summarized in the statement of owners' equity, another document that is periodically produced to provide a comprehensive financial snapshot of the firm.

***The Results:*** Despite the potential impact of withdrawals for owners' equity, Leiderhosen Lagers LLP appears to be a very healthy and prosperous company for the two Bavarian brothers. The strong financial performance indicates an above-average level of management, the final characteristic necessary when considering company acquisition. Beer City Brands made a successful bid, investing its capital in a promising enterprise that netted them greater geographic reach, financial profitability and some stellar brands to help them further solidify their role as a brewing industry up-and-comer.

And that level of success, after all, is what it's all about.

Future Value of $1

Interest Rate

| Number of Years | 1% | 2% | 3% | 4% | 5% | 6% | 7% | 8% | 9% | 10% | 12% | 14% | 15% | 16% | 18% | 20% | 24% | 28% | 32% | 36% |
|---|---|---|---|---|---|---|---|---|---|---|---|---|---|---|---|---|---|---|---|---|
| 1 | 1.0100 | 1.0200 | 1.0300 | 1.0400 | 1.0500 | 1.0600 | 1.0700 | 1.0800 | 1.0900 | 1.1000 | 1.1200 | 1.1400 | 1.1500 | 1.1600 | 1.1800 | 1.2000 | 1.2400 | 1.2800 | 1.3200 | 1.3600 |
| 2 | 1.0201 | 1.0404 | 1.0609 | 1.0816 | 1.1025 | 1.1236 | 1.1449 | 1.1664 | 1.1881 | 1.2100 | 1.2544 | 1.2996 | 1.3225 | 1.3456 | 1.3924 | 1.4400 | 1.5376 | 1.6384 | 1.7424 | 1.8496 |
| 3 | 1.0303 | 1.0612 | 1.0927 | 1.1249 | 1.1576 | 1.1910 | 1.2250 | 1.2597 | 1.2950 | 1.3310 | 1.4049 | 1.4815 | 1.5209 | 1.5609 | 1.6430 | 1.7280 | 1.9066 | 2.0972 | 2.3000 | 2.5155 |
| 4 | 1.0406 | 1.0824 | 1.1255 | 1.1699 | 1.2155 | 1.2625 | 1.3108 | 1.3605 | 1.4116 | 1.4641 | 1.5735 | 1.6890 | 1.7490 | 1.8106 | 1.9388 | 2.0736 | 2.3642 | 2.6844 | 3.0360 | 3.4210 |
| 5 | 1.0510 | 1.1041 | 1.1593 | 1.2167 | 1.2763 | 1.3382 | 1.4026 | 1.4693 | 1.5386 | 1.6105 | 1.7623 | 1.9254 | 2.0114 | 2.1003 | 2.2878 | 2.4883 | 2.9316 | 3.4360 | 4.0075 | 4.6526 |
| 6 | 1.0615 | 1.1262 | 1.1941 | 1.2653 | 1.3401 | 1.4185 | 1.5007 | 1.5869 | 1.6771 | 1.7716 | 1.9738 | 2.1950 | 2.3131 | 2.4364 | 2.6996 | 2.9860 | 3.6352 | 4.3980 | 5.2899 | 6.3275 |
| 7 | 1.0721 | 1.1487 | 1.2299 | 1.3159 | 1.4071 | 1.5036 | 1.6058 | 1.7138 | 1.8280 | 1.9487 | 2.2107 | 2.5023 | 2.6600 | 2.8262 | 3.1855 | 3.5832 | 4.5077 | 5.6295 | 6.9826 | 8.6054 |
| 8 | 1.0829 | 1.1717 | 1.2668 | 1.3686 | 1.4775 | 1.5938 | 1.7182 | 1.8509 | 1.9926 | 2.1436 | 2.4760 | 2.8526 | 3.0590 | 3.2784 | 3.7589 | 4.2998 | 5.5895 | 7.2058 | 9.2170 | 11.703 |
| 9 | 1.0937 | 1.1951 | 1.3048 | 1.4233 | 1.5513 | 1.6895 | 1.8385 | 1.9990 | 2.1719 | 2.3579 | 2.7731 | 3.2519 | 3.5179 | 3.8030 | 4.4355 | 5.1598 | 6.9310 | 9.2234 | 12.166 | 15.916 |
| 10 | 1.1046 | 1.2190 | 1.3439 | 1.4802 | 1.6289 | 1.7908 | 1.9672 | 2.1589 | 2.3674 | 2.5937 | 3.1058 | 3.7072 | 4.0456 | 4.4114 | 5.2338 | 6.1917 | 8.5944 | 11.805 | 16.059 | 21.646 |
| 11 | 1.1157 | 1.2434 | 1.3842 | 1.5395 | 1.7103 | 1.8983 | 2.1049 | 2.3316 | 2.5804 | 2.8531 | 3.4785 | 4.2262 | 4.6524 | 5.1173 | 6.1759 | 7.4301 | 10.657 | 15.111 | 21.198 | 29.439 |
| 12 | 1.1268 | 1.2682 | 1.4258 | 1.6010 | 1.7959 | 2.0122 | 2.2522 | 2.5182 | 2.8127 | 3.1384 | 3.8960 | 4.8179 | 5.3502 | 5.9360 | 7.2876 | 8.9161 | 13.214 | 19.342 | 27.982 | 40.037 |
| 13 | 1.1381 | 1.2936 | 1.4685 | 1.6651 | 1.8856 | 2.1329 | 2.4098 | 2.7196 | 3.0658 | 3.4523 | 4.3635 | 5.4924 | 6.1528 | 6.8858 | 8.5994 | 10.699 | 16.386 | 24.748 | 36.937 | 54.451 |
| 14 | 1.1495 | 1.3195 | 1.5126 | 1.7317 | 1.9799 | 2.2609 | 2.5785 | 2.9372 | 3.3417 | 3.7975 | 4.8871 | 6.2613 | 7.0757 | 7.9875 | 10.147 | 12.839 | 20.319 | 31.691 | 48.756 | 74.053 |
| 15 | 1.1610 | 1.3459 | 1.5580 | 1.8009 | 2.0789 | 2.3966 | 2.7590 | 3.1722 | 3.6425 | 4.1772 | 5.4736 | 7.1379 | 8.1371 | 9.2655 | 11.973 | 15.407 | 25.195 | 40.564 | 64.358 | 100.71 |
| 16 | 1.1726 | 1.3728 | 1.6047 | 1.8730 | 2.1829 | 2.5404 | 2.9522 | 3.4259 | 3.9703 | 4.5950 | 6.1304 | 8.1372 | 9.3576 | 10.748 | 14.129 | 18.488 | 31.242 | 51.923 | 84.953 | 136.96 |
| 17 | 1.1834 | 1.4002 | 1.6528 | 1.9479 | 2.2920 | 2.6928 | 3.1588 | 3.7000 | 4.3276 | 5.0545 | 6.8660 | 9.2765 | 10.761 | 12.467 | 16.672 | 22.186 | 38.740 | 66.461 | 112.13 | 186.27 |
| 18 | 1.1961 | 1.4282 | 1.7024 | 2.0258 | 2.4066 | 2.8543 | 3.3799 | 3.9960 | 4.7171 | 5.5599 | 7.6900 | 10.575 | 12.375 | 14.462 | 19.673 | 26.623 | 48.038 | 85.070 | 148.02 | 253.33 |
| 19 | 1.2081 | 1.4568 | 1.7535 | 2.1068 | 2.5270 | 3.0256 | 3.6165 | 4.3157 | 5.1417 | 6.1159 | 8.6129 | 12.055 | 14.231 | 16.776 | 23.214 | 31.948 | 59.567 | 108.89 | 195.39 | 344.53 |
| 20 | 1.2202 | 1.4859 | 1.8061 | 2.1911 | 2.6533 | 3.2071 | 3.8697 | 4.6610 | 5.6044 | 6.7275 | 9.6463 | 13.743 | 16.366 | 19.460 | 27.393 | 38.337 | 73.864 | 139.37 | 257.91 | 468.57 |
| 21 | 1.2324 | 1.5157 | 1.8603 | 2.2788 | 2.7860 | 3.3996 | 4.1406 | 5.0338 | 6.1088 | 7.4002 | 10.803 | 15.667 | 18.821 | 22.574 | 32.323 | 46.005 | 91.591 | 178.40 | 340.44 | 637.26 |
| 22 | 1.2447 | 1.5460 | 1.9161 | 2.3699 | 2.9253 | 3.6035 | 4.4304 | 5.4365 | 6.6586 | 8.1403 | 12.100 | 17.861 | 21.644 | 26.186 | 38.142 | 55.206 | 113.57 | 228.35 | 449.39 | 866.67 |
| 23 | 1.2572 | 1.5769 | 1.9736 | 2.4627 | 3.0715 | 3.8197 | 4.7405 | 5.8715 | 7.2579 | 8.9543 | 13.552 | 20.361 | 24.891 | 30.376 | 45.007 | 66.247 | 140.83 | 292.30 | 593.19 | 1178.6 |
| 24 | 1.2697 | 1.6084 | 2.0328 | 2.5633 | 3.2251 | 4.0489 | 5.0724 | 6.3412 | 7.9111 | 9.8497 | 15.178 | 23.212 | 28.625 | 35.236 | 53.108 | 79.496 | 174.63 | 374.14 | 783.02 | 1602.9 |
| 25 | 1.2824 | 1.6406 | 2.0938 | 2.6658 | 3.3864 | 4.2919 | 5.2474 | 6.8485 | 8.6231 | 10.834 | 17.000 | 26.461 | 32.918 | 40.874 | 62.668 | 95.396 | 216.54 | 478.90 | 1033.5 | 2180.0 |
| 26 | 1.2953 | 1.6734 | 2.1566 | 2.7725 | 3.5557 | 4.5497 | 5.8074 | 7.3964 | 9.3992 | 11.918 | 19.040 | 30.166 | 37.856 | 47.414 | 73.948 | 114.47 | 268.51 | 612.99 | 1364.3 | 2964.9 |
| 27 | 1.3082 | 1.7069 | 2.2213 | 2.8834 | 3.7335 | 4.8223 | 6.2139 | 7.9881 | 10.245 | 13.110 | 21.324 | 34.389 | 43.535 | 55.000 | 87.259 | 137.37 | 332.95 | 784.63 | 1800.9 | 4032.2 |
| 28 | 1.3213 | 1.7410 | 2.2879 | 2.9987 | 3.9201 | 5.1117 | 6.6488 | 8.6271 | 11.167 | 14.421 | 23.883 | 39.204 | 50.065 | 63.800 | 102.96 | 164.84 | 412.86 | 1004.3 | 2377.2 | 5483.8 |
| 29 | 1.3345 | 1.7758 | 2.3566 | 3.1187 | 4.1161 | 5.4184 | 7.1143 | 9.3173 | 12.172 | 15.863 | 26.749 | 44.693 | 57.575 | 74.008 | 121.50 | 197.81 | 511.95 | 1285.5 | 3137.9 | 7458.0 |
| 30 | 1.3478 | 1.8114 | 2.4273 | 3.2434 | 4.3219 | 5.7435 | 7.6123 | 10.062 | 13.267 | 17.449 | 29.959 | 50.950 | 66.211 | 85.849 | 143.37 | 237.37 | 634.81 | 1645.5 | 4142.0 | 10143. |
| 40 | 1.4889 | 2.2080 | 3.2620 | 4.8010 | 7.0400 | 10.285 | 14.974 | 21.724 | 31.409 | 45.259 | 93.050 | 188.88 | 267.86 | 378.72 | 750.37 | 1469.7 | 5455.9 | 19426. | 66520 | * |
| 50 | 1.6446 | 2.6916 | 4.3839 | 7.1067 | 11.467 | 18.420 | 29.457 | 46.901 | 74.357 | 117.39 | 289.00 | 700.23 | 1083.6 | 1670.7 | 3927.3 | 9100.4 | 46890. | * | * | * |
| 60 | 1.8167 | 3.2810 | 5.8916 | 10.519 | 18.679 | 32.987 | 57.946 | 101.25 | 176.03 | 304.48 | 897.59 | 2595.9 | 4383.9 | 7370.1 | 20555 | 56347 | * | * | * | * |

Future Value of an Annuity of $1

Interest Rate

| Number of Years | 1% | 2% | 3% | 4% | 5% | 6% | 7% | 8% | 9% | 10% | 12% | 14% | 15% | 16% | 18% | 20% | 24% | 28% | 32% | 36% |
|---|---|---|---|---|---|---|---|---|---|---|---|---|---|---|---|---|---|---|---|---|
| 1 | 1.0000 | 1.0000 | 1.0000 | 1.0000 | 1.0000 | 1.0000 | 1.0000 | 1.0000 | 1.0000 | 1.0000 | 1.0000 | 1.0000 | 1.0000 | 1.0000 | 1.0000 | 1.0000 | 1.0000 | 1.0000 | 1.0000 | 1.0000 |
| 2 | 2.0100 | 2.0200 | 2.0300 | 2.0400 | 2.0500 | 2.0600 | 2.0700 | 2.0800 | 2.0900 | 2.1000 | 2.1200 | 2.1400 | 2.1500 | 2.1600 | 2.1800 | 2.2000 | 2.2400 | 2.2800 | 2.3200 | 2.3600 |
| 3 | 3.0301 | 3.0604 | 3.0909 | 3.1216 | 3.1525 | 3.1836 | 3.2149 | 3.2464 | 3.2781 | 3.3100 | 3.3744 | 3.4396 | 3.4725 | 3.5056 | 3.5724 | 3.6400 | 3.7776 | 3.9184 | 4.0624 | 4.2096 |
| 4 | 4.0604 | 4.1216 | 4.1836 | 4.2465 | 4.3101 | 4.3746 | 4.4399 | 4.5061 | 4.5731 | 4.6410 | 4.7793 | 4.9211 | 4.9934 | 5.0665 | 5.2154 | 5.3680 | 5.6842 | 6.0156 | 6.3624 | 6.7251 |
| 5 | 5.1010 | 5.2040 | 5.3091 | 5.4163 | 5.5256 | 5.6371 | 5.7507 | 5.8666 | 5.9847 | 6.1051 | 6.3528 | 6.6101 | 6.7424 | 6.8771 | 7.1542 | 7.4416 | 8.0484 | 8.6999 | 9.3983 | 10.146 |
| 6 | 6.1520 | 6.3081 | 6.4684 | 6.6330 | 6.8019 | 6.9753 | 7.1533 | 7.3359 | 7.5233 | 7.7156 | 8.1152 | 8.5355 | 8.7537 | 8.9775 | 9.4420 | 9.9299 | 10.980 | 12.135 | 13.405 | 14.798 |
| 7 | 7.2135 | 7.4343 | 7.6625 | 7.8983 | 8.1420 | 8.3938 | 8.6540 | 8.9228 | 9.2004 | 9.4872 | 10.089 | 10.730 | 11.066 | 11.413 | 12.141 | 12.915 | 14.615 | 16.533 | 18.695 | 21.126 |
| 8 | 8.2857 | 8.5830 | 8.8923 | 9.2142 | 9.5491 | 9.8975 | 10.259 | 10.636 | 11.028 | 11.435 | 12.299 | 13.232 | 13.726 | 14.240 | 15.327 | 16.499 | 19.122 | 22.163 | 25.678 | 29.731 |
| 9 | 9.3685 | 9.7546 | 10.159 | 10.582 | 11.026 | 11.491 | 11.978 | 12.487 | 13.021 | 13.579 | 14.775 | 16.085 | 16.785 | 17.518 | 19.085 | 20.798 | 24.712 | 29.369 | 34.895 | 41.435 |
| 10 | 10.462 | 10.949 | 11.463 | 12.006 | 12.577 | 13.180 | 13.816 | 14.486 | 15.192 | 15.937 | 17.548 | 19.337 | 20.303 | 21.321 | 23.521 | 25.958 | 31.643 | 38.592 | 47.061 | 57.351 |
| 11 | 11.566 | 12.168 | 12.807 | 13.486 | 14.206 | 14.971 | 15.783 | 16.645 | 17.560 | 18.531 | 20.654 | 23.044 | 24.349 | 25.732 | 28.755 | 32.150 | 40.237 | 50.398 | 63.121 | 78.998 |
| 12 | 12.682 | 13.412 | 14.192 | 15.025 | 15.917 | 16.869 | 17.888 | 18.977 | 20.140 | 21.384 | 24.133 | 27.270 | 29.001 | 30.850 | 34.931 | 39.580 | 50.894 | 65.510 | 84.320 | 108.43 |
| 13 | 13.809 | 14.680 | 15.617 | 16.626 | 17.713 | 18.882 | 20.140 | 21.495 | 22.953 | 24.522 | 28.029 | 32.088 | 34.351 | 36.786 | 42.218 | 48.496 | 64.109 | 84.852 | 112.30 | 148.47 |
| 14 | 14.947 | 15.973 | 17.086 | 18.291 | 19.598 | 21.015 | 22.550 | 24.214 | 26.019 | 27.975 | 32.392 | 37.581 | 40.504 | 43.672 | 50.818 | 59.195 | 80.496 | 109.61 | 149.23 | 202.92 |
| 15 | 16.096 | 17.293 | 18.598 | 20.023 | 21.578 | 23.276 | 25.129 | 27.152 | 29.360 | 31.772 | 37.279 | 43.842 | 47.580 | 51.659 | 60.965 | 72.035 | 100.81 | 141.30 | 197.99 | 276.97 |
| 16 | 17.257 | 18.639 | 20.156 | 21.824 | 23.657 | 25.672 | 27.888 | 30.324 | 33.003 | 35.949 | 42.753 | 50.980 | 55.717 | 60.925 | 72.939 | 87.442 | 126.01 | 181.86 | 262.35 | 377.69 |
| 17 | 18.430 | 20.012 | 21.761 | 23.697 | 25.840 | 28.212 | 30.840 | 33.750 | 36.973 | 40.544 | 48.883 | 59.117 | 65.075 | 71.673 | 87.068 | 105.93 | 157.25 | 233.79 | 347.30 | 514.66 |
| 18 | 19.614 | 21.412 | 23.414 | 25.645 | 28.132 | 30.905 | 33.99 | 37.450 | 41.301 | 45.599 | 55.749 | 68.394 | 75.836 | 84.140 | 103.74 | 128.11 | 195.99 | 300.25 | 459.44 | 700.93 |
| 19 | 20.810 | 22.840 | 25.116 | 27.671 | 30.539 | 33.760 | 37.379 | 41.446 | 46.018 | 51.159 | 63.439 | 78.969 | 88.211 | 98.603 | 123.41 | 154.74 | 244.03 | 385.32 | 607.47 | 954.27 |
| 20 | 22.019 | 24.297 | 26.870 | 29.778 | 33.066 | 36.785 | 40.995 | 45.762 | 51.160 | 57.275 | 72.052 | 91.024 | 102.44 | 115.37 | 146.62 | 186.68 | 303.60 | 494.21 | 802.86 | 1298.8 |
| 21 | 23.239 | 25.783 | 28.676 | 31.969 | 35.719 | 39.992 | 44.865 | 50.442 | 56.764 | 64.002 | 81.698 | 104.76 | 118.81 | 134.84 | 174.02 | 225.02 | 377.46 | 633.59 | 1060.7 | 1767.3 |
| 22 | 24.471 | 27.299 | 30.536 | 34.248 | 38.505 | 43.392 | 49.005 | 55.456 | 62.873 | 71.402 | 92.502 | 120.43 | 137.63 | 157.41 | 206.34 | 271.03 | 469.05 | 811.99 | 1401.2 | 2404.6 |
| 23 | 25.716 | 28.845 | 32.452 | 36.617 | 41.430 | 46.995 | 53.436 | 60.893 | 69.531 | 79.543 | 104.60 | 138.29 | 159.27 | 183.60 | 244.48 | 326.23 | 582.62 | 1040.3 | 1850.6 | 3271.3 |
| 24 | 26.973 | 30.421 | 34.426 | 39.082 | 44.502 | 50.815 | 58.176 | 66.764 | 76.789 | 88.497 | 118.15 | 158.65 | 184.16 | 213.97 | 289.49 | 392.48 | 723.46 | 1332.6 | 2443.8 | 4449.9 |
| 25 | 28.243 | 32.030 | 36.459 | 41.645 | 47.727 | 54.864 | 63.249 | 73.105 | 84.700 | 98.347 | 133.33 | 181.87 | 212.79 | 249.21 | 342.60 | 471.98 | 898.09 | 1706.8 | 3226.8 | 6052.9 |
| 26 | 29.525 | 33.670 | 38.553 | 44.311 | 51.113 | 59.156 | 68.676 | 79.954 | 93.323 | 109.18 | 150.33 | 208.33 | 245.71 | 290.08 | 405.27 | 567.37 | 1114.6 | 2185.7 | 4260.4 | 8233.0 |
| 27 | 30.820 | 35.344 | 40.709 | 47.084 | 54.669 | 63.705 | 74.483 | 87.350 | 102.72 | 121.09 | 169.37 | 238.49 | 283.56 | 337.50 | 479.22 | 681.85 | 1383.1 | 2798.7 | 5624.7 | 11197.9 |
| 28 | 32.129 | 37.051 | 42.930 | 49.967 | 58.402 | 68.528 | 80.697 | 95.338 | 112.96 | 134.20 | 190.69 | 272.88 | 327.10 | 392.50 | 566.48 | 819.22 | 1716.0 | 3583.3 | 7425.6 | 15230.2 |
| 29 | 32.450 | 38.792 | 45.218 | 52.966 | 62.322 | 73.689 | 87.346 | 103.96 | 124.13 | 148.63 | 214.58 | 312.09 | 377.16 | 456.30 | 669.44 | 984.06 | 2128.9 | 4587.6 | 9802.9 | 20714.1 |
| 30 | 34.784 | 40.568 | 47.576 | 56.084 | 66.438 | 79.058 | 94.460 | 113.28 | 136.30 | 164.49 | 241.33 | 356.78 | 434.74 | 530.31 | 790.94 | 1181.8 | 2640.9 | 5873.2 | 12940.2 | 28172.2 |
| 40 | 48.886 | 60.402 | 75.401 | 95.025 | 120.79 | 154.76 | 199.63 | 259.05 | 337.88 | 442.59 | 767.09 | 1342.0 | 1779.0 | 2360.7 | 4163.2 | 7343.8 | 22728 | 63977 | * | * |
| 50 | 64.473 | 84.579 | 112.79 | 152.66 | 209.34 | 290.33 | 406.52 | 573.76 | 815.08 | 1163.9 | 2400.0 | 4994.5 | 7217.7 | 10435 | 21813 | 45497 | * | * | * | * |
| 60 | 81.669 | 114.05 | 163.05 | 237.90 | 353.58 | 533.12 | 813.52 | 1253.2 | 1944.7 | 3034.8 | 7471.6 | 18535 | 29219 | 46057 | * | * | * | * | * | * |

Present Value of $1

Interest Rate

| Number of Years | 1% | 2% | 3% | 4% | 5% | 6% | 7% | 8% | 9% | 10% | 12% | 14% | 15% | 16% | 18% | 20% | 24% | 28% | 32% | 36% |
|---|---|---|---|---|---|---|---|---|---|---|---|---|---|---|---|---|---|---|---|---|
| 1 | 0.9901 | 0.9804 | 0.9709 | 0.9615 | 0.9524 | 0.9434 | 0.9346 | 0.9259 | 0.9174 | 0.9091 | 0.8929 | 0.8772 | 0.8696 | 0.8621 | 0.8475 | 0.8333 | 0.8065 | 0.7813 | 0.7576 | 0.7353 |
| 2 | 0.9803 | 0.9612 | 0.9426 | 0.9246 | 0.9070 | 0.8900 | 0.8734 | 0.8573 | 0.8417 | 0.8264 | 0.7972 | 0.7695 | 0.7561 | 0.7432 | 0.7182 | 0.6944 | 0.6504 | 0.6104 | 0.5739 | 0.5407 |
| 3 | 0.9706 | 0.9423 | 0.9151 | 0.8890 | 0.8638 | 0.8396 | 0.8163 | 0.7938 | 0.7722 | 0.7513 | 0.7118 | 0.6750 | 0.6575 | 0.6407 | 0.6086 | 0.5787 | 0.5245 | 0.4768 | 0.4348 | 0.3975 |
| 4 | 0.9610 | 0.9238 | 0.8885 | 0.8548 | 0.8227 | 0.7921 | 0.7629 | 0.7350 | 0.7084 | 0.6830 | 0.6355 | 0.5921 | 0.5718 | 0.5523 | 0.5158 | 0.4823 | 0.4230 | 0.3725 | 0.3294 | 0.2923 |
| 5 | 0.9515 | 0.9057 | 0.8626 | 0.8219 | 0.7835 | 0.7473 | 0.7130 | 0.6806 | 0.6499 | 0.6209 | 0.5674 | 0.5194 | 0.4972 | 0.4761 | 0.4371 | 0.4019 | 0.3411 | 0.2910 | 0.2495 | 0.2149 |
| 6 | 0.9420 | 0.8880 | 0.8375 | 0.7903 | 0.7462 | 0.7050 | 0.6663 | 0.6302 | 0.5963 | 0.5645 | 0.5066 | 0.4556 | 0.4323 | 0.4104 | 0.3704 | 0.3449 | 0.2751 | 0.2274 | 0.1890 | 0.1580 |
| 7 | 0.9327 | 0.8706 | 0.8131 | 0.7599 | 0.7101 | 0.6651 | 0.6227 | 0.5835 | 0.5470 | 0.5132 | 0.4523 | 0.3996 | 0.3759 | 0.3538 | 0.3139 | 0.2791 | 0.2218 | 0.1776 | 0.1432 | 0.1162 |
| 8 | 0.9235 | 0.8535 | 0.7894 | 0.7307 | 0.6768 | 0.6274 | 0.5820 | 0.5403 | 0.5019 | 0.4665 | 0.4039 | 0.3506 | 0.3269 | 0.3050 | 0.2660 | 0.2326 | 0.1789 | 0.1388 | 0.1085 | 0.0854 |
| 9 | 0.9143 | 0.8368 | 0.7664 | 0.7026 | 0.6446 | 0.5919 | 0.5439 | 0.5002 | 0.4604 | 0.4241 | 0.3606 | 0.3075 | 0.2843 | 0.2630 | 0.2255 | 0.1938 | 0.1443 | 0.1084 | 0.0822 | 0.0628 |
| 10 | 0.9053 | 0.8203 | 0.7441 | 0.6756 | 0.6139 | 0.5584 | 0.5083 | 0.4632 | 0.4224 | 0.3855 | 0.3220 | 0.2697 | 0.2472 | 0.2267 | 0.1911 | 0.1615 | 0.1164 | 0.0847 | 0.0623 | 0.0462 |
| 11 | 0.8963 | 0.8043 | 0.7224 | 0.6496 | 0.5847 | 0.5268 | 0.4751 | 0.4289 | 0.3875 | 0.3505 | 0.2875 | 0.2366 | 0.2149 | 0.1954 | 0.1619 | 0.1346 | 0.0938 | 0.0662 | 0.0472 | 0.0340 |
| 12 | 0.8874 | 0.7885 | 0.7014 | 0.6246 | 0.5568 | 0.4970 | 0.4440 | 0.3971 | 0.3555 | 0.3186 | 0.2567 | 0.2076 | 0.1869 | 0.1685 | 0.1372 | 0.1122 | 0.0757 | 0.0517 | 0.0357 | 0.0250 |
| 13 | 0.8787 | 0.7730 | 0.6810 | 0.6006 | 0.5303 | 0.4688 | 0.4150 | 0.3677 | 0.3262 | 0.2897 | 0.2292 | 0.1821 | 0.1625 | 0.1452 | 0.1163 | 0.0935 | 0.0610 | 0.0404 | 0.0271 | 0.0184 |
| 14 | 0.8700 | 0.7579 | 0.6611 | 0.5775 | 0.5051 | 0.4423 | 0.3878 | 0.3405 | 0.2992 | 0.2633 | 0.2046 | 0.1597 | 0.1413 | 0.1252 | 0.0985 | 0.0779 | 0.0492 | 0.0316 | 0.0205 | 0.0135 |
| 15 | 0.8613 | 0.7430 | 0.6419 | 0.5553 | 0.4810 | 0.4173 | 0.3624 | 0.3152 | 0.2745 | 0.2394 | 0.1827 | 0.1401 | 0.1229 | 0.1079 | 0.0835 | 0.0649 | 0.0397 | 0.0247 | 0.0155 | 0.0099 |
| 16 | 0.8528 | 0.7284 | 0.6232 | 0.5339 | 0.4581 | 0.3936 | 0.3387 | 0.2919 | 0.2519 | 0.2176 | 0.1631 | 0.1229 | 0.1069 | 0.0930 | 0.0708 | 0.0541 | 0.0320 | 0.0193 | 0.0118 | 0.0073 |
| 17 | 0.8444 | 0.7142 | 0.6050 | 0.5134 | 0.4363 | 0.3714 | 0.3166 | 0.2703 | 0.2311 | 0.1978 | 0.1456 | 0.1078 | 0.0929 | 0.0802 | 0.0600 | 0.0451 | 0.0258 | 0.0150 | 0.0089 | 0.0054 |
| 18 | 0.8360 | 0.7002 | 0.5874 | 0.4936 | 0.4155 | 0.3503 | 0.2959 | 0.2502 | 0.2120 | 0.1799 | 0.1300 | 0.0946 | 0.0808 | 0.0691 | 0.0508 | 0.0376 | 0.0208 | 0.0118 | 0.0068 | 0.0038 |
| 19 | 0.8277 | 0.6864 | 0.5703 | 0.4746 | 0.3957 | 0.3305 | 0.2765 | 0.2317 | 0.1945 | 0.1635 | 0.1161 | 0.0829 | 0.0703 | 0.0596 | 0.0431 | 0.0313 | 0.0168 | 0.0092 | 0.0051 | 0.0029 |
| 20 | 0.8195 | 0.6730 | 0.5537 | 0.4564 | 0.3769 | 0.3118 | 0.2584 | 0.2145 | 0.1784 | 0.1486 | 0.1037 | 0.0728 | 0.0611 | 0.0514 | 0.0365 | 0.0261 | 0.0135 | 0.0072 | 0.0039 | 0.0021 |
| 25 | 0.7798 | 0.6095 | 0.4776 | 0.3751 | 0.2953 | 0.2330 | 0.1842 | 0.1460 | 0.1160 | 0.0923 | 0.0588 | 0.0378 | 0.0304 | 0.0245 | 0.0160 | 0.0105 | 0.0046 | 0.0021 | 0.0010 | 0.0005 |
| 30 | 0.7419 | 0.5521 | 0.4120 | 0.3083 | 0.2314 | 0.1741 | 0.1314 | 0.0994 | 0.0754 | 0.0573 | 0.0334 | 0.0196 | 0.0151 | 0.0116 | 0.0070 | 0.0042 | 0.0016 | 0.0006 | 0.0002 | 0.0001 |
| 40 | 0.6717 | 0.4529 | 0.3066 | 0.2083 | 0.1420 | 0.0972 | 0.0668 | 0.0460 | 0.0318 | 0.0221 | 0.0107 | 0.0053 | 0.0037 | 0.0026 | 0.0013 | 0.0007 | 0.0002 | 0.0001 | * | * |
| 50 | 0.6080 | 0.3715 | 0.2281 | 0.1407 | 0.0872 | 0.0543 | 0.0339 | 0.0213 | 0.0132 | 0.0085 | 0.0035 | 0.0014 | 0.0009 | 0.0006 | 0.0003 | 0.0001 | * | * | * | * |
| 60 | 0.5504 | 0.3048 | 0.1697 | 0.0951 | 0.0535 | 0.0303 | 0.0173 | 0.0099 | 0.0057 | 0.0033 | 0.0011 | 0.0004 | 0.0002 | 0.0001 | * | * | * | * | * | * |

Present Value of an Annuity of $1

Interest Rate

| Number of Years | 1% | 2% | 3% | 4% | 5% | 6% | 7% | 8% | 9% | 10% | 12% | 14% | 15% | 16% | 18% | 20% | 24% | 28% | 32% |
|---|---|---|---|---|---|---|---|---|---|---|---|---|---|---|---|---|---|---|---|
| 1 | 0.9901 | 0.9804 | 0.9709 | 0.9615 | 0.9524 | 0.9434 | 0.9346 | 0.9259 | 0.9174 | 0.9091 | 0.8929 | 0.8772 | 0.8696 | 0.8621 | 0.8475 | 0.8333 | 0.8065 | 0.7813 | 0.7576 |
| 2 | 1.9704 | 1.9415 | 1.9135 | 1.8861 | 1.8594 | 1.8334 | 1.8080 | 1.7833 | 1.7591 | 1.7355 | 1.6901 | 1.6467 | 1.6257 | 1.6052 | 1.5656 | 1.5278 | 1.4568 | 1.3916 | 1.3315 |
| 3 | 2.9410 | 2.8839 | 2.8286 | 2.7751 | 2.7232 | 2.6730 | 2.6243 | 2.5771 | 2.5313 | 2.4869 | 2.4018 | 2.3216 | 2.2832 | 2.2459 | 2.1743 | 2.1065 | 1.9813 | 1.8684 | 1.7663 |
| 4 | 3.9020 | 3.8077 | 3.7171 | 3.6299 | 3.5460 | 3.4651 | 3.3872 | 3.3121 | 3.2397 | 3.1699 | 3.0373 | 2.9137 | 2.8550 | 2.7982 | 2.6901 | 2.5887 | 2.4043 | 2.2410 | 2.0957 |
| 5 | 4.8534 | 4.7135 | 4.5797 | 4.4518 | 4.3295 | 4.2124 | 4.1002 | 3.9927 | 3.8897 | 3.7908 | 3.6048 | 3.4331 | 3.3522 | 3.2743 | 3.1272 | 2.9906 | 2.7454 | 2.5320 | 2.3452 |
| 6 | 5.7955 | 5.6014 | 5.4172 | 5.1421 | 5.0757 | 4.9173 | 4.7665 | 4.6229 | 4.4859 | 4.3553 | 4.1114 | 3.8887 | 3.7845 | 3.6847 | 3.4976 | 3.3255 | 3.0205 | 2.7594 | 2.5342 |
| 7 | 6.7282 | 6.4720 | 6.2303 | 6.0021 | 5.7864 | 5.5824 | 5.3893 | 5.2064 | 5.0330 | 4.8684 | 4.5638 | 4.2883 | 4.1604 | 4.0386 | 3.8115 | 3.6046 | 3.2423 | 2.9370 | 2.6775 |
| 8 | 7.6517 | 7.3255 | 7.0197 | 6.7327 | 6.4632 | 6.2098 | 5.9713 | 5.7466 | 5.5348 | 5.3349 | 4.9676 | 4.6389 | 4.4873 | 4.3436 | 4.0776 | 3.8372 | 3.4212 | 3.0758 | 2.7860 |
| 9 | 8.5660 | 8.1622 | 7.7861 | 7.4353 | 7.1078 | 6.8017 | 6.5152 | 6.2469 | 5.9952 | 5.7590 | 5.3282 | 4.9464 | 4.7716 | 4.6065 | 4.3030 | 4.0310 | 3.5655 | 3.1842 | 2.8681 |
| 10 | 9.4713 | 8.9826 | 8.5302 | 8.1109 | 7.7217 | 7.3601 | 7.0236 | 6.7101 | 6.4177 | 6.1446 | 5.6502 | 5.2161 | 5.0188 | 4.8332 | 4.4941 | 4.1925 | 3.6819 | 3.2689 | 2.9304 |
| 11 | 10.3676 | 9.7858 | 9.2526 | 8.7605 | 8.3064 | 7.8869 | 7.4987 | 7.1390 | 6.8052 | 6.4951 | 5.9377 | 5.4527 | 5.2337 | 5.0286 | 4.6560 | 4.3271 | 3.7757 | 3.3351 | 2.9776 |
| 12 | 11.2551 | 10.5753 | 9.9540 | 9.3851 | 8.8633 | 8.3838 | 7.9427 | 7.5361 | 7.1607 | 6.8137 | 6.1944 | 5.6603 | 5.4206 | 5.1971 | 4.7932 | 4.4392 | 3.8514 | 3.3868 | 3.0133 |
| 13 | 12.1337 | 11.3484 | 10.6350 | 9.9856 | 9.3936 | 8.8527 | 8.3577 | 7.9038 | 7.1889 | 7.1034 | 6.4235 | 5.8424 | 5.5831 | 5.3423 | 4.9095 | 4.5327 | 3.9124 | 3.4272 | 3.0404 |
| 14 | 13.0037 | 12.1062 | 11.2961 | 10.5631 | 9.8986 | 9.2950 | 8.7455 | 8.2442 | 7.7862 | 7.3667 | 6.6282 | 6.0021 | 5.7245 | 5.4675 | 5.0081 | 4.6106 | 3.9616 | 3.4587 | 3.0609 |
| 15 | 13.8651 | 11.8493 | 11.9379 | 11.1184 | 10.3797 | 9.7122 | 9.1079 | 8.5595 | 8.0607 | 7.6061 | 6.8109 | 6.1422 | 5.8474 | 5.5755 | 5.0916 | 4.6755 | 4.0013 | 3.4834 | 3.0764 |
| 16 | 14.7179 | 13.5777 | 12.5611 | 11.6523 | 10.8378 | 10.1059 | 9.4466 | 8.8514 | 8.3126 | 7.8237 | 6.9740 | 6.2651 | 5.9542 | 5.6685 | 5.1724 | 4.7296 | 4.0333 | 3.5026 | 3.0882 |
| 17 | 15.5623 | 14.2919 | 13.1661 | 12.1657 | 11.2741 | 10.4773 | 9.7632 | 9.1216 | 8.5436 | 8.0216 | 7.1196 | 6.3729 | 6.0472 | 5.7487 | 5.2223 | 4.7746 | 4.0591 | 3.5177 | 3.0971 |
| 18 | 16.3983 | 14.9920 | 13.7535 | 12.6593 | 11.6896 | 10.8276 | 10.0591 | 9.3719 | 8.7556 | 8.2014 | 7.2497 | 6.4674 | 6.1280 | 5.8178 | 5.2732 | 4.8122 | 4.0799 | 3.5294 | 3.1039 |
| 19 | 17.2260 | 15.6785 | 14.3238 | 13.1339 | 12.0853 | 11.1581 | 10.3356 | 9.6036 | 8.9501 | 8.3649 | 7.3658 | 6.5504 | 6.1982 | 5.8775 | 5.3162 | 4.8435 | 4.0967 | 3.5386 | 3.1090 |
| 20 | 18.0456 | 16.3514 | 14.8775 | 13.5903 | 12.4622 | 11.4699 | 10.5940 | 9.8181 | 9.1285 | 8.5436 | 7.4694 | 6.6231 | 6.2593 | 5.9288 | 5.3527 | 4.8696 | 4.1103 | 3.5458 | 3.1129 |
| 25 | 22.0232 | 19.5235 | 17.4131 | 15.6221 | 14.0939 | 12.7834 | 11.6536 | 10.6748 | 9.8226 | 9.0770 | 7.8431 | 6.8729 | 6.4641 | 6.0971 | 5.4669 | 4.9476 | 4.1474 | 3.5640 | 3.1220 |
| 30 | 25.8077 | 22.3965 | 19.6004 | 17.2920 | 15.3725 | 13.7648 | 12.4090 | 11.2578 | 10.2737 | 9.4269 | 8.0552 | 7.0072 | 6.5660 | 6.1772 | 5.5168 | 4.9789 | 4.1601 | 3.5693 | 3.1242 |
| 40 | 32.8347 | 27.3555 | 23.1148 | 19.7928 | 17.1591 | 15.0463 | 13.3317 | 11.9246 | 10.7574 | 9.7791 | 8.2438 | 7.1050 | 6.6418 | 6.2335 | 5.5482 | 4.9966 | 4.1659 | 3.5712 | 3.1250 |
| 50 | 39.1961 | 31.4236 | 25.7298 | 21.4822 | 18.2559 | 15.7619 | 13.8007 | 12.2335 | 10.9617 | 9.9148 | 8.3045 | 7.1327 | 6.6605 | 6.2463 | 5.5541 | 4.9995 | 4.1666 | 3.5714 | 3.1250 |
| 60 | 44.9550 | 34.7609 | 27.8656 | 22.6235 | 18.9293 | 16.1614 | 14.0392 | 12.3766 | 11.0480 | 9.9672 | 8.3240 | 7.1401 | 6.6651 | 6.2492 | 5.5553 | 4.9999 | 4.1667 | 3.5714 | 3.1250 |

# Glossary

**Account**   The form used to record financial activities such as additions and deductions to individual assets, liabilities, revenue, expense and owners' equity.

**Accounting Cycle**   Principle accounting procedures, conducted in sequence, to process transactions during the accounting period.

**Accounting Equation**   The fundamental building block of any accounting system used to describe the relationship between assets, liabilities and owners' equity: Assets = Liabilities + Owners' Equity.

**Account Payable**   A liability created by a purchase made on credit; it counts as a debt owed by the company.

**Account Receivable**   Revenue owed by the customer, posted as a claim against that customer for purchase made from the company on credit.

**Accrual Basis Accounting**   An accounting process in which revenues are recognized in the period earned and expenses recognized in the period incurred regardless of cash transference patterns.

**Adjusting Entry**   An entry to the books at the end of the accounting period to recognize an internal transaction and keep the general ledger current.

**Aging Bucket**   The total receivables in each aging period, i.e.: the 30-day aging bucket contains all receivables 30 days past due.

**AICPA**   An acronym for the American Institute of Certified Public Accountants, the national professional organizations for CPAs.

**Amortization**   Expense attributed to the estimated decline in usage of a tangible asset. The term also refers to allocation of a bond premium and discount over the lifetime of a bond issue.

**Articles of Incorporation**   Also known as the company charter, the articles outline the standards and parameters for business founders and owners of a corporate entity and are subject to approval by the appropriate authorities.

**Asset**   Real property owned by a business.

**Balance Sheet**   One of any business's primary financial statements, it lists assets, liabilities and owners' equity as of a specific date.

**Bond**   An interest-bearing note corporations use to raise capital on a long-term basis.

**Bookkeeping**   Recording of financial data used to run a business in a manner prescribed through basic accounting principles.

**Boot**   The balance owed investors when a new asset replaces an old asset.

**Budget**   A formal plan for a company's future development, expressed in financial terms and goals.

**Business Plan**   The outline of the company's strategy and the action steps needed to accomplish its corporate and fiscal goals, a business plan covers at least one year's duration and often as many as five years' duration.

**Business Transaction**   A formal or informal event affecting the business that must be properly recorded for accounting purposes.

**Capital**   The equity shared by owners in a business enterprise.

**Capital Expenditure**   A major purchase on behalf of the business that contributes to the effectiveness of that business.

**Capital Growth**   An increase in value of a market investment.

**Capital Lease**   A specific type of lease with criteria that demand it be treated as a purchased asset on a company's books.

**Cash**   Any exchange medium, most often government-issued currency or coin, that a bank will accept at face value.

**Cash Basis Accounting**   An accounting process through which revenue is recognized in the period in which cash is received, and expenses accounted for when cash is disbursed.

**Cash Flow**   The movement of money in and out of the business. Cash flow does not determine profitability, market share or any form of equity; it just chronicles actual funds movement.

**Chart of Accounts**   A complete listing of the accounts used to record revenue and expense by the business.

**Common Stock**   An ownership class of corporate stock, it represents a basic level of ownership with limited privileges.

**Continuous Budgeting**   A method by which a budget is constantly updated to always project 12 months out; also known as a *rolling budget*.

**Contra Account**   An account designed and used to offset another account.

**Control System**   The standards and methodology used by companies to detect and address inconsistencies and problems that arise in operations.

**Controller**  The chief accountant of an organization, one who manages other accountants.

**Cost of Goods Sold**  The actual cost of manufactured products, a price that includes all direct and many indirect expenses.

**CPA**  An acronym that stands for Certified Public Accountant, a financial professional who meets state requirements to practice his or her trade as a CPA.

**Credit**  The right side of any account and any entry made to that side of the account.

**Debit**  The left side of any account and any entry made to that side of the account.

**Deficit**  A debit balance applied to the retained earnings account.

**Depreciation**  The decrease in value through decrease in usefulness of company assets.

**Direct Expense**  An expense that can be credited directly to a specific department or operation in the execution of its business.

**Dividend**  A distribution of earnings to stockholders from the corporation.

**Double-entry Accounting**  The accounting system that records increases and decreases in all accounts in such a way that debits always equal credits.

**Earnings per Share (on common stock)**  The profitability ratio determined by the ownership for common stock shares.

**Economic Order Quantity (EOQ)**  The optimum quantity of inventory items to be ordered at one time.

**Equity**  The right or claim (ownership) to business properties by legal owners of that business and those properties.

**Expense**   The consumption of assets or services in conducting a business. Commonly referred to as a contributor to the cost of doing business.

**FASB**   The common acronym for the Financial Accounting Standards Board, the body charged with oversight of accounting standards and principles.

**FICA**   Formally, the Federal Insurance Contributions Act, taken from each paycheck and used to finance health and disability programs for the elderly (MediCare).

**FIFO**   A common acronym that describes inventory management procedure of first-in, first-out. The principle is based on the assumption that the cost of goods sold should be charged against revenue in the order in which those costs were incurred.

**Financial Accounting**   The branch of accounting that provides the financial information and statements necessary to run any business. It's also subject to transactional recording procedures defined by generally accepted accounting principles, also known as GAAP.

**Fiscal Year**   The annual accounting period during which a company's budget runs. Many fiscal years run concurrent with the calendar year, but that's not a requirement.

**Fixed Expense**   An operating cost that remains constant despite fluctuations in activity volume.

**GAAP**   The acronym for Generally Accepted Accounting Principles that serve as the guide for financial statement preparation.

**General Ledger**   The overall source of economic and transaction information for the company, the general ledger consists of a main ledger and numerous sub ledgers, plus supporting transaction documents that, taken together, paint a complete financial profile of the company.

**Goodwill** An intangible or undefined asset that is the natural byproduct of some other asset or business advantage, including such things as product superiority, competitive advantage and managerial skills.

**Gross Pay** The total amount earned by employees per pay period prior to deductions being taken.

**Gross Profit** The excess of net revenue from sales over the cost of merchandise sold.

**Gross Profit Analysis** The method by which the effect of changes in sales quantity and unit prices affect profitability.

**Horizontal Analysis** The measure of percentage increases and decreases as shown in comparative financial statements.

**Income Statement** A revenue and expense summary for a business for a certain period of time.

**Indirect Expense** An expense incurred by a company or business unit that is not under the direct influence of the department or operation against which it is incurred.

**Intangible Asset** A long-term asset that is useful to a business, has no physical specification and is not held for sale like other assets. A prime location for a business may be considered an intangible asset.

**Interim Statement** A financial statement used for information purposes that covers less than the assigned fiscal period, usually one year.

**Internal Accounting Controls** Procedures, records and methodologies to safeguard financial records and the assets they represent.

**Inventory** Supplies and merchandise on hand that contribute to the company's ability to achieve its financial goals.

**Invoice**  A bill submitted by the seller to the buyer for items purchased.

**Job Cost Sheet**  A ledger account in which costs charged to a particular job are recorded.

**Journal**  A record in which a transaction's effects are recorded.

**Journal Entry**  The entry of pertinent transaction data into a journal. Specifics include account numbers, transaction dates, credit and debit activities, who the transaction is with and who prepared it.

**Journalizing**  The recording of transactions in a journal.

**Liability**  A debit to a business operation.

**LIFO**  An inventory costing method that assumes the most recent merchandise costs incurred are charged against revenue. LIFO stands for "last in, first out."

**Liquidation**  The process by which a partnership goes out of business.

**Long-term Investment**  An investment not intended as a ready source of cash. It's listed on the "investments" section of the balance sheet.

**Long-term Liability**  A liability not due for a year or more.

**Lower of Cost or Market**  A method by which inventory or investments are assigned the lowest value of either their cost or the current market prices.

**Managerial Accounting**  A branch of accounting that uses estimated and historical data to provide management with operational information.

**Marketable Security**  A security investment that can be easily sold to convert its value to liquid assets.

**Market Value Method** A method by which product costs are allocated based on market sales values.

**Master Budget** The comprehensive budget plan that encompasses all individual budgets within a company.

**Matching** The accounting principle that says all revenues should be matched to expenses incurred in earning those revenues during the same time period.

**Maturity Value** Amount due when a note matures or at its due date.

**Merger** The joining of two companies based on the acquisition of assets of one company by the other.

**Mixed Cost** A cost with both fixed and variable characteristics. It may be referred to as a semi-fixed or semi-variable cost.

**Multiple-step Income Statement** An income statement with a variety of subsections that show intermediate balances before determining net income.

**Net Income** The final figure on an income statement after all revenues and expenses have been counted. It's the proverbial "bottom" bottom line.

**Net Loss** The final figure on an expense statement when expenses exceed revenues.

**Net Pay** Also known as "take home pay," it's the gross pay minus payroll deductions.

**Net Realizable Value** The amount at which merchandise able to be sold only at prices lower than cost should be valued. The value is arrived at by subtracting direct costs of disposition from the selling price.

**Net Worth**   A report of the owners' equity in the business once all expenses have been taken care of.

**Note Payable**   A written promise to pay representing an amount owed by the business.

**Note Receivable**   A written promise to pay, representing an amount owed *to* the business.

**Operating Lease**   The type of lease accounted for as an operating expense rather than a capital expense. Thus, future lease obligations and rights to use the lease asset aren't recognized in the accounts.

**Opportunity Cost**   Income that derives from the best alternative to a proposed use of resources, specifically cash.

**Other Expense**   An expense not directly associated with operations.

**Other Income**   Revenue from sources outside the realm of the primary business.

**Owners' Equity**   The rights and financial amounts due to the business's owners.

**Paid-in Capital**   The investment capital supplied by a company's stockholders.

**Par**   The arbitrary monetary value given a share of stock and printed on the stock certificate.

**Participating Preferred Stock**   Preferred stock subject to the awarding of dividends exceeding the specified amount given through its preferential rights.

**Partnership**   An unincorporated business owned by two or more individuals, definitely not a corporation.

**Payroll**   The total amount paid employees for a given pay period.

**Payroll Register** A form used to summarize and report payroll data figures, usually columnar in its design.

**Periodic Inventory System** A system of accounting in which sales revenue is recorded as the sale is made and the cost of merchandise on hand at the accounting period's end is determined through physical inventory.

**Perpetual Inventory System** An inventory accounting system that constantly discloses the inventory a company has on hand.

**Physical Inventory** A detailed listing of merchandise on hand.

**Plant Asset** A tangible asset, generally fixed in nature, owned by a company.

**Point of Sale Method** A revenue recognition methodology wherein revenue is realized when the title of ownership passes to the buyer.

**Pooling of Interest Method** An accounting methodology that controls the affiliation of two corporations in which voting stock from one firm is exchanged for substantially all voting stock from the other firm.

**Post-closing Trial Balance** A trial balance prepared once all temporary accounts have been closed.

**Posting** The method by which debits and credits are transferred from separate journals to their respective accounts.

**Pre-emptive Right** The shareholders' right to purchase additional shares of a stock issue to maintain the same level of financial interest in a corporation.

**Preferred Stock** A class of stock that has preferential rights over common issue stock.

**Premium** The amount by which the sales price of stock exceeds its par value. Also, the amount of excess of a bond issue's price over its face amount.

**Present Value**   The estimated worth of cash to be paid or received at some future date.

**Price-Earnings Ratio**   The ratio between the market price of a common stock share and its annual earnings per share.

**Process Cost System**   A cost system that accumulates for each process within a manufacturing facility.

**Profitability**   The company's ability to earn income.

**Profit Center**   An area of operations in which management is empowered and even required to earn profits for the firm and make the necessary decisions that affect revenue accumulation and expense preservation.

**Profit Margin**   Computed as an element of an investment's rate of return that factors operating income to sales.

**Promissory Note**   A written promise to pay the amount that is owed.

**Purchase Discount**   Discounts given to purchasers for an early payment of an invoice. This is treated financially as a contra account to Purchases.

**Purchase Order**   The form issued by a company's purchasing department to vendors that certifies payment of a particular order.

**Purchase Requisition**   The form filed by individual departments that alerts the purchasing department that a certain purchase needs to be made.

**Purchase Returns/Allowances**   A reduction in the amount spent for purchases by the return of unwanted merchandise to the supplier, also treated as a contra account to Purchases.

**Rate Earned on Stockholders' Equity**   A profitability measure computed by dividing total stockholders' equity into net income.

**Rate of Return on Investment (ROI)**   Generally considered a measurement of managerial efficiency.

**Real Account**   An account that appears on the balance sheet.

**Realization**   Earnings from the sale of assets when a partnership is liquidated.

**Report Form (Balance Sheet)**   The form of balance sheet that shows liability and owners' equity sections below the asset section.

**Residual Value**   The recovery cost or remaining value of an asset at the time it stops rendering service.

**Retained Earnings**   Net income after expenses retained by a corporation.

**Revenues**   Gross income retained by the business and as a result of conducting its business.

**Revenue Expenditure**   An expenditure that benefits only the current accounting period.

**Reversing Entry**   An entry into the books that reverses a specific adjustment to the books to correct the entry from the previous period.

**Safety Stock**   Inventory held on reserve for unforeseen circumstances, which doesn't become part of the overall revolving stock.

**Sales Discounts**   Discounts granted to the buyer by the seller for early payment of the invoice.

**Securities and Exchange Commission (SEC)**   The federal agency that regulates and oversees accounting and procedures for corporations whose securities are traded through interstate commerce.

**Single-step Income Statement**   An income statement in which all expenses have been deducted from the total revenues realized.

**Sole Proprietorship**  A business owned by a single individual.

**Solvency**  A company's ability to pay its debts when they come due.

**Special Journal**  A journal in which a single type of transaction is recorded.

**Stated Value**  The value assigned by a company's board of directors to each share of no-par stock.

**Statement of Financial Condition**  An individualized statement of financial condition, including estimated values for assets, liabilities, income tax on undepreciated assets, and net worth.

**Statement of Owners' Equity**  A summary of charges in the owners' equity category of a financial statement.

**Stock Dividend**  Distribution of a company's stock to its shareholders.

**Stockholders**  The company's owners, all of whom own shares of common and/or preferred stock.

**Stockholders' Equity**  The share of ownership stockholders have in a company.

**Stock Outstanding**  The stock currently in the hands of shareholders.

**Stock Split**  The planned reduction in the par value of common stock and the issuance of a corresponding number of shares.

**Straight-line Depreciation**  A depreciation method by which there are equal charges assigned periodically during the life of the asset.

**Subsidiary Ledger**  A ledger containing information on specific types of accounts that interacts with the general ledger.

**Sum-of-the-Year's-Digits Depreciation**   A method by which declining periodic depreciation charges are made throughout the life of an asset.

**T Account**   The basic balance sheet form applied to an individual account and resembling the letter T.

**Taxable Income**   The earnings amount on which income tax is based.

**Trade Discount**   An allowable reduction based on the list price of goods for sale.

**Treasury Stock**   Company stock that has been reacquired by the corporation.

**Trial Balance**   A summary listing the names and balances in each account.

**Unearned Revenue**   Revenue received in advance of being earned from an accounting point of view.

**Units-of-Production Depreciation**   A depreciation method calculated based on the expected productivity of an asset.

**Variable Costing**   The process by which the value of materials is computed based only on the variable costs that go into the production of each unit.

**Variable Expense**   Expenses that fluctuate in amount, based on activity and production volume.

**Vertical Analysis**   An analysis of a financial statement's component parts in relation to the sum of those parts.

**Voucher**   A document that serves as evidence of the provider's ability to pay cash for an item or service.

**Voucher Register**   A list of all vouchers issued.

**Working Capital**   The excess of assets over liabilities available for use at a certain time.

**Work Sheet**   A document used to assist in preparation of financial statements.

**Zero-based Budgeting**   A budgeting methodology that requires management to start from zero as if there had been no financial activity within their working units during previous accounting periods.

# Index